RAISING

# RAISING CAIN

*Protecting the Emotional Life of Boys*

DAN KINDLON, PH.D.
*and*
MICHAEL THOMPSON, PH.D.
WITH TERESA BARKER

MICHAEL JOSEPH
LONDON

MICHAEL JOSEPH

Published by the Penguin Group
Penguin Books Ltd, 27 Wrights Lane, London w8 5tz, England
Penguin Putnam Inc., 375 Hudson Street, New York, New York 10014, USA
Penguin Books Australia Ltd, Ringwood, Victoria, Australia
Penguin Books Canada Ltd, 10 Alcorn Avenue, Toronto, Ontario, Canada m4v 3b2
Penguin Books (NZ) Ltd, Private Bag 102902, NSMC, Auckland, New Zealand

Penguin Books Ltd, Registered Offices: Harmondsworth, Middlesex, England

First published in the United States of America by Ballantine 1999
Published in Great Britain by Michael Joseph 1999
1  3  5  7  9  10  8  6  4  2

Set in 12/14¾pt Monotype Bembo
Typeset by Rowland Phototypesetting Ltd, Bury St Edmunds, Suffolk
Printed in England by Clays Ltd, St Ives plc

A CIP catalogue record for this book is available from the British Library

ISBN 0–718–14371–X

# Contents

# Acknowledgements

### Dan

The genesis of this book was in a discussion I had with my wife, Catalina Arboleda, who is a brilliant clinical psychologist, and our friend Mary Challinor, who works with Josh Horwitz at Living Planet Books. I thank Catalina and Mary for giving me the initial encouragement to write this book. I must also acknowledge the perspiration of two doctoral students from Harvard's psychology department who served ably as my research assistants. Eric Petersen was a great help in locating research literature and in helping me think about biological and anthropological issues related to boys. The ebullient Sara Mednick combed the stacks of the Harvard libraries, conducted and transcribed interviews, and pointed me toward scientific sources that I might have otherwise overlooked. In the final stages of writing, Olawunmi Mobolade, a Harvard undergraduate, also helped with library research. I thank my colleagues at the Project for Human Development in Chicago Neighborhoods, particularly Tony Earls and Steve Buka, for their support during the writing of this book. I benefited from conversations about boys with two experienced and capable public school teachers: my brother, Tim, and his wife, Jane. Many teachers and administrators at the St Sebastian's school helped shape my thinking over the years. I cannot acknowledge them all but would like to mention Jerry Ward, Alden Mauck, Charlie Riepe, Mike Lajoie, Leslie Altman, Jean Lynch, Morris Kittler, Michael Nerbone, Pat Colton and Bill Burke. Apart from her professional input, which included many conversations about the many drafts of this book, I must also acknowledge Catalina Arboleda's role as patient wife and mother to our darling children, Julia and Diana, to whom I owe a debt of gratitude for putting up with me while I worked on 'the book'. I also owe Diana a debt of thanks for sharing her thoughts about her experience of boys and for allowing me to use her precious Rosetta Stone pencil sharpener.

## Michael

I have benefited from the wisdom of students, parents and educators in many schools. However, I particularly want to thank five school communities, one all boys and four co-ed, with whom I have had special relationships over many years: Rick Melvoin, headmaster, and the administrators and faculty at the Belmont Hill School, Belmont, Massachusetts; Cathy Gately and the faculty at the Charles River School in Dover, Massachusetts; Betty Brown and the faculty at the Langley School in McLean, Virginia; Tom Northrup, the faculty, and the Hill School community in Middleburg, Virginia; Catherine Peterson and the faculty of the Capitol Hill Day School in Washington, D.C. I have thrived from relationships in the independent school world provided me by my work with Peter Relic, Linda Gibbs and Kathleen Johnson of the National Association of Independent Schools. I have been influenced by the writings of Richard Hawley and Tony Jarvis and publications of the Boys' School Coalition.

Public speaking comes naturally to me; writing is a lot tougher. My dear friend, Ned Hallowell, and my dear cousin Bonnie Bryant Hiller, both successful authors in their own right, have been encouraging me for many years to write a book. I appreciate the push they gave me. I want to thank Catherine O'Neill Grace, Dick Barbieri, and Michael Brosnan for their support of my essay-writing, which led up to this book. Larry Cohen, Ph.D., wise writer and experienced psychologist, did research work for me and provided a sounding board for many of my thoughts in their formative stages. Michelle Antony, Tom Needham and Ann Northrup read early drafts of the book and made helpful comments. Throughout the writing, I have had the generous support of my wider family, especially Amy and Peter Thompson. And throughout this sometimes difficult process I have had the love, the steadiness and the valuable insights of my wife, Theresa McNally. She and my children, Joanna and Will, have uncomplainingly made many sacrifices the family of an author has to make. I cannot thank them enough. Joanna skimmed the galleys of the book and declared, 'I'm not mentioned anywhere!' That's true, this is a book on boys, but my experience as a husband and father of both a boy and a girl is everywhere in this book.

There are also five people we would like to jointly acknowledge. Our agent, Gail Ross, was an infallible source of wisdom, experience and style. We cannot imagine a more enjoyable and knowledgeable companion to lead us through the maze of the New York publishing world. We would like to thank our perspicacious editor, Ginny Faber, for putting her faith in our ideas and then, through her continual challenging and questioning, forcing us to better articulate them. A jointly authored book of this scope presented a host of difficult editing problems. Ginny's level of commitment went far beyond what was required, and her warmth and good humour were an effective antidote for the stress-related symptoms that accompany book-writing. Her assistant, Jason Zuzga, was a delightful and highly competent companion, especially during the last stages of reference checking. We also profited greatly from his perspective as a reader. Teresa Barker is an extraordinary journalist and writer. She had the unenviable task of marrying our very different writing styles and threw her heart and soul into the task. Her level of professionalism was inspirational and was crucial in getting us over some very rough places. Moreover, having both Teresa's and Ginny's sensitive and cogent insights as mothers of boys made this a better book. Josh Horwitz of Living Planet Books must be acknowledged for his invaluable help at every stage of *Raising Cain*'s development. Simply put, without him this book would not and could not have been written.

Finally, and most importantly, we wish to thank all the boys we have worked with over the course of our professional careers. We hope that we have faithfully represented the lessons they have taught us.

# Introduction

We are two male psychologists who have specialized in treating boys for more than thirty-five years of our combined practice. From the earliest days in our training, we have been sent the angry boys, the boys who kick things, and especially the boys who don't talk. We have played pool and basketball with our patients and called it therapy. We have talked with boys while building Lego structures with them. We have discussed family problems with boys as we lined up plastic soldiers preparing for a major battle. We have left our offices to make trips across the street to the Store 24 to purchase junk food and returned to the office to eat it, discussing the relative merits of different soft drinks in our efforts to make contact. We have conducted therapy sessions walking the streets or sitting in pizza parlours, in diners, in cars. We have had boys jump on our couches and leap to the floor with alarming thumps. We have had colleagues from downstairs call to complain about the amount of noise going on in our therapy sessions. All we could do was apologize: we're very sorry. Of course, therapy should be quiet. It should involve talking, not jumping. But we're doing therapy with boys here!

Perhaps it was inevitable that we would be drawn to work at all-boys schools in Massachusetts. At our two excellent schools, where boys are respected and well educated, we have, nonetheless, seen boys who have come to our offices angrily, reluctantly, and often on orders from the headmaster. We have had some coaches bring us boys and drop them off at the door for therapy who have themselves been too uncomfortable to stay and talk. Other teachers have brought unhappy students to our offices, and we have had to interview the teacher about a boy's unhappiness as the boy sat silent, because he was unable to articulate his own pain. We have seen boys sitting furious and silent with their families, boys whom we had to interview in the car park of the building because they wouldn't get out of the car to come to a family session.

In short, we have struggled for many years, in many ways and with mixed success, to help sad, anxious, and angry boys to tell us about their inner lives. We have waited patiently for those five minutes out of a fifty-minute session when a boy might say, 'My father criticizes me all the time. My grades went up from Cs to Bs in two courses and down in another, and all he could talk about was the course I had done worse in. Why would a father say something like that to a kid?' We sometimes have to wait weeks or months for that brief window of emotional disclosure when a boy suddenly shows us his sadness and bewilderment, which had previously been masked by silence or anger.

Our experiences with and our worries about boys have compelled us to write this book. We want to help people who love boys – their parents, teachers, and mentors – to see past the opaque surface of boys' lives to their inner lives. Their joy and their struggles. We want you – our reader – to understand the ways boys suffer and what causes them emotional pain. It is vital that parents and teachers do not take boys at face value, even though they sometimes insist, furiously, that we do so. They often present us with an apparently simple set of needs: Ninja Turtles, Nike shoes, exciting and violent video games, and support for their athletic ambitions. It may seem that every boy wants to 'be like Mike' (Michael Jordan). But it isn't so. Boys want different and complicated and conflicting things. Some want to 'be like Will' (Shakespeare); others yearn to be like Bill (Gates) or Al (Einstein); while still others want to be like Walt (Whitman). How can we respond to the needs of these extremely varied boys when our views of their inner lives are often so shallow?

If, as the poet contends, 'the child is father of the man', then it's doubly important that we unearth the true nature of our boys – look at them with eyes unclouded by cultural prejudice and listen to them with open minds and open hearts. Because if there's one thing we've learned, it's that, unless we give him a viable alternative, today's angry young man is destined to become tomorrow's lonely and embittered middle-aged man.

We are writing this book together because we share a feeling of alarm and urgency about the fate of boys. Though we have some-what different training and areas of expertise, we found that we had independently reached the same conclusions about how our culture is railroading boys into lives of isolation, shame, and anger. This book's inquiry has been guided by two basic questions: what do boys need to become emotionally whole men? And what is the cost to boys of a culture that suppresses their emotional life in service to rigid ideals of manhood?

For the most part, we will be using the editorial 'we' in this book. But when we delve into particular case histories from our individual practices, we will identify which one of us was involved and relay that story in the 'I' voice.

By way of introducing the two 'I's who will be leading this guided tour through the inner lives of boys, we'd like to tell you a little about ourselves – the kinds of boys we were and the men we became.

## Michael Thompson

My wisdom about boys – such as it is – has come from working with them in schools and in my private practice. After I graduated from college thirty years ago, I was a middle school teacher in a state school, a high school teacher in a public school, then a school counsellor, and finally a clinical psychologist working on the South Side of Chicago and in Cambridge, Massachusetts. These professional experiences have shaped my views about the nature of boyhood, but whatever understanding of boys I possess is also built on my personal experience growing up as a boy.

My own boyhood might seem to disqualify me from commenting on the common experience of boys because it was so unusual in its setting and opportunities. My family lived on the Upper East Side of New York City; my father had been born to wealth and had owned two polo ponies when he was growing up. I attended elite public schools with the sons of the successful and famous. I was taken regularly to see Broadway musicals, the opera, and to hear Leonard Bernstein's concerts for young people at Carnegie Hall. But then again, I was just a boy.

When I was eleven, my friend Tony Franz and I were up in his flat on the twelfth floor overlooking Park Avenue, surrounded by his parents' collection of Picasso paintings, the largest such private collection in the world. We thought it would be a good idea to throw wads of wet toilet paper out the window on to the windscreens of passing taxicabs, and so we had gathered some toilet paper rolls and a bowl of water and were making some pretty satisfactory hits. It never occurred to us how dangerous and terrifying such paper explosions might be for the taxi drivers and their passengers. That thought did, however, cross the mind of one of New York's finest, who spotted our window, counted up the floors, and demanded of the doorman in Tony's building that he be allowed to come up to the flat. It was in that museum-like setting that the policeman caught us, walking quietly into the flat and tapping us on the shoulders. I can vividly recall the terror and shame of our apprehension.

I had a driven, ambitious father, a successful architect and engineer who spent his entire life *en charrette* – an expression from the French architectural world meaning 'working against deadline and eating from a food cart in the office'. Gifted in his professional life, he lived a troubled and unconscious personal life. He had lost both his father and his closest brother when he was nine years old and was a mountain of unexpressed grief. All his life he was visibly terrified of strong feeling. He couldn't sustain intimacy, and as my brother and I grew up, he seemed increasingly baffled by the complexity of his sons. I began to feel more emotionally grown-up than my father by the time I was thirteen years old.

Despite all of this – despite the fact that I *never* played catch with my father (I don't think he had ever played baseball or football in his life) and that we were often confounded and enraged by each other – he managed to offer me some gifts that have helped me become a loving man. Was it his playfulness? Was it that he loved cooking pancakes in exotic shapes and loved board games and puzzles? Perhaps it was the fact that he would get into the pool and play games with the children while other fathers sat drinking and reading the paper.

My mother, a person of deep feeling and great sadness to whom I owe my capacity for empathy, used to say, 'I had to keep Michael and his father apart because they always fought.' I wish she hadn't intervened and managed our relationship in the way she did. She didn't understand our competition, our conflict, and our need to throw ourselves at each other. We were always making attempts at intimacy, right up until his death. My father is gone now. He died during the writing of this book, but I am often reminded of Geoffrey Wolff's remark in *The Duke of Deception*: 'My mind is never completely empty of my father.'

I also had an older brother named Peter, who was huge on my horizon. He was always bigger as we grew up, and we were intensely competitive with each other. My memory is that he beat me up most days of my young life and that one time, when we were fourteen and sixteen, we were in such a rage that we really wanted and tried to kill each other – me with a huge glass ashtray in my hand, he with a full bottle of Scotch. I'll never forget how satisfying it was to arrive at the age of seventeen and realize that I was now bigger than he was. He is one of my closest friends today. We take out our Cain-like impulses on the tennis court, which works just fine.

Now that I am a father myself, with a thirteen-year-old daughter and an eight-year-old son, my life feels like a delicate balancing act. I'm always worried about my son, Will, a boy who shuns athletics and loves Lego and art projects. He does not naturally run with the boy pack. And I'm constantly dancing on the edge of hypocrisy because I spend so much time at work, flying around the country telling parents to spend more time with their children. I am humbled and not a little bit frightened by the parallels I sometimes glimpse between my life and my own father's propensity for burying himself in his work.

If I could achieve my purpose in writing this book, it would be that I would be able to use my experiences as a man, my memories of my boyhood, and my experience as a therapist of boys and men to help parents to understand their sons better. I'd like to open the door of my office to reveal how adolescent boys struggle with sadness and show how often they channel that sadness into contempt for others and into self-hate. Most important, I would like to illuminate the inner life of boys for their parents so that they do not back away from their sons, hurt and bewildered by changes they do not understand. I want to show parents how to develop an emotional language with their sons that is boy-flavoured, deep, and enduring – a channel of communication that can help boys negotiate the cruel power struggles of adolescence.

# Dan Kindlon

I spend much of my professional life as a professor and researcher at the Harvard School of Public Health studying child and adolescent behaviour problems, particularly fighting and violence. Like a broker on the floor of the stock exchange, I watch the numbers and track the grim bull market trends for interpersonal violence, suicide, and substance abuse. Behind these numbers are real children, the large majority of them boys.

What the statistics don't tell us is what's going on inside of these guys. From my work with boys in schools, I know that too many boys fall into the trap of embracing the image of stoic masculinity they see in the mainstream media – a template that has been adopted as the inflexible code of their peer group. These boys are driven by psychological self-protection; they feel that they must be respected and will work hard to maintain a masculine persona that they feel will achieve that end. So much of their energy is devoted to sustaining this defensive perimeter, seeing threats where they don't exist and staging pre-emptive strikes against any feared incursions into their fortress of solitude. These sad facts are clear to those of us who work with boys, but too often the people who need to understand boys most, their parents and teachers, don't. They see only boys' anger without understanding its roots in their fear of exposure and vulnerability.

In my clinical practice, I keep getting lulled into thinking that times have changed. They have, but not enough. There seem to be more men willing to admit vulnerability, to relish the role of nurturing father, to hold a vision of masculinity that allows strength and caring to exist side by side. But then, I see boys in schools or in my therapy office who hide their fear behind a false bravado of drinking prowess or exploitative sex. When I look at their peers, I see that they are not in the minority. I see too many boys who just try to 'tough it out' on their own, boys who will not form meaningful connections with others because they have been led to believe that feelings equal weakness – and because they have never learned how to think or behave otherwise. And I still see too many men who are unable to be the kind of fathers they want to be. Often these men are hostile to, and critical of, their sons – despite their desire to behave otherwise – pushing their boys further and further inside a tight box of impossible expectations and denied feelings.

When I try to identify the single missing item in most boys' emotional toolbox, it usually comes down to flexibility. Adolescence is by definition a time of rapid change, and flexibility is the most important tool for growth. Many of the boys I see are so strait-jacketed by their sense of manhood that they can't enjoy being boys. Looking back at my own boyhood, I can see the advantage I was afforded by the flexibility to identify with both my father and my mother.

I grew up in a family of three boys and lived the early part of my life happily engaged in boyish pursuits, mostly outdoors, playing some version of war or baseball. But I was also intellectually curious and read voraciously – often books about war or baseball, but also about scientists, physicians, and explorers. Taking an honest look at myself now, I notice that I have not put away my boyhood fascinations. Among the twenty or so books strewn on and around my nightstand, three have the word *Gettysburg* in the title, and six more describe other battles or other wars.

Part of this interest in the history of warfare stems from my father's being a combat veteran of World War II. As a young child, I was fascinated by the army, asking my dad innumerable questions about how many Germans he had killed or what it was like to ride on a tank. In awe of his experiences, I would often sneak into his bedroom to gaze at the medals resting in felt-lined boxes he kept in a drawer among his socks. I knew intuitively that these ribbons were important, private evidence of his manhood.

If you had asked the six-year-old me about the man he wanted to become, the answer would certainly have included 'soldier'. But when my time came to go to war, in Vietnam, I saw the world in a different way. Instead of considering whether I would enlist in the army or the marines, I pondered whether I could truthfully answer the draft board's questions and still end up with conscientious objector status. Because I was unable to listen to my father talk about America's duty to fight Communism, our conversations turned warlike.

As a psychologist, I can't help but speculate about the connection between my current reading list and my ongoing struggle with the issues raised for me by Vietnam and by my father. As I continue to pore over descriptions of men in combat, I wonder whether I'm trying to penetrate the mysterious allure of battle – and to recover a deep common experience with my dad.

My father introduced me to my other boyhood passion – baseball. Comiskey Park and Wrigley Field, the cathedrals of major league baseball for boys in Chicago, felt far more holy to me than the church we attended every Sunday. Like Michael, I also had an older brother, Tim, whom I sought to emulate. His early years were dominated by a love of baseball, and although younger, smaller, and less talented, I was happy to follow along as best I could. At the advanced age of forty-five, I still play in a competitive softball league, and the only thing I really wanted to buy with the advance money from this book was a machine that pitches softballs to me in my backyard.

War and baseball – it's almost a cliché of boyhood passions. But thanks to my close connection with my mother, I got to explore beyond the confines of the classic male mould. I have many happy memories of cooking with my mother and of her teaching me to sew (I still like to cook but never really got the hang of sewing). Perhaps most valuable of all, because I spent time with my mother in these casual domestic pursuits, I have always felt relaxed and at home in the presence of women. Beginning with those hours in the kitchen, I learned how to talk to them and how to listen.

The flexibility afforded by these dual role models has allowed me to move freely between disparate worlds as an adult. This has served me well as a therapist to teenagers, as I have found it relatively easy to slip out of my adult skin and into a variety of teenager identities, whether popular or not, smart or academically challenged, a good kid or a troublemaker. And because emotional flexibility has been valuable to me, I try to encourage boys to move more freely through the inner world of their emotions, to be more honest with themselves about what they are feeling and why.

I am a father now, with two wonderful young daughters. When I think about the kinds of boys and men they'll come to know, the stakes for boys' emotional development become much more than professional for me. I don't want my girls to be reaching out to someone who's protecting himself behind a shield of anger and defensiveness. I don't want them to love a boy who cannot be intimate because he can't trust anyone. I don't want them to put their hearts out to someone whose preferred mode of dealing with emotional pain is drowning it in a six-pack of beer. I want the boys – and men – in my daughters' lives to be full emotional partners: empathic, expressive, and accountable. I want my daughters to know men who have retained their exuberant boyishness, but not at the expense of a lost emotional life.

We believe that boys, beginning at a young age, are systematically steered away from their emotional lives towards silence, solitude, and distrust. How this happens is the central subject of this book. We want to stress that this is *not* a book against girls or an effort to promote the interests of boys over those of girls. Nor is it an attempt to 'turn boys into girls' by helping them become more attuned to their emotional lives. Our premise is that both genders will be better off if boys are better understood – and if they are encouraged to become more emotionally literate.

*Raising Cain* is a book about boys and, we hope, a rich one. If you are looking for an easy answer to the question 'What makes boys the way they are?' you'll have to look elsewhere. What you will find in these pages is a perspective on boys you may never have had before. As therapists, we can offer you a glimpse through our privileged window into the inner lives of boys as they struggle to inhabit the 'Big Impossible' of manhood. As men, we have made (and are still making) that halting journey ourselves.

We started out to write a prescriptive book, with lots of bulleted suggestions about how to become better parents. In the end, we found that the best advice we had to offer was simply to understand boys as they truly are – rather than as they appear or as we wish them to be. Our deepest wish is to pull aside the curtain boys so tenaciously draw around themselves and offer you a look inside their hearts and minds. If we succeed, we hope that you will see more clearly the ways in which our culture conspires to limit and undermine their emotional lives. We hope you will understand boys better, and above all, we hope you will enjoy them more. In our work as therapists, we have loved working with so many kinds of boys. We have been dazzled by their energy, impressed by their inarticulateness, touched by their confusion, and sometimes simply blown away by their ability to cut right through the artifice of gender stereotypes and tell us what it is like to be human . . . and a boy.

# 1. The Road Not Taken: Turning Boys away from Their Inner Life

A young man is so strong, so mad, so certain, and so lost.
He has everything and he is able to use nothing.
Thomas Wolfe, *Of Time and the River*

Luke, thirteen, pauses at the office door, undecided whether to take his baseball cap off or leave it alone; he pulls it off and steps into the room – the school psychologist's office.

'Come on in, Luke. Have a seat in the big chair.'

An oversized, ancient, leathery brown Naugahyde chair dwarfs all but the largest athletes at this all-boys school. Some boys sink deep into the chair as if hoping to distance themselves from scrutiny; others sit stiffly on its edge, clearly uncomfortable with the unnerving assignment to look inward. In our work with boys at schools and in private practice, we see this body language all the time. Boys approach their emotions with much the same awkwardness, alternately sinking into the depths or sitting stiffly on the edge of feelings that threaten to overwhelm them.

Luke's a 'good kid'. He plays drums in the school band and makes fair grades, though they've dropped lately. At school he's not part of the popular clique, but he does have friends. He's not in the sporty crowd and mostly steers clear of them. So what brings him here? In the past few months Luke has grown increasingly sarcastic and sullen, and especially argumentative with his father. A few evenings ago, concerned about his grades, his parents turned down his request to participate in an optional after-school activity. Luke flew into a rage. Stormed off to his room. Slammed doors. Kicked a hole in his bedroom wall. His mother was stunned by the violent outburst, his father was livid, but they left him alone to cool off. The next morning

Dad left early for work, Luke had a headache and took a sick day off from school, and his mother called the school to see if anyone there might know what's troubling him. Luke's adviser suggested the counselling visit.

Now here we sit, and Luke is both nervous and angry at the prospect of talking about any of this, but most especially about his feelings. He has pushed himself back and sideways into the chair as far as he can go. His KEEP OUT sign is clearly posted.

The declining grades and the escalating hostility at home – especially the explosive outburst – are red flags of concern to everyone but Luke. 'I'm fine,' he says defiantly, while his eyes flash with anger at having been sent here at all.

As we talk, my questions cruise the perimeter of his life: academics, music, friendships, family. His answers are curt, cautious, and begrudging, punctuated with shrugs and a steely expression intended to keep the conversation from moving any closer than that outer edge. He doesn't have an explanation for his recent behaviour, and although he reluctantly agrees that talking about feelings might help, he shies away from it. 'I just need to work harder,' he says, shifting the focus to his grades. 'I don't need help. I'm not crazy,' he says. 'My parents are the ones with the problem.'

But we're here to talk about Luke's feelings. He offers a candid, perfunctory assessment of home and school life: his eight-year-old sister is an idiot. His older brother is a jerk. His father, a businessman, isn't around much – gone early, home late most days. His mother treats him like a five-year-old and pisses him off with all her questions. And although he has friends and likes a few of his teachers, for the most part, school sucks. That about covers it.

'About the other night. The rage and that hole in the bedroom wall. You must have been pretty angry to do that?'

Luke looks wary, and even a little scared. He shrugs.

'You look sad. Do you feel sad?'

Luke quickly looks down, and I see that his eyes are beginning to well up with tears. Clearly he is hurting, but it is masked in the toughness that fills his voice: 'I don't know. Maybe, I guess.'

'Let's see if we can figure out what's making you feel so bad.'

★

Every troubled boy has a different story, but their stories share a disturbing theme, a theme of emotional ignorance and isolation. Each day we try to connect with boys like Luke, who are unversed in the subtleties of emotional language and expression and threatened by emotional complexity. When we ask them to open up, most, like Luke, respond with the same 'fight-or-flight' response we all have to threatening situations. We see boys who, frightened or saddened by family discord, experience those feelings only as mounting anger or an irritable wish that everyone would 'just leave me alone'. Shamed by school problems or stung by criticism, they lash out or withdraw emotionally.

Parents are often at a loss to figure out how best to help. A boy's world is full of contradictions. One mother asks how she can offer wise counsel to her eight-year-old son, when her advice to 'use words' instead of physical aggression only earns him teasing and abuse from his peers. Another wants to know how she can get through to her brooding eleven-year-old when he fends off her attempts to make conversation: 'Now everything's an argument – we argue more than we talk – and even when I know something's bothering him, he won't talk about his feelings – just like my husband.' A father asks how he is supposed to help his teenage son when the boy 'won't listen' or is openly hostile.

A boy longs for connection at the same time he feels the need to begin to pull away, and this opens up an emotional divide. This struggle between his need for connection and his desire for autonomy finds different expression as a boy grows. But regardless of their age, most boys are ill-prepared for the challenges along the road to becoming an emotionally healthy adult. Whatever role biology plays (and that role is by no means clear) in the way boys are characteristically different from girls in their emotional expression, those differences are amplified by a culture that supports emotional development for girls and discourages it for boys. Stereotypical notions of masculine toughness deny a boy his emotions and rob him of the chance to develop the full range of emotional resources. We call this process, in which a boy is steered away from his inner world, the emotional *mis*education of boys. It is a training away from healthful attachment and emotional understanding and expression, and it affects even the youngest boy, who learns quickly, for instance, that he must hide his feelings and silence his fears. A boy is left to manage conflict, adversity, and change in his life with a limited emotional repertoire. If your toolbox contains only a hammer, it's not a problem as long as all your equipment is running right or repairs call only for pounding. But as tasks grow more complex, the hammer's limitations become clear.

## Emotional Literacy: Education versus Ignorance

If you ask a boy the question 'How did that make you feel?' he very often won't know how to respond. He'll talk instead about what he did or plans to do about the problem. Some boys don't have the words for their feelings – *sad* or *angry* or *ashamed*, for instance. A large part of our work with boys and men is to help them understand their emotional life and develop an emotional vocabulary. We begin by helping them increase their clarity about their feelings and those of others – recognizing them, naming them, and learning where they come from. We try to teach them *emotional literacy* – the ability to read and understand our emotions and those of others.

This process is much like learning to read. First we master the letters and sounds of the alphabet, then we use that knowledge to decode words and sentences. As we begin to comprehend and appreciate increasingly complex thoughts, we are able to communicate more effectively with others. Eventually, reading connects us to a larger world, beyond our own, of experiences and ideas.

Similarly, learning emotional literacy involves recognizing the look and feel of our emotions, then using this skill to better understand ourselves and others. We learn to appreciate life's emotional complexity, and this enhances all our professional and personal relationships, helping us to strengthen the connections that enrich our lives.

We build emotional literacy, first, by being able to identify and name our emotions; second, by recognizing the emotional content of voice and facial expression, or body language; and third, by understanding the situations or reactions that produce emotional states.[1] By this we mean the link between loss and sadness, between frustration and anger, or threats to pride or self-esteem and fear. In our experience with families, we find that most girls get lots of encouragement from an early age to be emotionally literate – to be reflective and expressive of their own feelings and to be responsive to the feelings of others. Many boys do not receive this kind of encouragement, and their emotional *il*literacy shows, at a young age, when they act with careless disregard for the feelings of others at home, at school, or in the playground. Mothers are often shocked by the ferocity of anger displayed by little boys, their sons of four or five who shout in their faces, or call them names, or even try to hit them. One of the most common complaints about boys is that they are aggressive and 'seem not to care'. We have heard the same complaint from veteran teachers who are stunned by the ferocity of boy anger and disruption in their classes. Too often, adults excuse this behaviour as harmless 'immaturity', as if maturity will arrive some day – like puberty – to transform a boy's emotional life. But we do boys no favour by ignoring the underlying absence of awareness. Boys' emotional ignorance clearly imposes on others, but it costs them dearly, too. Lacking an emotional education, a boy meets the pressures of adolescence and that singularly cruel peer culture with the only responses he has learned and practised – and that he knows are socially acceptable – the typical 'manly' responses of anger, aggression, and emotional withdrawal.

When we first began working with and speaking about boys, a large part of our task was to convince sceptical parents and educators of a truth we knew from our years of experience as therapists: that boys suffer deeply as a result of the destructive emotional training our culture imposes upon them, that many of them are in crisis, and that all of them need help. Perhaps because men enjoy so much power and prestige in society, there is a tendency to think that boys are guaranteed future success and to diminish the importance of any problems they might experience in childhood. There is a tendency to presume that a boy is self-reliant, confident, and successful, not emotional and needy. People often see in boys signs of strength where there are none, and they ignore often mountainous evidence that they are hurting.

Our audiences are no longer sceptical. The change would be more heartening if not for the tragic events that have enlightened them in a few short years. Killings or other violent acts by emotionally troubled adolescent boys have heightened public awareness and sparked widespread discussion of 'the boy problem' in schools and communities across the country.

Statistics state the case boldly. In the United States about 95 per cent of juvenile homicides are committed by boys. Boys are the perpetrators in four out of every five crimes that end up in juvenile court. They account for almost nine out of ten alcohol and drug law violations. Suicide is the second leading cause of death among boys in their mid- to late teens (accidents and homicides occupy the first and third spots). The vast majority of 'successful' suicides are boys. Compared to a girl the same age, a fifteen-year-old boy is seven times more likely to die by his own hand.

Although murder is an almost exclusively male enterprise, most boys don't kill despite feelings of anger and pain. Most boys are quieter students of emotional suffering. They long for love, acceptance, and approval from their parents and peers. They struggle for self-respect. They act impulsively, moved by emotions they cannot name or do not understand. Boys exercise their emotional ignorance in cruel treatment of one another or girls. Their inner turmoil is expressed in academic failure, depression, drug addiction, alcoholism, troubled relationships, or delinquency.

At a school's introductory seminar for parents, the headmaster asked parents of daughters to take an active role in discouraging cliques and social competition among their girls. In contrast, the social trials of boys in junior high school were dismissed with a good-natured thumbs-up: 'We don't worry so much about boys at this age because they are a lot more resilient and straightforward about it all,' the headmaster said. 'They get mad, they push each other around a little to blow off steam, and then it's done. They don't hold grudges.'

Yet boys do struggle with the same painful feelings of failure and rejection and not fitting in that we so easily attribute to girls. When they can't hold the pain any longer, they act on it. At any age, boys cut off from meaningful relationships miss critical opportunities for emotional growth. There is plenty of reason to be concerned: a confused young boy grows into an angry, emotionally isolated teenager, and, predictably, into a lonely middle-aged man at risk for depression.

What do boys need to become emotionally literate? We think the answer is clear. Boys need an emotional vocabulary that expands their ability to express themselves in ways other than anger or aggression. They need to experience empathy at home and at school and be encouraged to use it if they are to develop conscience. Boys, no less than girls, need to feel emotional connections. Throughout their lives, but especially during adolescence, they need close, supportive relationships that can protect them from becoming victims of their turbulent, disowned emotions. Most important, a boy needs male modelling of a rich emotional life. He needs to learn emotional literacy as much from his father and other men as from his mother and other women, because he must create a life and language for himself that speak with male identity. He must see and believe that emotions belong in the life of a man.

### *Dan with Mario, Robbie, Jack, and Friends*

I sit in a small, rectangular room with a group of eight twelve-year-old boys. Characteristic of their age, they are a varied lot. One, Mario, is taller and physically more mature than the rest, already well along on the journey through puberty. His straight, jet-black hair hangs at a severe angle across his forehead. In my youth this would have been considered a bad haircut, but for Mario and the others it is fashion. His friend Jack looks like a baby by comparison. A head full of soft, fine blond hair and vivid blue eyes give him an undeserved look of innocence. Jack is sharp-tongued and witty, the dominant personality in the group. Mario sometimes vies with him for leadership but more often serves as his lieutenant. A third boy, Robbie, whose trials are the focus of today's discussion, has a physical package that lies somewhere in between Jack and Mario. With a soft, pudgy build, he shows none of the budding athleticism of the other boys, but he is also taller than everyone but Mario. His mouse-brown hair is cut seemingly at random, and his clothes look as if he has slept in them.

These boys are not gathered in my office today for group therapy – at least not in the traditional sense. None has been diagnosed with a particular emotional problem. They are not especially 'bad' boys, poor students, or troublemakers. They make good-enough grades. In fact, there is nothing unusual about any of them. And that's why they're here. They represent a cross section of their class, and they have been picked by their headmaster to talk with me about the cruel teasing that has become so commonplace at their school as to seem unremarkable.

They all take part in the drama. Jack most often plays the role of the attacker. If he can find a flaw in someone, real or imagined, he'll point it out, turn it into a nickname, hammer it home at every opportunity, and enlist others to join in the fun. Mario is often at his side, the combination of his imposing size and Jack's sharp wit making them an almost irresistible force. Most boys in their class find themselves in the uneasy middle. Sometimes they are targets; sometimes they are the attacker. It is the way of the jungle. Only the strong survive. Robbie finds himself among a handful of boys who have been a frequent target of teasing. The other day he broke down crying and ran out of the room when he was teased by some boys in his maths class for failing a quiz.

I am trying to engage them in a discussion about how teasing can hurt. My initial questions are directed to Robert and Ernesto, who are friends.

'Is it ever all right to tease someone?'

Robert: 'Sure. I tease Ernesto all the time, and he teases me back. But we're still friends.'

'What do you tease each other about?'

Robert: 'I don't know. I'll tease him about his shoes.' (Everyone looks at Ernesto's old, very plain box-like shoes and laughs. Clearly they are familiar with the topic. Buoyed by their laughter, Robert's explanation gains vigour.) 'You know how, like, they're so old. His shoes are home-made, you know. His dad made them for him. His whole family has home-made shoes, even his sister.'

'Does it bother you, Ernesto, when Robert teases you like this?'

Ernesto: 'My shoes *aren't* home-made. I like my shoes.'

Robert: 'Yeah, right! They're like made of wood or something.'

Ernesto: 'Dr Kindlon, you know how Robert's mum packs him a cheese sandwich every day? That's because she has all this welfare cheese at home, and that's all she'll give him for lunch. His sister gets, like, McDonald's every day, but she saves the welfare cheese for him.'

'Okay. What does everybody else think about this? Is it okay to tease like this between friends?'

Jack: 'Yeah, it's funny. Nobody minds.'

'When isn't it okay? How do you know when you've hurt someone's feelings? When you've gone too far?'

There is silence and long vacant stares. Although I should know better by now, I am surprised by their lack of understanding of how their words and actions affect one another.

'Does teasing ever hurt?'

Several boys admit that it does.

'Then how can you tell whether you've hurt someone? How about with Robbie? You were all in the lesson with him the other day. What about that?'

More silence. They don't have a clue. They're not faking it to look cool or tough. They don't know how to read Robbie and don't even sense that they should. Another boy from the uneasy middle, Randy, offers a response, finally, that singles him out as the deepest emotional thinker in the group, yet none too confident in this intuitive realm. His answer is a question: 'You know you've gone too far when somebody starts to cry?'

'Sure, that's right. But wouldn't it be better if we knew how to stop teasing before we made somebody cry? Does someone have to cry before you suspect that what you're saying might be hurting him? How else might you know that a person's upset?'

More silence. This is really hard for these boys, even the ones who usually have all the answers in class. They squirm in their seats uncomfortably trying to come up with something that will get them out of this discussion. It's no use. They're stumped.

If a boy this age were unable to decipher the alphabet or read any better than this, every adult in his life would recognize that he needed help. But emotional illiteracy is so pervasive among boys that no one notices until something drastic happens. It takes playground shouting, a hole kicked in a wall, a drunk-driving arrest, or a suicide for a boy's emotional needs to get anyone's attention. For adults, the question might be: 'Do boys have to cry – or run or crash or kill, even kill themselves – before we suspect that something is wrong, that they might be hurting?'

Is it any wonder, then, that so many boys seem so emotionally bereft or limited? How can they be so oblivious to others' feelings? What happens to boys that denies them full access to the world of feelings?

## All Boys Are Born with Emotional Potential

One of the most common disclaimers we hear from mothers talking about a problem their son is having is this: 'I know my son is sensitive, but . . .' The inference is, of course, that most boys aren't sensitive and that her son is somehow different because he is. That's something our culture would have us believe, but it's not true. All boys have feelings. They're often treated as if they don't. They often act as if they don't. But all boys are born with the potential for a full range of emotional experience.

When researchers compare men and women or boys and girls on their emotional awareness, understanding, and expression, males almost invariably finish second. If boys and girls are given a series of pictures of faces showing different expressions, boys generally will be less accurate in their identification of the emotions that are being displayed. In therapy one of the most common complaints we hear from women about men is that men so often seem oblivious to the hurt, anger, or emotional needs of others. Many men readily acknowledge that the generalization is true: they do prefer to avoid emotional people and situations. That doesn't mean, however, that males lack the 'wiring' for expressing or understanding emotion. Newborn boys, on average, are actually more emotionally reactive than girls. For example, studies show that baby boys cry more than baby girls when they are frustrated or upset.

Despite those expressive beginnings, the overall pattern is that – with the possible exception of anger, regarding which the research results are inconclusive – *as boys get older, they express less emotion.* This is true when they are observed in natural settings or when they are observed watching slides or film of emotionally arousing situations. Leslie Brody, a leading authority on gender differences, describes this as a 'developmental shift in which males become less facially expressive of emotions with age, whereas females become more so'.[2]

So boys don't show as much emotion. But does that mean that boys actually *feel* less? Research suggests that they may feel more. When heart rate or skin conductance – sweaty palms – are measured in emotionally arousing situations, there is no consistent pattern of differences between girls' and boys' responses. Studies that have shown a difference suggest that males may react to a greater, not lesser, degree. Other research findings suggest that when boys get emotionally aroused, they may do less well at managing their emotion. In an intriguing study by Richard Fabes and Nancy Eisenberg at the University of Arizona, researchers played a tape of a baby crying to a group of five- and six-year-old boys and girls and monitored their physiological and behavioural reactions.[3] Specifically, they noted whether the child tried to eliminate the troubling sound by turning off the speaker or to soothe the baby in a manner that had been demonstrated previously by an adult – talking to the baby over the speaker.

The results? The girls were less upset by the crying. They made greater efforts to calm the baby and less often moved to turn the speaker off. Boys whose heart rate showed that they were quite stressed by the crying also were quick to 'turn off' the crying with a flip of the speaker switch. These distressed boys were also more likely to act aggressively towards the baby – telling it to 'shut up', for instance. Boys whose heart rate showed a lower stress level were more likely to comfort the infant. The researchers theorized that children – in this case, boys – who are more easily stressed by emotional responses may prefer to avoid them. In other words, boys who have trouble managing their own emotions may routinely tune out the cues of other people's upset.

## Boy Biology: No Simple Answers

In the wake of a 1998 playground killing in Jonesboro, Arkansas, a journalist asked us about 'the nature–nurture question', whether the boys' violence was genetic or the result of how they'd been raised. Her implicit assumption was that boys are prone to violence because of their biology. Certainly, male hormones were present at the scene: every boy has them. But we think the intensity of discussion about boy biology obscures the more meaningful and urgent issue of how we raise boys in this culture.

We answered the reporter's question with an apocryphal anecdote about a famous professor of psychology who said that he had studied the nature–nurture question with great care, reading all the literature, and had finally come to a conclusion: nature wins – by a score of 53 per cent to 47 per cent. When we mentioned this to the reporter, she laughed, seeing both the humour and the truth contained in the statement – that clearly everything we do is influenced heavily by both. Then we asked her why it is that there is always such an exclusive, determined hunt for a biological culprit? The reporter paused again and said, 'Well, people are looking for simple answers.'

But human behaviour defies simple explanation, whether we're talking aggression or tenderness. What is clear is that every behaviour is influenced by multiple forces, from biology to community. The 'nature or nurture' debate sidesteps the genuine complexity of these issues. Rather than making it a contest between the two, current thinking highlights the inextricable link between biology and experience, and it is now widely recognized that environmental factors can affect the structure of our brain.[4] An extreme example is a trauma victim whose body releases stress hormones over a long period, which cause physical damage to parts of the brain, which in turn will affect how he behaves. On the other hand, brain functioning can be enhanced by various learning experiences, such as exposure to an environment rich with the experience of letter shapes and sounds. These experiences will shape his brain – new neurons may actually be created – and a child will end up with a greater ability to read than he 'was born with'. The bottom line: heredity isn't destiny.

There are, however, two clear biological differences between boys and girls that have been shown to have an impact on development and behaviour.[5] The first, which we discuss more fully in chapter 2, is that girls' verbal abilities, on average, mature faster than boys': they talk earlier and more fluently. Boys tend to catch up later, but in the early years, especially, feminine superiority in this area is readily apparent to parents, teachers, and researchers. The second difference is that boys tend to be more physically active than girls, moving faster and staying in motion longer. As we shall see, this propensity for activity and the consequences of it shape a boy's every experience and the way others experience him.

Other than these, there are not many developmental differences that are clearly biological in origin. Even the celebrated superiority of boys in maths skills cannot be reduced to boy biology. Many studies of gender difference in maths performance show that overall the *girls* tend to do slightly better.[6] We are fascinated when sex differences in brain functioning or biochemistry are discovered. If, for example, a researcher finds in a neuroimaging study that slightly different parts of the brain light up for men and women when they are doing a rhyming game, the findings make headlines. But when another similar study finds no sex differences, it often doesn't get reported. It's not news. The greater attention paid to the gender differences skews our view of reality. If one had to sum up all the scientific work on sex differences in one finding, it would be that male and female humans are a lot more the same than they are different.

When research does offer us fascinating glimpses into the science of boys and gender differences, the information is too often misrepresented to the public or oversimplified, then accepted as a truth – however flawed – about boys.

Testosterone, for example, has become a buzzword for masculinity and a popular explanation for all boy attributes. A parent tells us that her two sons 'fight constantly', but she feels it's futile to intervene. 'It must be testosterone,' she says with a shrug. Referring to some rowdy students in her gym class, a teacher says: 'They're just testosterone-crazy boys.'

Testosterone's reputation, however, goes far beyond any grounding in scientific literature. A recent review of scientific studies of pre-adolescent and early adolescent boys concludes that the research literature 'provides no evidence of an association between testosterone and aggressive behaviour'.[7] One example, a study done at the Bronx Children's Psychiatric Center in New York, measured the testosterone levels of the centre's most violent young boys.[8] The researchers found that none of the boys had blood levels of testosterone that were outside the normal range or were significantly different from those of a group of non-aggressive patients of the same age and race to whom they were being compared.

Although scientists have yet to discover the extent to which testosterone shapes brain development before birth, we know that before and after puberty, the amount of testosterone in the bloodstream does not cause aggression. For example, all normal boys experience a huge surge of testosterone in early adolescence, but they do not all display increased aggression. Gender differences in aggressive behaviour can be observed as early as eighteen months and throughout early childhood, and yet testosterone is present in boys *and* girls in roughly the same amounts before the age of ten.

Blood levels of testosterone are not stable. Although a man may inherit a certain baseline level of testosterone, the level was never meant to be locked in place. Levels vary considerably over the course of a day, and, most important, they vary according to what happens to a person. For example, research shows that if a man wins a tennis match, or even a chess game, his level of testosterone rises and remains elevated for some time. The loser? His testosterone level falls. The typical action of a hormone is to change over time in response to environmental events – testosterone is no different. In many cases, where high levels of testosterone are measured, they are the *effect* of aggression rather than the cause of it.

Anthropologists offer evidence that further discounts the power of testosterone's role in aggression.[9] The Semoi of Malaysia are one of the most peaceful societies known. Men don't fight one another; husbands don't beat their wives; parents don't hit their children. What's more, the Semoi children seldom fight among themselves. Assault, rape, and murder are virtually unknown. The Semoi believe that aggression is very dangerous and that aggressive thoughts or even unfriendliness put a person at greater risk for getting sick or having a bad accident. Thus, their children learn from a very early age that non-violence is the way of the world.

Within North America, culturally distinct groups such as the Hutterite Brethren, the largest and most successful Christian communal group in the United States, or the Amish, have been astonishingly peaceful, perhaps more so than any other of the peaceful societies known to anthropology. For example, over 350 years no Hutterite living within his own community has slain another community member.

A destiny of aggression isn't born, it's made, most notably in societies like ours in which aggressive impulses are allowed free rein. We can raise boys to be non-violent if we so choose.

## Closer to Home: Training Boys for Toughness

Although there is a lot of lip-service being paid to the new age of the 'sensitive male', stereotypic images of masculinity are still with us. Whereas boys used to emulate John Wayne or James Dean (who now seem quaint by comparison), today's boys see even more exaggerated images of stoic, violent, impossibly powerful supermen on movie, television, computer, and video screens. The media serves up as role models Neanderthal professional wrestlers; multimillionaire professional athletes in trouble with the law, demanding 'respect' from fans and the press; and angry, drug-using, misogynist rock stars.

Even boys who are not allowed to watch violent movies or play violent video games, but who watch television sports, will nevertheless consume a steady diet of commercials in which a man is not a man unless he drives a tough truck and drinks lots of beer. These are not visions of manhood that celebrate emotional introspection or empathy. We are often invited to schools to talk with students when incidents or behaviours have roused the concern of parents or teachers. At one such meeting at an all-boys school the topic was drinking, which, on an average weekend, reached epic proportions among the teenagers. The boys talked openly about hangovers, passing out, fights, drunk driving, and casual sex, but this behaviour did not appear to worry them. Instead, they spoke with pride about the amount of alcohol they could consume.

Our culture co-opts some of the most impressive qualities boys can possess – their physical energy, boldness, curiosity, and action orientation – and distorts them into a punishing, dangerous definition of masculinity.

Evidence of the maladaptive nature of this vision of masculinity comes from one of the most revealing windows on boys' attitudes, the National Survey of Adolescent Males, in which researchers interviewed a large, representative group of fifteen- to nineteen-year-old boys in the United States.[10] Funded in the early days of the HIV crisis, the survey focused on risk-related sexual behaviour. Boys were asked, for example, whether they used condoms. To find out how strongly they believed in a 'masculinity ideology' – the attitude that manhood is primarily based on strength, stoicism, toughness, and dominance over women – researchers asked the boys how much they agreed with the statements:

- It is essential for a guy to get respect from others.
- A guy will lose respect if he talks about his problems.
- A young man should be physically tough even if he's not big.
- A husband should not have to do housework.

The survey results showed that the more boys agreed with the masculinity ideology statements, the more those statements corresponded to the boys' own views, the more likely they were to drink beer, smoke pot, have unprotected sex, get suspended from school, and 'trick' or force someone into having sex. In fact, the most significant risk factor for a boy's involvement in unprotected sex was his belief in this set of 'hypermasculine' traditional male attitudes. This mind-set spelled trouble for boys whether they were black or white, rich or poor, city kid or suburbanite.

Popular culture is a destructive element in our boys' lives, but the emotional miseducation of boys begins much earlier and much closer to home. Most parents, relatives, teachers, and others who work or live with boys set out to teach them how to get along in the world and with one another. In the process of teaching them one thing, however, we often teach them another, quite different thing that ultimately works against their emotional potential. Traditional gender stereotypes are embedded in the way we respond to boys and teach them to respond to others. Whether unintentionally or deliberately, we tend to discourage emotional awareness in boys. Scientists who study the way parents shape their children's emotional responses find that parents tend to have preconceived stereotypic gender notions even about infants[11] (like the father we know who bragged to us that his son didn't cry when he was circumcised). Because of this, parents provide a different emotional education for sons as opposed to daughters.

This has been shown to be true in a variety of contexts.[12] Mothers speak about sadness and distress more with their daughters and about anger more with sons. And it shows. Another study observing the talk of pre-school-aged children found that girls were six times more likely to use the word *love*, twice as likely to use the word *sad*, but equally likely to use the word *mad*. We know that mothers who explain their emotional reactions to their pre-school children and who do not react negatively to a child's vivid display of sadness, fear, or anger will have children who have a greater understanding of emotions.[13] Research indicates that fathers tend to be even more rigid than mothers in steering their sons along traditional lines. Even older siblings, in an imitation of their parents, talk about feelings more frequently with their two-year-old sisters than with their two-year-old brothers.

Here's how this gender socialization can look in its mildest, most ordinary form: Brad is four years old and has a question about everything. His mother fields most of these questions because she's with him more often than his dad, and even when the whole family is together, she typically is the more verbally responsive of the two. She tries to answer all questions with equal attention, but what she doesn't fully realize is that she, like any parent, subtly shapes the kinds of questions her child asks.

'Mummy, why do I have to sit in a car seat if you don't?' he asks. She responds with a talk about the safety advantages, how it is against the law for children to ride in a car unless they ride in a car seat. Because of the attention she pays to this question, Brad feels rewarded for asking about how things work and is thereby encouraged to do it again sometime.

But in the park, when Brad points to a small boy who is crying and asks his mother why, she is more likely to give a much shorter and less animated answer. 'I don't know, Brad, he just is. Come on, let's go. It's not polite to stare.'

The truth is, Brad's mother may not know why the little boy is crying, and she is teaching her son appropriate manners when she instructs him not to stare. But her short answer is less engaging, less informative, and less rewarding for her son. It subtly discourages him from thinking any further about why someone cries or what might have moved this particular child to tears. Her quick closure on the inquiry also may convey her own discomfort with the subject – a message that boys frequently 'hear' when fathers give short shrift to questions or observations about emotions.

We know that mothers who explain their emotions to preschoolers, and who don't react negatively to a child's emotional display, have children who have a greater understanding of emotions. Yet studies of parent interactions with both boys and girls suggest that, when a girl asks a question about emotions, her mother will give longer explanations. She's more likely to speculate with her daughter about the reasons behind the emotion or to validate or amplify her daughter's observation: 'Yes, honey, he does look very sad. Maybe he's got a little hurt or he's lost his toy.' The message the daughter gets is that it's okay to be concerned about another's feelings; her natural concern and empathy are reinforced.

Boys experience this kind of emotional steering constantly.

When six-year-old Jack and his family moved into their new house, one of the three children had to take the downstairs bedroom, separate from the others on the first floor. It was not his seven-year-old sister, Kate, who got the assignment, or his four-year-old sister, Amy. It was Jack. When Jack expressed a little uneasiness at sleeping alone on the ground floor, his father said to him, 'Oh, you're a big guy; you can handle it. Your sisters are scared to sleep alone.'

In much the same way, when boys express ordinary levels of anger or aggression, or they turn surly and silent, their behaviour is accepted as normal. If, however, they express normal levels of fear, anxiety, or sadness – emotions most often seen as feminine – the adults around them typically treat them in ways that suggest that such emotions aren't normal for a boy.

### The Story of Cain: Could There Have Been a Different Ending?

The biblical story of Cain and Abel, in which a jealous Cain kills his brother, endures as a parable of sibling rivalry, but it offers much more than that.[14] We see in Cain's story a reflection of the emotional life of boys today – a boy's desire to be loved and respected, and his propensity to respond to humiliation and shame with anger and violence rather than reflection and communication.

This short tale in the Book of Genesis opens simply enough. The brothers, both eager to please the Lord, each make an offering, Cain from the fruits of his labour in the fields and Abel a prized lamb from his flock. The Lord expresses pleasure with Abel's offering but pays no heed to Cain's. The scripture doesn't explain why the Lord responded so differently to each boy's offering, but Cain feels humiliated. In the story, Cain is visibly distressed – 'his countenance fell' – and yet he utters no words to express his feelings.

'Why are you so distressed, and why is your face fallen?' is the Lord's sharp response to Cain in the biblical script. In other words, 'Get over it!' And he gives Cain a stern lecture admonishing him to do right and be uplifted. The Lord reminds him: 'Sin couches at the door; its urge is toward you. Yet you can be its master.' There is no further discussion, and Cain remains silent, though surely he must be hurting at the rebuke and seething with anger as he draws his brother out to the field and slays him. When the Lord, well aware of Cain's murderous act, asks him what has become of Abel, Cain replies, 'I do not know. Am I my brother's keeper?' The Lord confronts him with his lie and banishes Cain to the land of Nod, away from his family and any future he might have envisioned. When confronted with the unalterable consequences of his action,

Cain cries out with self-pitying remorse, 'My punishment is greater than I can bear!' Although the Lord places a mark upon Cain to protect him from harm in exile, with his family shattered and his brother dead, Cain is burdened for life.

Conspicuously absent from the story are the boys' biological parents, Adam and Eve, with whom Cain might have talked or from whom he might have received calming counsel. As Elie Wiesel asks in *Messengers of God*, 'Could they not have reasoned with [the two brothers], explained to them calmly but firmly what life, particularly collective life, was all about?'

Cain's story describes every boy's desire to please – especially to please his father – and the sequence of ill-managed emotional reactions that lead to a tragic ending. We see a reflection of boys today in Cain's disappointment and shame at his heavenly father's rejection, his anger at feeling disrespected, his silenced voice in the turmoil of feeling, the absence of empathy or emotional reflection, and his impulsive act of anger.

For us, Cain's story resonates in the lives of boys today when we see them distanced from their own feelings and insensitive to the feelings of others, so clearly suffering the consequences of an impoverished emotional life.

Before Cain kills his brother, God reminds him: 'Sin couches at the door; its urge is toward you. Yet you can be its master.' How different Cain's story might have been had he been able to draw upon inner resources, emotional awareness, empathy, and moral courage, for instance, to master the moment. But this emotional education was missing for Cain, and it continues to be the missing piece in the lives of most boys today.

### Protecting the Emotional Life of Boys

In our work as therapists, we have seen boys suffer terrible losses – the death of a parent or sibling, a serious injury or catastrophic illness – and yet struggle successfully to reclaim a life and a future for themselves. We've seen others snap under the pressure of what could only be termed a bad day. The difference between boys who overcome adversity and those who surrender to it always comes down to the emotional resources they bring to the challenge.

Boys often find an emotional mentor in a favourite teacher or coach, but parents have a unique and powerful influence on a boy's view of himself and on his willingness to engage in learning emotional language and literacy. Parents can model emotional connectedness and empathy. They can listen to boys' feelings without judging them, hear their problems without dictating solutions. We have to come to grips with the fact that all boys have an inner life, that their hearts are full. Every boy is sensitive, and every boy suffers. This is a scary idea for many adults, who, consciously or unconsciously, don't want to acknowledge a boy's emotional vulnerability. But when we do acknowledge it, and we use this understanding to advance our own emotional education as parents and teachers of boys, we can help them meet the shadows in their lives with a more meaningful light.

If we teach our sons to honour and value their emotional lives, if we can give boys an emotional vocabulary and the encouragement to use it, they will unclench their hearts.

## 2. Thorns among Roses: The Struggle of Young Boys in Early Education

> What else can you tell a boy who likes flying, sparrows, tumbling and being amazed?
>
> Kuris Lambkin

It is mid-morning in Ms Alvarez's kindergarten class, and fifteen children – six boys and nine girls – sit in a circle on the carpet in a cosy corner of the room waiting for her to begin reading.

On one side of the circle, the girls sit shoulder to shoulder, some with legs crossed, some with hands clasped in their laps, some waiting quietly, expectantly, others chatting happily as they wait for a sign that Ms Alvarez is ready to begin. Beside them sits a boy, Daniel, equally self-possessed, relaxed, and waiting. Daniel is the best reader in the class; he spends hours at home and at school poring over books. For him story time is the happiest time of his day. As one kindergarten girl told a visitor, 'All of the girls in my class can read, even chapter books, but none of the boys can, only Daniel.'

A few feet away from Daniel sit four boys who are a study in contrast. Justin leans sideways on to Will's chest; Will is collapsing on to Bashir's shoulder; while Bashir leans into Ryan, who is doing all he can not to tip over. Surprisingly, this falling tableau does not turn into a total collapse; it seems frozen in space. The boys seem content with it; they will rest in this partially upright pig-pile for a long time, waiting for Ms Alvarez to begin reading. They are doing their best to comply with the rules of the classroom, and she knows it. Yet she cannot start reading until Christopher comes to join the circle.

Christopher is standing by the supply shelves, idly sifting through the crayons in a plastic box. He had been playing when Ms Alvarez had rung the bell and called for story time. On his way to putting the toys back in their box, he had run his finger through the chalk swirls on the blackboard, leaving a satisfying green line, bumped into Justin as Justin walked towards the circle, and stopped to pick up the plastic pears and tomatoes in the play kitchen. Finally, he had arrived at the supply shelves, lost in thought.

'Christopher, are you going to join us?' asks Ms Alvarez. Her question catches his attention. He looks over, but he doesn't move.

'Christopher, we're waiting,' she says, firmly. Christopher hesitates, stares, then drops the crayons and starts to make his way across the room. In the meantime, the domino boys have begun to collapse. Justin has fallen into Will, and Will is beginning to try to push him out of his lap and on to the floor. 'Will, don't push Justin,' says Ms Alvarez. 'Well, he's on top of me,' complains Will. 'Justin, please sit up and leave some space between you. Will, there's no need to push him. Let him do it by himself,' she says firmly. Then, 'Christopher, everyone is waiting to read. Would you join us, please?'

Christopher negotiates the last few feet to the circle and sits down expectantly. Then Bashir decides to lie on his back, and only his knees and shoes are now part of the circle. He is staring at the ceiling. 'Bashir, would you sit up like everyone else?' Bashir hauls himself up. 'Good,' Ms Alvarez says. 'Now we're ready to read.'

Though the entire process of getting the boys to sit quietly in the reading circle has only taken two to three minutes, it is hard not to be annoyed at Justin and Christopher. They do waste a disproportionate amount of class time every day. The gender split is obvious; the girls bring energy and exuberance to the circle, too, but it is contained; they readily follow instructions. How does the activity of these boys impose upon these girls? What is the impact on Daniel, who waits patiently alongside the girls, aware that he is not one with these other boys? And what about the bumping, jostling, wrestling boys? Or the distractible Christopher? What lessons do they learn from being reprimanded at story time or any time their behaviour or skills set them apart? As mothers often recall about their sons' school years: 'I have a wonderful son, but he spent a lot of time on the bench outside the headmaster's office.' What *is* it about boys? These are the questions that occupy teachers and parents and dominate discussions about boys in school.

In recent years the public discussion of fairness in schools has focused almost exclusively on girls and the ways they have been shortchanged in a system that favours boys. As right as the concern for girls is, we are disturbed by the dialogue when it seems to pit boys against girls in the quest for fairness. The unchallenged assumption is that, if girls are suffering in school, then boys are not. Yet research, statistics, and our own experience as school psychologists and with boys and men in private therapy contradict this.

From kindergarten through middle school, a boy spends more than a thousand hours a year in school, and his experiences and the attitudes of the teachers and other adults he encounters there are profoundly shaping. The average boy faces a special struggle to meet the developmental and academic expectations of a primary school curriculum that emphasizes reading, writing, and verbal ability – cognitive skills that normally develop more slowly in boys than in girls. Some boys are ahead of the others on that developmental curve, and some girls lag behind, but when we compare the average boy with the average girl, the average boy is developmentally disadvantaged in the early school environment.

Junior schools are largely feminine environments, populated predominantly by women teachers and authority figures, that seem rigged against boys, against the higher activity level and lower level of impulse control that is normal for boys. As one disappointed five-year-old boy remarked unhappily at the end of his first day of school: 'You can't *do* anything!' The trouble wasn't really that he couldn't do anything, of course, but that everything he loved to do – run, throw, wrestle, climb – was outlawed in the classroom. In this setting a boy's experience of school is as a thorn among roses; he is a different, lesser, and sometimes frowned-upon presence, and he knows it.

A teacher described her classroom, a typical school day, and her instructional style to us, insisting that the emphasis on compliant behaviour and sit-down reading and language arts activities was not a feminine template but reflective of a 'human agenda'. 'I don't think of my classroom as a girl place or a boy place. I think it is a human place, a civilized place,' she said. 'It just happens that it's easier for girls to adapt to it.'

As much as she would like the school environment to be just a place where instruction and expectations present both boys and girls with the same opportunity for success, the fact that it's clearly easier for girls to adapt to it means that, in some unseen way, the expectations reflect girls' abilities and sensibilities.

This is the reason that David Trower, the headmaster of the all-boys Allan Stephenson School in New York City, says, 'If boys need the protection of the single-sex environment at all, they need it most in elementary school because of the developmental disparity.'

We are not suggesting that boys are good and schools are bad, or that teachers don't care about boys. Quite to the contrary, much of what we know about boys' difficulties in school is confirmed by the many caring, creative teachers we know who struggle with the unique challenge of working with boys in the school setting. We know, too, that there are boys whose talents or temperaments make them exceptions, but if we're going to talk about the ways in which boys' life experiences complicate their emotional development or compromise it, we have to talk about the hidden hurt that the early school years inflict on so many boys.

Studies that track children's development through the school years suggest that, by the age of eight, a child has established a pattern of learning that shapes the course of his or her entire school career.[1] We see this clearly with boys: the first two years in school are a critical moment of entry into that world of learning, but boys' relative immaturity and the inability to fit in that they so often experience in school set them up to fail. Many boys who are turned off to school at a young age never refind the motivation to become successful learners. Even among those who press on to achieve success later in life, the emotional scars of those troubled years do not fade.

Karl was a frequent no-show at his two sons' school plays and other activities. A successful corporate consultant, he found it difficult to get away from the office at the end of the day and certainly couldn't break away for the midday plays and chorus concerts at the school. He steered clear of parent–child conferences, despite the teachers' efforts to accommodate his schedule.

Karl wanted to be a good father, a responsible parent, but he felt ill at ease and impatient at these school functions. As his wife began to pressure him to come more often, he went dutifully, but his negative, hostile attitude towards his sons' teachers made the conferences uncomfortable for everyone. Finally, his wife told him not to bother.

In a heated exchange of words, he recalled later, he was surprised by his wife's angry accusation that he didn't care about his children's education. His own response surprised him almost as much. His first thoughts weren't about his work or the office or deadlines – or even his children. They were about his feelings: shame, resentment, and anger that had smouldered for more than forty years.

'I walk into a school building, and I can feel my chest get tight,' he explained later. 'It's a place that's up to no good. I had a difficult time in school when I was a kid over stuff I had no control over. What I learned in school was that, in some essential ways that matter to other people, I didn't measure up. Now, as far as I'm concerned, all the kid art on the wall doesn't change the fact that school is a place where kids suffer, and it makes me angry to have to pretend otherwise, to have to sit there and make small talk with teachers who are part of the problem – smug, small-minded, inflexible people who think they're qualified to sit in judgement of children, and in judgement of me as a parent, when I know they're not. It's a sham.'

Never mind that Karl's boys were successful students with talented, enthusiastic teachers. Neither time nor success had dimmed the hurt and anger of those years, and visits to schools forced him to revisit painful memories of his own childhood. When Karl walked into a school building, he was forty-eight going on eight years old.

Whether they have achieved enormous success in life or are struggling to make their way, we hear similar stories from countless men for whom school was a painful endurance test.

This is the struggle we witness in boys who, often by the age of eight, have already disengaged their energy from the task of learning, tuned out of school, and written it off as a place where they can't do anything right. Others achieve but feel the same alienation of spirit. They bide their time and perform satisfactorily, but experience no joy in learning and, like the others, lose the greater potential of these best learning years of their life.

More than two thousand years ago, the Hebrew sage Hillel advised that 'a person too anxious about being shamed cannot learn'. Today many boys face a steady diet of shame and anxiety throughout their primary school years. From it they learn only to feel bad about themselves and to hate the place that makes them feel that way. Emotionally estranged from their life in school, these are boys already in deep trouble before they've even learned to spell the word.

## Michael with Alan: A Boy's-Eye View of School and Teachers

Alan's mother called me to say that he was having a tough year at school. He'd been angry at several teachers, and despite his high IQ, his grades had dropped to an all-time low for him, from As and Bs to Bs and Cs. Furthermore, he had 'hated' school periodically throughout the year – a stronger version of the unhappiness he had expressed occasionally since kindergarten. A school administrator had recommended that Alan be given psychological testing and perhaps some therapy because he seemed, at moments, to be so withdrawn and angry. The administrator told Alan's mother that he was worried that Alan might be depressed. She asked me to provide an independent opinion of her son's situation. Because Alan's family lived far outside Boston, I knew I couldn't be his therapist, but I could review his records and talk with Alan to hear his own views.

I learned later that Alan had been reluctant to talk with me, but he gave no indication of that the day we met. This twelve-year-old with a marvellous smile, freckles, and a wiry athlete's body was an articulate spokesperson for the average boy in school. He was polite and responsive, but from the beginning he grappled with the questions I asked about school. Since teachers had been the focal point of his anger of late, we started there. Which teachers did he like, and which didn't he like?

He remembered his class teacher from two years ago: 'She was just nice, and she had a sense of humour, and she didn't get mad very easily.'

He didn't like his social studies teacher from the year before, he said. She seemed perpetually angry, to hear him describe her, and 'she was always getting mad at me over little things'.

'Like what?'

'Lots of things. Like when I'd come to class without my pencil. Or . . . no . . . I know . . . we had these little assignment books that we had to keep track of on a field trip. We went to a museum, and we were at a fountain outside, and my little book fell in. Stuff like that.'

'Was she that way with other boys and girls in the class?'

'Well, she was harder on boys because they do things, I guess. I don't think she's ever really liked me. We don't get along very well.'

He recalls others who he believes did not like him. One teacher stands out in his mind. Alan was seven and that was the year his slight learning disability in spelling became clear. This particular teacher discouraged him from writing poetry until he could spell better, he says.

'When you have had a teacher who has really liked you, how have you known?'

'Well, they don't get mad at me that easily. Just . . . they're easy to be around. They're like Mr Clarkson . . . He pays attention, and he has more stuff you want to learn about.'

We discuss the 'stuff' Alan likes to learn about and some of his favourite teachers and the qualities he liked about them. There aren't many more. To dig a little deeper, I turn the focus of the questions away from Alan's feelings about himself and ask instead about teachers and boys in general.

'Is it difficult for boys to have all women teachers?'

'They're pretty used to it,' he says of boys.

'Is it easier for boys to have men teachers?'

'Yeah. They understand us more or something. They understand what we're trying to say.'

'What do women have trouble understanding about boys?'

'They don't like to be gotten mad at.'

Alan makes a simple point – that boys don't like being yelled at and yet that makes up a large part of their lives.

I'm reminded of a wise librarian – a woman – who lamented

once: 'Adults feel justified in yelling at boys because they are so "bad" all the time.'

The assumption is that yelling helps, especially in communicating dissatisfaction to boys, and that boys don't suffer from it as much as girls might. That is not my experience. Boys typically don't show that they suffer from yelling because being a boy requires that they do not show it. But it hurts.

I ask Alan what aspects of school he finds most satisfying. Not surprisingly, it is sports.

'I know this may sound stupid, but why are sports so much more satisfying than anything else you do?'

'It's fun. It's something you can get better at by working hard . . . I don't know. You can excel in an area – like if you really like hockey, you can do that. If you really like soccer, you can do that. I look forward to sports every day. It is kind of like a big organized break where you get to *do* stuff.'

'But you're learning in school, aren't you?'

'Yeah, but running around is better than sitting. I have all these sitting classes all morning, and then I get to stand in art and in science when we go outside.'

He talks some more about classes he likes – not many – and those he doesn't like, and it is clear that, whatever sophisticated planning has gone into curriculum design at Alan's school, the distinction between a good class and a bad class, from his point of view, has a lot to do with the freedom it offers to stand up and walk around.

In his weary review of life at school, Alan has described the nature of the problem so many boys have there. In essence, they sit all morning, and they have to keep track of those little books and not drop them in the water. And if they can't move around, they feel trapped and turned off to anything the teacher might have to offer.

In my previous experience working with children on the South Side of Chicago, I saw so many boys whose education had already been so scarred by the time they were seven that they were truly done with schools – and as good as done for in life because the gangs were ready to snap them up. And yet, when school is not like this, not 'charged' with tension the way their family lives and neighbourhoods are, it becomes a 'neutral' place where children can feel their own success. To the extent that a child is able to hook on to school as a place of achievement and support, school becomes a lifeline.

The interesting thing about Alan is that the same principle applies, even though he comes from a caring, educated, and affluent family. If school becomes a negatively 'charged' environment, he will come to dislike it as a place where his personal achievement simply doesn't count for much. In this setting a boy's experience of school is as a thorn among roses; he is a different, lesser, and sometimes frowned-upon presence, and he knows it. Alan is at that point now, and he is at risk for taking his soul out of school.

## The 'Differentness' of Boys: When Assets Become Liabilities

Jane mused on the differences she had observed in the way that ten-year-old boys and girls worked on projects in her industrial arts class. Every year, as the first project of the year, she offered the children their choice of working on a model bridge or a catapult. Typically, the girls chose to build the bridge and set about organizing the group effort very cooperatively, listening to one another's ideas, drawing rough sketches, and then working together to carefully construct the bridge. The boys, she said, typically chose the catapult, but their work didn't begin cooperatively. Instead, each boy would hurry off to throw together his own best idea for a catapult that could hurl a rock; there was no sharing or listening to one another's ideas. They sprawled across floor, chairs, and tables; lunged at materials; and yelped each time they stabbed themselves with pencils or got stung by a backfiring rubber band. In the rush, they usually built a catapult that didn't work, but they seemed unfazed by the setback. As they experimented with failure and the better catapults emerged in competition, the group began to coalesce as well, with each boy learning from the others' mistakes and the boys eventually cooperating to produce the best-of-all catapult.

It would be easy to criticize the boys for the predictable failure of their hurried and flawed first-round catapults, easy to shame them by comparing their rambunctious work style to the calmer, more efficient style of the girls. But this teacher saw something different. In addition to the well-executed planning and building by the groups of girls, she recognized in the boys a risk-taking energy and an enthusiasm that were of real value to the class.

Most educators – like Ms Alvarez in her kindergarten class – strive to make school a place where boys and girls alike can grow to be responsible, caring individuals and enthusiastic learners. But we know that there are days when even caring teachers like Ms Alvarez, who believes absolutely in the potential of each of her boys, wishes that boys weren't so different or that the parents of boys raised them differently; days when parents raising just girls wish the same thing; and days when parents raising girls *and* boys are saying to one another, 'You know, they *really are different!*'

The 'differentness' of boys is not inherently bad, but it does present a challenge to teachers, to the school culture, and to boys themselves.

Boys generally are an active lot, and often impulsive. Their energy is contagious, especially among other boys, and that physical energy can translate into a kind of psychological boldness. They often are the risk takers, seemingly oblivious to the potential hurt of a fall or sting of a reprimand. Whether their choices might eventually prove to be brave or reckless, boys are often in the middle of an action before they consider the consequences.

Boys are direct; they act and speak in simple terms. Their more slowly developing language skills are apparent in their often blunt and unsophisticated humour or their preference for action over negotiation – grabbing the box of crayons rather than negotiating a turn for using them. Boys' emotional immaturity allows them to celebrate themselves unabashedly, strutting, boasting, clamouring to be noticed. They're not terribly concerned about pleasing others. When the fabled little boy declared that the emperor wore no clothes, he spoke with the candour characteristic of boys.

Boys' need to feel competent and empowered leads them to express a keen power-based, action-oriented sense of justice, fairness, good and evil. Spiderman, Batman, Ninja Turtles – heroic action figures dominate the landscape of young boys because they want so much to be seen in heroic proportions – to be big instead of small, to have power in the world instead of the role of powerless child, and to be the arbiter of right and wrong rather than a negotiator or an observer.

Boys and girls alike bring energy, curiosity, and a desire for competence to their lives at school, but those gifts come wrapped in gender patterns that are recognizably different, as teachers and parents so frequently tell us. How many playful, imaginative girls will use their energies to fashion guns out of twigs or toast? How many playful, imaginative boys will use their energies to pretend they're beautiful, wild horses running across the plains?

The average boy's gifts are wrapped in high activity, impulsivity, and physicality – boy power – and the value of these gifts depends on the teacher, the boy, and the moment. These qualities serve boys beautifully in the playground, where there is room and respect for bold strokes of action and impulse. In the classroom, however, alongside girls – who are typically more organized, cooperative, and accomplished school learners – those 'boy qualities' quickly turn from assets to liabilities. Even among those who aren't considered problem boys, many teachers identify the ordinary boy pattern of activity, attitudes, and behaviours as something that must be overcome for a boy to succeed in school.

## Gender Differences: Worlds Apart in a Classroom Together

Two important developmental distinctions define boys' readiness for the tasks of primary school and help explain their generally inferior performance compared with girls. First, boys mature more slowly than girls. Second, boys are more active and slower to develop impulse control than girls. This developmental pace appears largely biological, influenced by parents and teachers only to the extent that they provide support for that growth or fail to do so. Current scientific thinking about the nature–nurture debate highlights the inextricable link between biology and experience.[2] A boy's early ease with throwing a ball or climbing may begin with developmental readiness, but his skill and interest grow when he finds encouragement for his hobby at home. A girl's greater ease with reading and language also appears to begin with an early neurological advantage, enhanced when she is encouraged in her reading habit. These influences – some biological, some cultural – combine to nurture a child's developmental progress. Nurture and nature cannot be separated.

The fact that girls mature earlier than boys means that they frequently achieve cognitive milestones at younger ages.[3] They generally learn names for things sooner, such as the names of colours, and how to do simple counting. Because of this, girls are more ready when, in the first year at school, teachers commence with the first serious attempts to teach reading. The fact that many boys start out behind girls in these pre-reading skills means that boys are more likely to be miscategorized as learning disabled in the early years of school.

In terms of activity level – and by this we mean motor activity, as in moving one's body around while running or walking – not many studies find sex differences until pre-school. Or put slightly differently, gender differences in activity level between boys and girls become more pronounced as children approach school age. Recent research suggests that the main differences between boys and girls occur in social interaction. Boys in a group behave quite differently than boys alone, and boys are stimulated by the challenges presented by other boys. As with any gender difference, there is a lot of overlap between the populations of boys and girls: thus, there are girls who are more active than many boys. But by school age, the average boy in a classroom is more active than about three-quarters of the girls, and the most active children in the class are very likely to be boys.[4] And even the more active girls don't seem to express their energy in the unrestrained way more characteristic of boys.

When we examine extremes of activity – hyperactivity, for instance – the sex differences become even greater.[5] Most research finds that two to four times as many boys are diagnosed with attention deficit–hyperactive disorder (ADHD) as are girls. For example, in a study of 8,258 children aged five to eleven in Tennessee, all students in sixteen schools in one heterogeneous county, almost 4 per cent of boys were diagnosed with the hyperactive-impulsive variety of ADD, whereas this was true for less than 1 per cent of girls. So every class of at least twenty-five students is likely to find itself with one hyperactive boy.

The profile of boys as troubled learners stands out clearly to anyone who spends any time in primary schools. As a seven-year-old girl commented ruefully one day: 'Why are the bad kids always boys?' Our own experience is mirrored in research that indicates that a boy is four times more likely to be referred to a school psychologist than is a girl.

Some researchers have suggested that the preponderance of boys among the learning disabled (60 to 80 per cent of learning disabilities occur in boys) would disappear if eight-year-old boys were taught in classes with six-year-old girls, because learning disabilities are diagnosed based on assessment of reading ability at a certain age compared with intellectual potential (IQ test results) at the same age. For decades, the Ethical Culture School in New York admitted five-year-old girls and six-year-old boys to kindergarten, because of the developmental disparity between boys and girls. The school eventually modified the practice because of the protests of that minority of parents who had very school-ready five-year-olds, but believes that the underlying wisdom of the earlier policy still holds. In the United States, the private Waldorf Schools (similar to Montessori schools in the UK), with an arts-based curriculum, don't even teach reading in the first few years. Why? A Waldorf headmaster once told us: 'If you start teaching it any earlier, it looks as if all your boys have reading disabilities.'

In short, the early age at which we teach reading favours girls, on average, and puts boys at a disadvantage. As a consequence, boys, on average, do not feel as able or as valued as the girls in the central learning tasks of primary school. In therapy with boys, we frequently hear them describe themselves as losers or failures, even when they are developing skills at a pace that is normal for boys their age. Boys who struggle with genuine learning disabilities face even greater obstacles to school success, and their disheartening struggle as students easily comes to define their lives as boys.

## Dan with Joe: A Paper Trail of Trouble to Come

In her phone call, Joe's mum tells me that she and her husband are worried about Joe. He has been having trouble in school and doesn't seem very happy. Lately, he has complained of stomach aches in the morning and begs to stay home. Joe is only six years old. It is April, and he is nearing the end of his first year at school. I am going to meet him in about an hour. I have his file open before me, and I read it while I eat my lunch. The folder contains some reports from his class teacher of that year and kindergarten teachers as well as a few pages of pre-school reports. It also has the completed question-naires that his parents mailed back to me. These contain information about his medical history, which I will include in my report of the neuropsychological evaluation I am about to perform. I find myself mentally writing the report while I read over the information.

Joe is the product of a full-term birth by Caesarean section. He weighed seven pounds seven ounces. His five-minute APGAR was a 9. Medical history is remarkable for frequent ear infections requiring prophylactic antibiotics between the ages of six and eighteen months.

The questionnaires also tell me about Joe's early development and behaviour at home and school. There is quite a bit of information. Putting together a diagnostic report always reminds me of doing a puzzle. The pieces come from different sources – parents, teachers, physicians – and the precise significance of each piece isn't entirely clear. Sometimes a boy's problems are fairly straightforward: the big picture is clear before you start, and you can see easily how the pieces fit. But with Joe, as with many boys, we're not sure what that big picture is.

Joe's mother reports that there were some areas in which his development lagged behind peers. Although he walked early, Joe did not speak until he was two, which he reportedly found very frustrating. He initially had quite a bit of difficulty separating from his mother at pre-school.

When I read the comments from his teachers, I sense that they like Joe. I am familiar with the school he attends, and over the years I have been uniformly impressed with the teaching staff. Because of this, I pay special attention to what the teachers have to say. I have arranged to call Joe's teacher at home tonight. For the purposes of diagnosis, the observations of a good teacher are invaluable.

By teacher report, Joe has difficulty working independently, and his attention to task is described as 'variable'. Maths skills are developing more rapidly than reading skills. Since February Joe has been in a language arts group, where he is beginning to acquire basic information about how letters and sounds go together. This work is not easy for Joe, but he has been making some progress, especially lately. Socially, he tends to keep to himself or interact with a small group of friends.

Although I haven't even seen Joe yet, I find myself thinking about his not-too-rosy prognosis. I know that my pessimism is due in part to my interaction with Alex, a fifteen-year-old boy who left my office a half hour ago. This was a boy who had been ground down by his years in school. He told me as much.

Alex thought of himself as 'stupid'. 'I can't do the work,' he told me. But his test scores told a different story. Alex wasn't stupid at all. He had just fallen further behind the pack each year, and now, like a tired marathon runner, he had pulled off the road. I couldn't help thinking that some day Joe would look like this – that in a few years a fifteen-year-old Joe would be sitting in my office, his folder as fat as Alex's.

Alex had been evaluated every three years since he was six, and his folder contained stacks of report cards, IQ scores, and reading comprehension test results. I dutifully added more paper to his file. It is part of my job. Parents, teachers, and special education directors all want to know the 'scores' – as if they would provide some magical insight into what is wrong, as if they were like the 'scores' one would get from a biopsy.

My mood is also fuelled by a conversation I had with a colleague a few weeks ago. We were talking about how busy we were and how many reports we had to write. I had been asking him how much detail he put into the 'Background and Medical History' section of his reports. For kids with thick folders, reading the information and summarizing it can be very time consuming. I found that his approach was very similar to mine; he had no shortcuts to offer. But then he said something tongue in cheek that contained too much brutal truth to laugh at: 'We probably shouldn't waste the time because the reports really all say the same thing: "Kid has trouble learning to read in his first year; starts to hate school; his self-esteem goes to hell; and when he's a teenager, he's pissed off or taking drugs." ' This is what we see.

Young Joe will walk through my door in a few minutes, and so I try to shake off my pessimism. I want to be able to see him separate from this apocalyptic vision. Like my colleague, I have read hundreds of these thick folders, and too many of them read this way. It is what I try to communicate in my meetings with parents and teachers, what I try to emphasize amid the ten or more pages of test scores, interpretation, and recommendations:

The most important thing to remember, the guiding principle, is to try to keep your son's self-esteem intact while he is in school. That is the real risk to his success and to his mental health. Once he's out of school, the world will be different. He'll find a niche where the fact that he can't spell well, or didn't read until he was eight, won't matter. But if he starts to hate himself because he isn't good at schoolwork, he'll fall into a hole that he'll be digging himself out of for the rest of his life.

## Wild Animals and Entitled Princes: Destructive Boy Archetypes

Teachers and parents are in a position to help boys find success at school, help them avoid the black hole of failure or help them get out of it, but only if they see that a boy is in need. Too often, a stereotyped view of boys becomes a barrier to meaningful responses to them in school.

'We expect too much of boys – and we don't expect enough,' said a teacher reflecting on the way our culture's view of boys often scrambles the messages they get from teachers and parents. 'On the one hand, we expect them to do things they're developmentally not ready to do and to be tough "little men" when they're really just little boys who still need good-bye hugs and affection. On the other hand, when they behave in cruel or thoughtless ways, we say, "Oh, boys will be boys," and don't hold them accountable – we let them off the hook over issues of respect and consideration for others.'

There are common views of boys that adversely influence how they are treated in school. We tend to regard them as wild animals out of control, dumb giants incapable of responsible behaviour, or entitled princes who aren't held accountable to the same moral standards as the rest of us.

Plato said that, of 'all wild beasts, the most difficult to manage' were boys. The trouble with this image as a classroom management philosophy is that it sets us up to view a boy's energy and activity as threatening, and we feel justified in responding with harsh action, correcting or reprimanding him more than necessary, or becoming ferociously controlling and determined to 'whip him into shape'. A boy's most common response to controlling behaviour is to *not* be controlled – to become confrontational or defiant.

Excusing boys as dim-witted giants might seem less harsh, but it is no less hurtful. This casts boys as physically capable but intellectually out to lunch – all action, no brains. When we view boys as intrinsically flawed, we expect less of them as learners, we feel justified in excusing or making allowances for inappropriate behaviour, and we may fail to establish the reasonable limits and expectations they need and are capable of meeting.

When we view boys as entitled princes, we assume that a boy's gender or talents entitle him to a future of leadership, success, and power; we excuse him from the labour of learning to live and work wisely with others; we protect him from the consequences of acting badly; and we hold him to a different, lesser standard of moral accountability in his actions and behaviour towards others.

When our responses are distorted by these stereotypes, boys suffer for it. If the school culture or teachers react to a boy in ways that suggest they are fearful of him, baffled by him, or uncomfortable with him, then he assumes that he is fearsome and somehow not quite right, even unlovable. If they excuse him from reasonable childhood expectations on the grounds that he is a man in the making and need not be bothered, then lessons of empathy and accountability are replaced by a creed of entitlement void of responsibility.

Boys who feel feared, discounted, or unduly revered in school suffer a kind of emotional isolation that only intensifies their own fears, feelings of unworthiness, or arrogant expectations of entitlement. In the early school years, these stereotypes not only create a shallow template for understanding boys and responding to them, they also create negative expectations at an age when a child reads unconscious expectations more easily than openly expressed ones and takes them to heart.

These stereotypes shortchange boys because they keep teachers and other adults from recognizing a boy's inner life and responding to him in meaningful ways. This happens in every realm of a boy's life to some degree, but it is particularly destructive in the school environment because so much of a boy's experience in school is shaped by the quality of his relationship with teachers.

## When Boy Activity Is Misinterpreted, Mismanaged

The crisis call came about three weeks into the new school year at a small co-ed public school in a suburb of Boston. 'Help! We have some of our worst ten-year-olds ever,' the desperate school director said. She rattled off a list of concerns. It was a small school, with only one class for each age group, and in our subsequent discussion with teachers, we learned that, due to a series of departures and arrivals of new students, the school had ended up with an extremely boy-heavy class of ten-year-olds: fourteen boys and six girls. The tenor of the class seemed more confrontational than it ever had felt before, and it was sometimes hard to maintain control. Said one teacher: 'It's just not nearly as *nice*.'

Clearly, this was the worst class of children this age that these teachers had ever experienced at this school, but was it a *bad* class, or was it just not like the others? As we explored the complaints and concerns, it became clear that *worst* meant was that it was very boy-flavoured. Nothing extreme – no threats or intimidation, no fistfights or vandalism – just an ordinary level of ten-year-old boy energy that expresses itself in greater activity than does ten-year-old girl energy. And that was the crux of the problem. The preponderance of boys in the class had introduced a new standard that made the teachers uncomfortable. The students picked up on that discomfort and reflected it back in their own behaviour towards one another, creating a climate of tension and tempers in the classroom.

Schools do need to maintain order, and boys can be difficult. This can be problematic, and every educator has to find a philosophical position with respect to the kind of disruption and disorder associated with the presence of boys. A teacher has to deal with boys' physical activity and disruption without always interpreting this behaviour as malevolent or animalistic, because boys turn to activity as an outlet for a host of emotions – especially when their feelings outstrip their language skills or other options.

### Music Room Mêlée Hits Sour Note of Aggression

At a small, private co-ed school in the north-east of America, we worked with administrators and teachers during the first year after the formerly all-girls school was opened to boys.

Traditionally, during the lunch hour the girls had eaten their lunch and then sat in the spacious cafeteria to talk. With the first wave of boys into the school, it became apparent that boy style was to eat lunch in ten minutes and immediately go outside. This worked fine during the autumn months, when the weather and lunchtime staffing allowed for the supervised outdoor break. When winter came, the boys and supervising staff took over the gym instead, but when faculty members balked at the lunchtime break assignment, the gym was closed.

A couple of days later, several boys took an unauthorized and unruly after-lunch run through the building, damaging some instruments in the music room.

Before talking with the boys and getting the facts straight about the extent of the damage, we heard two different tales of destruction. One was from the faculty members who, truth be told, weren't happy about the presence of boys at their school. The other report came from teachers who supported the co-ed environment.

The first version, told and retold by many of the unhappiest teachers, insisted that the boys had wilfully set about to vandalize the music room and did so to the tune of $2,000 in broken instruments.

The second version held that, after a short but energizing lunch, the boys had engaged in a spontaneous game of tag, used poor judgement in racing through the music room, and accidentally bumped three instruments. Teachers who told this version prefaced it with the opinion that school officials had screwed up in the first place by closing the gym and eliminating an acceptable space for boys – or anyone – to work off the excess energy after a morning of sitting in classes.

After discussing the matter with the boys themselves, we judged the second version to be the more accurate. Clearly, the boys' behaviour was unacceptable, and they were held accountable, but it was not an act of wilful aggression. Nor was it abnormal, antisocial, or fraught with violent psychological undertones. But it's easy to understand how the image of boys as rampaging vandals (the wild-animal stereotype) could spring to the minds of those who were predisposed to view the boy presence at their school as a negative. Any school day is full of similar, though less dramatic, misunderstandings regarding boys' motivations.

The emotional turmoil a boy feels – shame, anger, sadness – and his difficulty expressing those feelings may contribute to high activity and impulsiveness. A usually well-behaved eight-year-old boy described being reprimanded by his teacher for climbing a fence in an outdoor play area in the minutes after his team lost the day's football game. Later, when the teacher sat the boy down to discuss consequences, the embarrassed boy confessed that he'd been on the verge of tears, but to avoid crying in front of his classmates, he had run to the fence and climbed it.

A friend, forty-three, recalled that, when he was young, he had an obsessional habit of counting the letters of words and sorting them into groups. His teachers, family, and friends considered this an odd piece of behaviour but let him be. He never admitted to any of them that he immersed himself in this diversion to keep himself from crying in front of his classmates at school when he was upset. Here was a young boy with an impressive facility with words who chose to hide behind them, literally, rather than use them to express his emotional distress and his need for comfort. When boy activity is misinterpreted as aggression or wilfulness, a boy is punished twice: once for the 'wilful' act and again in the loss of opportunity to reflect on the emotional dimension of the moment. In our work in schools, we often serve an 'undercover' role in helping teachers and boys find a channel for communication that is free from the static of misunderstanding.

## Michael with John, Norman: Negativity as a Cover

In my school consultation work, I often try *not* to see a boy who is struggling with the school environment. I prefer to work through his teachers and his parents, helping them to understand the issues without labelling the boy as a 'patient' or a 'problem'. My meeting with a boy may alarm him or make him feel bad about himself, no matter how kind I am. This effect is called 'labelling', and mental health professionals have always been aware of the simple and potentially negative impact of seeing a child for a diagnostic session. Perhaps the effect is diminished a bit these days, because so many children are seen and tested, but it is always a bit shocking for a child to have to see a psychologist.

A teacher talked to me early in the new school year, already sensing trouble ahead for a seven-year-old boy in her class. John was relentlessly negative about school. In his first conversation with the teacher, he made his position clear. 'I don't want to go to school. No one plays with me. No one likes me,' he said. He had a whole set of adult-like mechanisms that were a bit baffling for the teacher because they were so confrontational and precocious: sarcasm, irony, trying to 'dis' things or shrug them off. When John called a boy in his class an idiot, his teacher took him out into the hall to speak with him privately.

'He *is* an idiot,' John snapped at her defiantly. 'Do you think if he had any brains he'd keep coming here every day?' But even as John lashed out with his angry words, she could see he was terrified to be standing in the hall having this confrontation with her.

In reviewing John's history with his teacher, I saw that John's reading skills were very poor. He had been the only total non-reader at the beginning of his first year at school, and he was still the least capable reader a year later when he was seven. Without any question, his life at school had become a series of traumas for him, in which he experienced his self-esteem as being attacked daily. He was aware that he lagged behind in reading and viewed himself as a loser.

John's situation required a change in strategy. He didn't appear to have a learning disability, but his slower developmental pace was going to keep him behind the pack. Indeed, because he was close enough to the group, the teacher had not wanted to single him out by praising his efforts too obviously or specifically. When John felt bad about reading, he felt bad about himself and exported that bad feeling in critical comments and defiant behaviour. The teacher and I decided that she needed to let John know that she understood his feelings and his need, that she needed to acknowledge his daily efforts and give him a lot of positive feedback. This the teacher did, and very soon she reported back that, when she praised John on his reading effort, he smiled more and his negative banter faded out. And I faded out as a consultant as well. John didn't need to have a meeting with a psychologist. That would simply have complicated his already cloudy feelings.

As John began to feel better about himself as a reader, he felt better about a lot of things. John's reading skills developed slowly over time, but his behaviour improved dramatically and quickly. He could cope with being a slow reader, but not with a vision of himself as a loser. With his teacher helping him feel competent and competitive – still in the game – John responded with a more positive attitude towards his work and his classmates. More confident of his potential for success, he no longer felt diminished or threatened by the success of others.

Norman was another boy I was consulted about but with whom I never met. Norman, a seven-year-old, was consistently negative and loud. If someone said he or she had been to the beach for a holiday, Norman would yell out, 'The beach sucks.' His teachers dreaded the new school year with him. They experienced him as a thin-skinned, self-centred, thoughtless little boy who expected to dominate his environment and everyone in it. Behaviour like Norman's can be very hard to sympathize with, but I suggested to the teachers that, instead of responding to him as a negative person, they could help him 'externalize' that negativity – define it as something separate from himself – and encourage him to rise up and defeat it.

This is a classic 'narrative therapy' technique in which, instead of locating the problem inside the boy, you place the problem outside the boy and stand at his shoulder, allied with him in his struggle against it. When Norman acted in those negative ways, for instance, I encouraged his teacher to say to him, 'I see that your bad mood has a grip on you today.' Or to say, when he was having a great day, 'How did you keep your bad mood from ruining your day at school today?' 'You must have tricked it. How did you do that?'

This was a boy who wanted to feel good about himself and his life, but he had felt powerless in the face of his negative feelings. His teachers, rather than seeing him as a negative boy, saw him as fighting an enemy that was trying to ruin his school experience. Every boy likes to fight an enemy; every boy likes to feel that he has allies. Norman's teacher was able to escape the trap of becoming Norman's enemy or seeing Norman as an entitled prince who was going to ruin her class for a year. It is particularly a boy thing to lead with this kind of negativity; many more boys do it in school than do girls. It is a challenge for every teacher to meet boy negativity with finesse and a deft response.

Despite the fact that boys are more active and impulsive than girls in the early years and that there appears to be some biological basis for this, we should remember that activity and impulsivity are also produced by other forces. We can all remember a time when we've been very anxious – waiting for the results of a medical test, pacing the floor while a loved one was undergoing an operation, standing in front of a large audience, or meeting some very important person for the first time – and remember how this anxiety was translated into jitteriness and pacing or talking without thinking. Or think of a baby pumping his arms and legs while he cries; at young ages there is a direct connection between the centres of emotion and the brain's control centre for movement, the motor cortex – and the infant's movements are a direct window on his emotional state.[6]

Similar principles are at work in all of us. We know that ease with verbal expression improves impulse control. So does emotional understanding, or being able to be conscious of your emotions and the reasons why you feel a certain way. When this literacy is absent, the emotions tend to be expressed through movement or action.

This developmental lack of ease with verbal expression, combined with the cultural edict against talking about feelings, channels boys' emotional energy into action. When boys are excited and happy, they often get loud and physical: they shout, they jump, they run, they push and shove one another around, they run it off. But when the emotions are painful, a good run isn't good enough. Physical activity can relieve some stress, but it doesn't eliminate the source of it, and for that reason, physical activity – whether it's running laps or punching a hole through the wall – isn't enough. It discharges the energy around the feeling but not the feeling itself. It lets off steam but doesn't turn off the burner under this emotional pressure cooker.

When school is not a good fit for a boy, when his normal expressions of energy and action routinely meet with negative responses from teachers and classmates, he stews in feelings of failure – feelings of sadness, shame, and anger, which can be very hard to detect beneath that brash exterior. Unable to 'talk out' the emotional pressure, boys typically act out through verbal or physical aggression that walls them off emotionally from others, straining or severing emotional connections to the people and circumstances they find painful. And the worse a boy behaves, the more he invites negative reactions from teachers and other adults.

## Medicating Boyhood: A Question of Culture, Philosophy

We can't discuss boys' compulsivity without talking about its most extreme form. For many years boys who were extremely distractible or extremely active were considered wilful, misbehaved, morally deficient, oppositional, or lazy. But in the past twenty years, with advances in the diagnosis and treatment of attention deficit disorder (ADD) and attention deficit–hyperactive disorder (ADHD), this litany of harsh, judgemental descriptors has dropped from use among teachers and in schools. Even without medication, such boys have found their situation vastly improved; there is now much greater empathy and understanding for boys who struggle to pay attention or to sit calmly and who have trouble understanding what everyone else gets with greater ease.

Over the years we have worked with many, many boys who suffer from ADD or ADHD and whose lives have been transformed through treatment with Ritalin or other drugs like Adderad. However, as the number of boys taking Ritalin (the drug of choice for treatment of ADD) has topped 1 million in the United States – tripling from 1990 to 1995 alone – we have begun to see an even more frantic new version of the old view of a boy as someone who needs 'fixing'.[7] In this fix-frenzied spirit of the times, ADD/ADHD is the explanation of choice for any boys who have trouble paying attention, and with that explanation comes the willingness – even an eagerness, on the part of some adults – to medicate boys, not just to make them clinically 'better', but to make them *better boys*. They want a boy who makes As instead of Bs, a boy who can focus on the seriousness of building his future rather than the frivolous pursuits of the afternoon. They want a boy who always listens up when he's told to do something, a boy who reliably remembers instead of forgets.

Many thoughtful parents with genuine concerns about whether their son 'has ADD' ask us, 'How do you tell?' After all, the list of symptoms of ADD or ADHD is identical to the list of complaints most parents have about most children at least some of the time: 'fidgets or squirms in seat, loses things, doesn't seem to listen when spoken to directly, interrupts or intrudes on others, has difficulty playing quietly'.[8] There is no simple answer to this question, and it is not even the best first question to ask. Attention problems don't generally show themselves in the same way as a typical medical condition. ADD isn't like the chicken pox; the question isn't 'Does he have it, or does he not?' There are gradations of ADD severity, and many other factors about the boy's personality, intellectual abilities, and environment will affect how problematic ADD is for him. Two boys could have the same 'degree' of ADD and be affected by it very differently.

All boys fit somewhere on a spectrum of distractibility, impulsivity, and hyperactivity. The fact that they are more physically restless and impulsive than girls makes many more boys than girls 'look' ADHD.

That leaves you with the question, which boy is just 'boy' and which boy is ADHD? How you answer that question and how you structure the environment around such a boy depends a lot on your training, the flexibility of the educational environment, and your view of boys. When statistics tell us that 20 per cent of the boy population must be medicated to 'fit' in their school environment, then clearly we have not, as a culture, accepted either the biological nature of boys or the kind of boys that we, as a culture, are training them to be. We find in our work with schools and families that ADD/ADHD has added a new opportunity for turning away from the inner life of a boy, a new detour away from more complex issues of a boy's emotional life, of parenting issues and teaching styles, in favour of a drug that offers the promise of quick improvement.

Parents can fall into this trap as easily as can teachers and educators, like the parents of eight-year-old Evan, who they believed was 'impulsive' because he sometimes didn't think carefully about a move when he was playing chess. Not a lot of eight-year-old boys could even sit through a whole game of chess. More typical was the case of the mother who said that her son had thrown a lamp at her and she thought he probably had ADD. When asked what she had done about the lamp incident, it became clear that she had done nothing and, what's more, that she rarely set any firm limits on her son's behaviour. It would be hard to tell if he had ADD until more active parenting was in place.

The parents of a sixteen-year-old boy in therapy, Mark, asked for an ADD work-up (diagnostic evaluation) because his grades had slipped and they were wondering about his 'organizational skills'. This boy was a highly motivated achiever. Mark studied very hard, sometimes late into the evening. He also wanted to excel at sports and usually had practice every day after school and a game at the weekend. He was also a good guitarist and had just started a rock band with some of his friends. As you can imagine, Mark didn't sleep much. When his parents made the request for the ADD evaluation, we felt that the only responsible reply was to suggest that we consider that option once they could demonstrate that he was getting close to eight hours of sleep every night.

Last, there are boys with other psychological conditions that get mislabelled as ADD. We have seen cases in which a parent or teacher wants us to check for ADD because a boy is having trouble concentrating and we find other factors that would clearly disrupt a boy's train of thought in maths class: there was a boy whose best friend had recently tested HIV-positive, a boy whose father had died of cancer with a strong genetic link, and a boy new to a school who was being unmercifully teased. These are fairly extreme cases, but they point out that, when thinking about ADD and normal boy behaviour, the first question to ask is, 'What are the reasonable expectations for a boy his age, and are there any plausible non-medical explanations for his behaviour?' Plausible explanations may include family and parenting issues or an inability to fit in for a boy in school, in the match of either teacher, school culture, or overall expectations.

Mitch Williams, a former major league baseball player who had the affectionate nickname of 'Wild Thing', once told a sportswriter that, when he was a kid, his parents had been told that he was hyperactive, that he had ADD. The writer asked, 'Did they put you on medication?' 'No,' Williams replied, 'my dad bought a farm.' Williams's father had a perspective that worked in his son's favour. He gave the boy an environment where his activity level did not present a problem.

We're not suggesting that all parents of active boys should move to the country, but only that it is important to think about the boy and his environment as a package. Even very active boys do quite well in a school with a high tolerance for a lot of movement. Alternatively, we have seen ADD-type distractible boys who fare very badly in an 'open' classroom environment because of their organization and attention problems. Children like this tend to need a great deal of structure and do better when they know exactly what is expected of them at all times. We have seen boys whose behaviour suddenly improves when they move to a class with a teacher who likes them and doesn't think they are wilfully bad. We've known boys who became 'normal' overnight when they moved from a school with a very demanding environment in which they were expected to do homework for two or three hours a night to a school with more moderate requirements.

This is not to say that we don't believe that there is a medical condition that makes it very difficult for some people to sit still and pay attention in a minimally stimulating environment. The discovery of Ritalin and other drugs prescribed for ADD has been a lifesaver for them and their families. But in the less clear cases – and these are the majority – in our experience it is evident that most of what is being called ADD today would not have been called ADD fifteen or twenty years ago and that much of it falls within the normal range of boy behaviour. We think it is very important to pause and think about the whole boy and the environment in which he finds himself before one jumps in with a diagnosis of ADD.

Then the challenge is to find the right combination of school environment, parental support, structure, and medication for boys with classic ADD and ADHD. And that's the challenge for all boys: to find the combination of support, empathy, appropriate structure, and expectations that works for boys, especially boys who are so significantly more distractible than their female classmates, boys whose level of spaciness or distractibility fits in least well in their school environment.

## Boys Will Work for Schools That Work for Boys

When normal boy activity levels and developmental patterns are accommodated in the design of schools, curricula, classrooms, and instructional styles, an entire stratum of 'boy problems' drops from sight. When a boy's experience of belonging at school is greater than his sense of differentness, then the burden of shame, inadequacy, and anger drops away, and he is free to learn.

Any school – co-ed or all-boys – can do this well or do it poorly.

If we look at all schools as laboratories for educational insights and strategies for engaging boys with developmentally appropriate challenges and learning opportunities, here is what we find:

Boys respond to a full range of academic, athletic, and extracurricular opportunities when the school culture supports their involvement. For instance, at an all-boys school, boys fill all the roles – artist, actor, athlete, editor, cook, cheerleader, and cellist – embracing experiences that often go to girls in a co-ed environment.

Boys can achieve a high standard of self-control and discipline in an environment that allows them significant freedom to be physically active. The headmaster of a boys school known for its high standards of conduct noted that running, wrestling, and other benign physical expressions of boy energy are commonplace there during 'downtime' between classes or other quieter activities. Not all boys wrestle whenever they have free time, but it helps every boy that this administrator welcomes a full range of boy behaviour as normal and healthy and creates an environment in which boys feel that acceptance.

Boys benefit from the presence of male teachers and authority figures as role models of academic scholarship, professional commitment, moral as well as athletic leadership, and emotional literacy. The presence of men can have a tremendously calming effect on boys. When boys feel full acceptance – when they feel that their normal developmental skills and behaviour *are* normal and that others perceive them that way – they engage more meaningfully in the learning experience.

These are the qualities that make some boys schools – with their largely male faculty and boy-centred curriculum – particularly effective learning environments for boys. But a more boy-friendly school environment can be created at any school where educators want it to happen. Teachers and headmasters at all-boys and co-ed schools share with us success stories that underscore the power of even small details to transform the school setting for boys and, in so doing, transform boys' experience and behaviour.

One boys school serves students their midmorning snack of milk and chocolate chip cookies outside well into the winter. The stated rationale is that the spot is centrally located on the campus. But the large open space also minimizes the effects of the inevitable bumping and shoving of groups of large boys.

The teacher of a co-ed kindergarten told us about her simple solution to 'the unmanageable-boys problem' that routinely overwhelmed the first two hours of her class each day until the eleven o'clock breaktime. One day, following the morning story time, she turned the children out for an early break before bringing them back in to do class work. The release of physical energy made it much easier for the boys to settle in to work afterwards, and both boys and girls were delighted with the early running-around time.

Other teachers have described rearranging the play areas in their classrooms to accommodate a greater range of boy activity with more open spaces or using the placement of desks as natural speed bumps to help reduce running with less nagging.

A year 4 teacher said she sends fidgety boys or girls on errands in the building for her. She places students who need her physical closeness in desks nearer to hers.

A kindergarten teacher told us how she uses hugs to welcome her students each day and has seen the transformative calming effect of that simple act on the most troubled and disruptive boys in the class. 'It's about communicating what's important to that child,' she explained. 'Kids pick up on how you feel about them as human beings. If they feel respected, if they feel liked and cared for, those boys are a piece of cake. These cold, angry boys melt in your hand because their basic needs are to be loved, cared for, respected. Boys have the same human needs as the girls.'

## Meeting the Challenge of Boy Energy, Boy Potential

History is full of great men who were notable misfits in the school environment. In *The Life and Death of Mahatma Gandhi*, author Robert Payne wrote that Gandhi was 'often boisterous' as a school-boy and that he later described school as 'the most miserable years of his life' and recalled that he 'was never more than a mediocre student[;] . . . he had no aptitude for lessons and rarely appreciated his teachers[;] . . . he had no gift for learning and might have done better if he had never gone to school.'

How can we 'ask more' and 'ask less' of boys in school in ways that respect who they are and each one's potential to grow up to be a decent, caring, successful man in his own way? This is the riddle that schools confront, the knot that schools have to untie every day. It can't be untied with a simple moral argument that concludes boys are 'worse' than girls, nor can it be that boys are wild and must be forcibly civilized.

At our local ice-skating rink, skaters of all ages and expertise are welcome, and so it makes an interesting mix on an average Saturday night. Ice tag – one of boys' favourite activities on the ice – is prohibited. This is a very good rule, a great rule, because if skaters played tag openly, they'd be darting in and out and sometimes going against the orderly flow of skaters, many of them less able, gliding in a single direction around the rink. Or they might disturb those figure skaters who take to the middle of the rink to practise or perform their graceful manoeuvres.

To enforce the ice tag ban, monitors – the equivalent of skating police – patrol the crowded ice rink to guard against unruly behaviour and roust rowdies from the rink. But boys love to play ice tag, and the ban on it only adds to the challenge of doing it so deftly that one avoids getting caught. Occasionally a girl joins in a tag game, but most often it's boys you see darting furtively through the gliding mass of leisurely skaters, clearly loving this marvellously intricate game of stops, starts, and smooth getaways. Inevitably, however, a few are collared by the monitors and escorted off the ice for a time-out. Just as inevitably, they return, refreshed and not at all discouraged from resuming their illicit game of speed and skill.

In a classroom setting, it can be hard to make this kind of allowance for 'defiance within reason', but the bold energy it represents is life-affirming. If you never had that, you'd miss it. It would be a diminished world if everyone skated in precisely the same way around the circle or if the only deviation allowed were to skate graceful, skilful turns in the centre of the ring. On the ice, in our schools, and in our lives, there is a need for some moments of anarchy, for a sprint of the spirit, not only for boys but for us all.

# 3. The High Cost of Harsh Discipline

The difference between coarse and refined abuse is the difference between being bruised by a club and wounded by a poisoned arrow.

Samuel Johnson

Matt's bedroom was down to the bare essentials for a thirteen-year-old boy: bed, desk, and chair. Gone were his favourite posters from the walls, his stereo, his electronic games, his stack of comic books and magazines, the dartboard, and the mini-basketball hoop formerly on his closet door. Gone, too, were privileges he had taken for granted a month ago: after-school time with friends, evening TV programmes, recreational computer time, and phone calls. Matt was in jail in his own home.

The communication in the family was also down to bare bones: 'Have you done your homework yet?' 'No.' 'When are you going to do it?' 'I'll do it. Don't worry about it; just get off my back.' In despair, the family had come to a family therapy session – mother, father, Matt, and his older sister, Mary.

'We've taken away everything there is to take, and things have only gotten worse,' says his mother, her voice tense with worry and exhaustion. She looks over at Matt, who is sitting with his arms folded tightly across his chest, staring straight ahead or down at the floor. Since all their disciplinary efforts had failed, they had come to family therapy, in hopes of a breakthrough. But Matt is having none of it. No one is going to get any information, any reaction from him. He is here under protest, and the bulkhead doors to his emotional life are going to stay shut until this ordeal is over.

His father speaks angrily: 'I've had it with all this coddling. It's gotten us nowhere. His grades have gone downhill; he's a disrespectful, stubborn kid at home; and now we find out he's been cutting classes. And the boys he's hanging out with are all in trouble or maybe even doing drugs.'

Matt glares at his father. The mention of his friends gets under his skin. 'You don't know anything about my friends,' he says through clenched teeth.

'I know enough to know that they are not helping you,' snaps his father.

'You don't know anything about me,' says Matt, his voice rising. 'You're never at home. At least Mum's got a clue. All you do is take stuff away. You think you can hurt me, but I don't give a fuck. You can take it all. Why don't you take the bed, too? I'll sleep on the floor.'

Mary jumps to her father's defence: 'Matt, how can you say things like that? Dad cares about you. How can you be so mean?'

'Oh, Miss Perfect. You don't even have friends. No one calls you. All you do is homework. You're a geek. You're just like Dad.'

Matt's parents have fallen into a common trap: they are trying to control his behaviour using power and coercion instead of love and reason, and all that this is producing is angry counterreaction and more 'acting-out' behaviour.

Only Matt's mother stays out of the conflict in the session. Though at times her anger and frustration show, mostly she is sad. 'This is making us so miserable,' she says. 'He's so unhappy, and so are we. Still, I'm not going to give up on him. I'm sure he feels like a failure, and everything we do makes him feel more like a failure. Sometimes . . . in one of those few rare times when he talks to me, I can see how bad he feels.' She starts to cry, and Mary reaches out to touch her.

Matt gets up from his chair and starts to walk around the room. It is clear that, if he doesn't move around, he is going to start to cry himself. 'Do you know how it feels to be the only fuck-up in this family?' he says. 'Christ, everybody here is perfect. None of *you* have ever had trouble in school!'

At last, here is an opening. Now everyone can see the sadness under Matt's anger. Everyone can see the contempt that he feels for himself and how painful that is for him. It's clear that simply punishing Matt isn't going to bring him back to his family or build his self-respect. Matt is a boy at risk, and he will need some pretty close monitoring and limits in order to be kept away from drugs and out of trouble. Matt's parents will need to work hard to extricate themselves from the pattern of escalating power plays in their attempts to control Matt's behaviour. Stepping up punishment is not the answer for this boy.

Harsh discipline – by which we mean both physical punishment in the form of hitting or spanking and verbal intimidation, which includes belittling, denigrating, scapegoating, and threatening – is not the answer for any child. Not ever. And yet boys are like lightning rods for harsh discipline, much more so than girls. Many parents acknowledge that they use a more severe disciplinary style with their sons than with their daughters. As we saw in chapter 2, teachers who feel put out with the boys in their class more often than with the girls will, as a result, respond to them more harshly. Parents and teachers will often discipline girls reluctantly, conveying an under-tone of regret and even, at times, expressing a concern that a 'sensitive' girl will 'take it too hard'.

Harsh discipline is presumed to help make a man out of a boy: he needs tough treatment to whip him into shape. The assumption is that boys are impervious to subtle suggestion and more resistant to abuse. This gender split reflects our underlying cultural belief that boys are made of 'different stuff' than girls. When it comes to their capacity for hurt and anger, this assumption is not true. If you are excessively cutting, unfair, or physically and verbally abusive with boys or with girls, they develop powerful, angry defences against the treatment, or they become traumatized. Men who have been hit, shamed, and humiliated as boys take it out on the world.

### Boys on the Receiving End of a Punishing Culture

The Native American Pawnees would prepare young boys for their warrior role by waking them up early and throwing them into the snow. Today, instead of the snowbank, we use harsh discipline, rigid expectations, and the threat of rejection to 'toughen up' a boy.

We impose a 'tyranny of toughness' on boys and men. Whatever else it means to be a boy in our culture, it means that your actions are more likely to be misinterpreted as threatening or disobedient, that you are more likely than the girl next door to be punished or treated harshly. For all of a boy's life, regardless of the nature of his transgressions, he is likely to receive swifter, harsher treatment than a girl would receive, and harsher than reason would justify.

When a man and a woman are convicted of the same crime, the harsher sentence is imposed on the man. The United States Justice Department statistics show that a man convicted of murder is twenty times more likely than a woman convicted of murder to receive the death penalty. In general, prison sentences are longer for men than for women, even when the circumstances of the crimes are comparable.[1]

Judges commit boys to juvenile detention centres more often than they commit girls, even when the offence is the same. For example, in drug offences, the kind most likely to result in detention, boys are 1.5 times more likely than girls to end up in custody.[2]

Interestingly, in research on inequality in punishment between boys and girls in state schools, the gender bias shows clearly, although the findings are couched within the more familiar context of racial discrimination. In a recent survey of administrators of state schools representing more than 25 million children in the United States, researchers found that African-American boys are the group most likely to receive corporal punishment – harsh physical discipline – at school, but for all ethnic groups, boys are much more likely than girls to be disciplined this way. African-American boys are 3.1 times more likely to be hit than African-American girls. And for every one white girl hit, nearly six white boys are hit. An Asian boy is eight times more likely to be hit than an Asian girl.[3]

Researchers also noted that 'it is a misconception to picture corporal punishment as necessarily simply involving a light smack on the posterior.' According to the American National Center for the Study of Corporal Punishment and Alternatives in Schools, corporal punishment is legal in nearly half the states, and it includes: punching, slapping, twisting children's arms, banging their heads on desks, ramming students up against lockers or a wall, kicking, and shaking. Instruments that have been used to inflict corporal punishment include switches, sticks, rods, ropes, wooden paddles, rubber hoses, leather straps and belts, straight pins, plastic baseball bats and arrows, books, and clipboards.

This harsher response towards boys occurs in families as well, where research suggests that, whereas boys are disciplined with corporal punishment somewhat more frequently than are girls, they are also disciplined with greater *severity*. In the 1950s – the days of romanticized Norman Rockwell portraits of family life – surveys showed that 99 per cent of parents used corporal punishment, and in 1985 the figure was still over 90 per cent. Although some research into the gender disparity finds only slightly more boys than girls receiving corporal punishment – with boys being hit 13.3 times a year compared to 11.5 times per year for girls – other findings suggest a greater disparity. Retrospective reports by college students show that 75 to 90 per cent recall having been spanked. A recent survey of more than thirteen thousand residents of Ontario, Canada, found that boys were 50 per cent more likely to be physically abused than were girls. Fathers, in particular, were much more likely to hit a teenage son than a teenage daughter.[4]

Despite a growing outcry against corporal punishment and some decline in its use, it is clear that a great many adults continue to spank, hit, or use threatening or abusive language as a way to exert control or demand compliance from their children – especially boys.

Physical punishment is only half the picture. Harsh or threatening words leave a mark on a child, too, and boys get an earful. Even parents who wouldn't think of striking a child acknowledge that in anger or frustration they say things or impose penalties that are meant to sting in the same way. And all of it does sting in much the same way: the spanking, hitting, smacking, yanking ways that some adults use to show a boy who's boss, as well as the shaming criticism, sarcasm, belittling, and other verbal intimidation or harsh penalties that so many parents use to discipline or direct a boy.

In a study of family interactions among visitors to a shopping centre, researchers noted that the most prevalent form of discipline used by parents and other adult supervisers was verbal aggression.[5] Again, boys were more harshly disciplined than girls. Parents and teachers often justify using harsher discipline with a boy for some very simple reasons: it gets his attention. It gets the message of disapproval across in clear, simple terms. And it defines who's boss in the relationship.

Where we see harsh discipline or abuse in boys' lives, we see boys struggle with shame, self-hatred, and anger. Many boys simply shut down emotionally at a young age and stay that way, unable to understand or express their feelings as they move into adult relationships in work, marriage, and family. Deeply shamed, sad, and angry boys don't just get over it with the passage of time. We know because we work with the angry, anxious, or depressed men so many of them grow up to be.

In family counselling with boys and their parents, and in school settings where we often are called in to consult on disciplinary cases, we see this pattern of unnecessarily harsh discipline and communication with boys and the negative or confrontational behaviour with which boys so often respond. When we look more closely into school or home problems *with* boys, or the emotional problems *of* boys, we almost always find excessive or misguided discipline as a contributor to the conflict.

## Boys as a Lightning Rod for Harsh Discipline

Classical psychoanalysis – the couch kind you see caricatured in movies and cartoons – is supposed to guide you through an exploration of the very deepest, darkest corners of your inner conflicts, impulses, desires, and unexpressed anger. It's one way to learn a lot about yourself. But if you really want a tour of your own dark impulses, have children; it, too, will put you in touch with all of your most uncontrolled and regrettable impulses. If you've ever had a rotten day at work, had to haggle with a domineering boss or an unreasonable ex-spouse, or suffered a nerve-racking commute home, then walked into the house to come face-to-face with your son's careless arrogance, you may remember your own four-star rage over something 'minor'. Most of us have been there.

Research shows that harsher, power-oriented punishment is more often triggered by a child's physical misbehaviour – destruction of property and lapses of self-control such as running into a street or hitting a sibling – than it is by other undesirable behaviour, such as whining or speaking inappropriately. Because boys tend to engage in more of this active, high-intensity behaviour than girls, and because they tend to mature more slowly, they also tend to have less self-control than girls of a similar age. A boy's apparent disregard for expectations, rules, and requests for compliance often drives the best-intentioned parents over the edge.

In one survey of parents of four- to ten-year-olds, it was found that physical punishment was most likely to be used in response to 'high-arousal transgressions' like running into the street or breaking something of value. When this group of 'normal' parents was compared to a group of parents who were in treatment because they had a history of physical abuse of their children, it was found that, in these high-arousal situations, normal parents were just as likely as abusive parents to use harsh punishments on their children.[6]

### Michael with Nick: Finding the Trouble in a 'Troublemaker'

Nick had been in and out of detention more often than any other boy in his class at the large co-ed school he attended. When his teacher explained his problems to me, his exasperation with Nick's behaviour was obvious: 'He's fourteen, but he behaves like a twelve-year-old. We had so many reports on how obnoxious he was to girls that we thought, for a time, that it was a case of systematic sexual harassment, but the truth is, he's just incredibly annoying to everyone. He's small, and the girls were teasing him a lot about his size. He doesn't know how to handle it, and he comes back with retorts about their bodies. Furthermore, he has broken more small rules than almost any other boy in the school. We had to suspend him from the bus for three weeks. Last week he threw water all over another boy's books and papers. We suspended him from school for a day. I've talked to him any number of times, and he's always contrite and promises to do better, but within a week, he's back at it again.'

'Why do you want him to see a psychologist?' I replied. 'I'm not sure I'll be able to do anything. What can I do that you haven't done? If he is truly immature, then we'll have to wait for development. Is he working to the standard level of his class?'

'He's a bit erratic and sloppy as a student, but he's very bright. His grades are decent. I just want to know if there is something else going on with him. I don't get any answers when I talk with him.'

Although Nick had come to see me at the teacher's request, he didn't skip the first appointment or require five reminders the way that many boys do. He arrived at my office and sat down respectfully, with an open face and a wish to please.

'Why did your teacher want you to see me?'

'I dunno. I guess 'cause of the thing last week . . . the water thing.'

'What was that?'

'Oh, I got into a water fight the other day and soaked some boy's books. The kid went running to the teacher, and the teacher got all bent out of shape.'

'Was it really a water fight – that is, did the other boy throw water, too?'

'No, he called me a . . . like he said something to me and it pissed me off, and I had a water bottle with me with one of those nozzle tips, so I squirted him with it, but . . . like it went all over his stuff. It wasn't a big deal. Everything would have dried out if he had waited a while.'

'Your teacher tells me you got suspended for that.'

'Yeah.'

'How did your parents react?'

'My mum wasn't too bad about it, not like she was about the bus, but my dad was pretty angry.'

'What happened about the bus?'

'Well, she had to drive me to school and pick me up in the afternoons, and she was pretty steamed.'

'That wasn't the first time that your teacher had called them, was it?'

'The school gets worked up over nothing.'

'Well, tell me about your life these days. Tell me about your mum and your dad. Any big changes in your life? I wonder whether you're angry about something. Do you hate this school? Do you want to get out of here?'

Eventually Nick's story emerges. His father has begun to travel on business in the last year and a half; his mother, who used to work part-time for his father, has taken a new job full-time, so she's no longer there in the afternoon when Nick gets home. While Nick's parents wondered how this might affect him, they also thought he might like it; after all, he was fourteen now and seemed to want more freedom. When they had talked to him about the new situation, Nick seemed okay about being a 'latchkey' kid. He had joked about how much take-out food they were going to be eating. When on the road, Nick's father tried to keep in touch by e-mail.

All the same, the problems had piled up. Nick was now missing deadlines on homework projects. Three times in one week he had gone to friends' homes after school without letting his parents know where he was, even though his mother had made a point of asking him to check in with her at work by phone before leaving the house. Every day brought some new drama, and Nick's mother had lost her characteristic margin of patience and humour. She was yelling at him more than she ever had in her life. She thought that a boy Nick's age should have more direction from his father, and she told her husband so, both in private and in front of Nick.

I asked Nick if he was worried about his parents' marriage.

'Nah . . . not really. I guess my mum's more pissed off at my dad than she was.'

'About his travel?'

'I guess.'

'Are you worried that they are going to get divorced?'

Nick stares at me as if I had opened some drawer I wasn't supposed to look in.

'No . . . I don't know . . . maybe a little.'

'Are you worried that it's partly your fault, because of all the trouble you've been in this year?'

Pause.

'I hadn't thought about it exactly like that, but maybe . . .'

'Do you miss seeing your dad? Do you miss your mum in the afternoons?'

'Well, it's not the same as it was.'

★

And so I embark on the questions that are the province of psychologists – the kinds of questions that educators could ask but often
don't, or when they do ask them, boys don't answer, or they answer
in a way that discourages the adult from asking more. Nick's status
as a pain in the neck has been blamed on immaturity, but to tag him
as immature and write him off as a jerk would be to ignore the
more important issues for Nick and everyone around him. If a
fourteen-year-old girl were the most annoying person in the year,
everyone would want to know what was going on inside her head.
If a boy of the same age is the most annoying person in the year,
many people simply say: 'Jesus, what an irritating kid. He needs
some discipline.' Many adults lack curiosity about the motivations
of boys. Rarely are they reluctant to throw the book at them.

## Boy Activity Pushes Buttons at School and at Home

The same raw energy and activity levels that often put boys at odds
with the school environment create similar tensions at home. A
toddler runs towards the street, a young boy hits another child or
runs recklessly through the house and causes damage, an adolescent
disregards the household rules or defies his parents' expectations.
From the time a boy is old enough to get around freely, many parents
view parenting as a struggle to determine whose will shall prevail.

In jest, a primate researcher who spends her days with apes told
us that, when she returns home to her three active sons, she sometimes
forgets whether she is at home or at the lab.

A father of four young sons recalls one particularly rambunctious
bath-time experience. As the three- and five-year-old boys squealed
and screamed in the tub, creating a 'tidal wave' in and around the
tub, the seven- and nine-year-old boys chased each other, snapping
towels at bare bottoms. As he and his wife took a deep breath and
prepared to enter the fray, he quipped: 'Take a good look, because
someday you're gonna miss this.'

But too many other parents do not appreciate the exuberance.
They find it annoying, insensitive, rude, or disrespectful. As one
father told us: 'I'm sick of seeing spoiled, disrespectful kids. You

have to show them you mean business.' Said another: 'Spanking is getting a bad name, but I think you have to let your son know that you have the ultimate weapon.'

A mother's plaintive note to an advice columnist described the discipline dilemma: 'I'm at my wits' end. I am the single mother of twin boys age 15. They drive me crazy. They don't do as well as they could in school and don't help out at home. I've nagged and yelled until I'm hoarse. I'd put them in a military academy, but can't afford it.'[7]

Either as an attempt to protect their sanity or because they feel that it is the right thing to do, some parents use discipline like a hammer to pound in their message of power: who's got it and who hasn't, who's big and who's small, who's paying for the garage door that the footballs have dented and who's causing the damage.

It has been said that violence is the product of an exhausted mind, and we find that to be true of parents and children alike. As was the case with Nick, boys become emotionally exhausted if they haven't developed the ease of expression that allows them to share their feelings and relieve some of the fear and isolation they feel. They can't 'talk about it' because they don't know how. Instead, they vent their feelings in actions that only serve to further aggravate the parent or teacher.

Not surprisingly, research indicates that harsh disciplinary practices increase significantly when parents feel stressed to begin with. For example, studies of families during the Great Depression found that financial hardship was particularly hard on fathers and that one of the results was harsher discipline – whipping or hitting, for instance – which, incidentally, was also found to be associated with angry and retaliatory child behaviour.[8] The stress of having few resources made the men irritable, and they took it out on their children. The children, in turn, became angry as well, and it showed in more explosive outbursts of their own. Financial, health, and other family concerns continue to be major sources of emotional stress for parents today. Almost always, when parents in therapy tell us about their episodes of poor parenting responses, stress is a factor. When parents carry around their own heavy load, they often take it out on their children.

We all get tired, overwhelmed, and angry at times. That's often at the centre of a boy's imperfect behaviour, and it's at the centre of a parent's imperfect response.

## The Lessons of Fear, Anger, and Weak Conscience

'I don't want to be a "hitting mum",' the mother of a four-year-old boy told us, 'but sometimes it seems like that's the only way I can get my son's attention and make it clear that I mean business.' She described a typical incident in which they were driving home from pre-school, her son in the passenger seat next to her. 'For some reason he was talking really loudly. I asked him to be quiet, but he only got worse. Pretty soon he was screaming as loud as he could. I yelled at him to stop, but he kept ignoring me. He was making me nuts. Finally I leaned over and slapped him. He got real quiet in a hurry.'

There is no doubt that a smack or a slap can stop a child in his tracks. If you spank a young boy, he'll generally stop his misbehaviour, but the quick fix is ineffective over time.

An adult's use of power to push or punish ignores the central emotional component of a boy's attitudes and actions. It fails to make a connection begging to be made. Instead of teaching responsible, moral behaviour, when we use harsh discipline, we pass up that 'teachable moment' – the window of opportunity for helping boys reflect on their actions and learn a better way. It is clear that a boy's experience of discipline is influential in shaping his conscience, for better or for worse.

When adults use these more coercive, power-oriented approaches, even among young boys, we see a greater likelihood that the discipline will backfire: the boy will respond with an aggressive counter-attack to retaliate. A parent may feel the incident is over when the boy stops the offending behaviour. But if the boy feels unfairly assaulted or shamed, the conflict remains alive for him until he resolves the feelings. That may take hours, days, or much longer. The intensity of the harsh discipline will escalate over time. It becomes like an arms race in which the adversaries each work to develop stronger weapons.

The child will resist a parent's rules and values and simply learn the harshness, which defeats a main goal of discipline – to guide a child towards more responsible behaviour.

Instead of fostering the development of internal controls, harsh discipline reinforces the idea that discipline comes from external forces – from parents, headmasters, the police, or the courts. Instead of leading a boy towards better decision making, it prevents him from internalizing the values – and learning the lessons of empathy, respect, and reason – that lead to responsible, moral behaviour and emotional accountability. Those lost links weaken the chain of conscience as a boy moves through life.

Scientists who study how we learn and remember describe two kinds of learning that are involved in the development of conscience – semantic learning and episodic learning.[9]

Semantic learning is the rule-based kind of learning we take away from an experience or from informational resources such as a lecture, an explanation, or a set of directions. Semantic learning gets a real workout in the school setting.

Episodic learning is highly sensory, and we tend to remember the experience in terms of its sound, feel, taste, smell, or visual images. If you spend a leisurely afternoon baking cookies with a child, he's likely to remember the way the heat from the oven fogged the kitchen window or the touch, smell, and taste of the cookies far more vividly than the recipe or the baking process.

Memories of emotional trauma are processed this way, too. Victims of physical or sexual abuse or survivors of disaster often have extremely vivid recollections of the sensory elements of the events surrounding the trauma – the visual images and the smells, textures, lighting, and sound associated with the events.

A thirty-six-year-old man recalls an incident from his early childhood when he and his older brother were whipped by their grandfather. 'I don't remember what we did wrong,' he says, 'but it must have been pretty bad. He took off his belt and came after us. We tried to run away, but he cornered us in my room. I can still see my brother trying to crawl under the bed to get away from him. It's like it happened yesterday. I don't think he hit us that many times, and truthfully, I don't even remember if it hurt all that much. I just remember being scared as hell.'

A parent has enormous power in a child's eyes. From their earliest memory, we tower over children in size and intelligence; we are giants, incredibly competent, and we rule their world. Imagine yourself facing a ten-foot-tall raging man and you have a sense of how the size differential feels to a child. We may explode in an angry tirade that lasts thirty seconds and then turn calmly to answer the telephone. But to a child, especially a young one, that anger thunders across a universe of time and space. In addition to feeling dwarfed by our size and inherent power, a child is further disadvantaged by the fact that he lacks the perspective and life experience to understand what's behind an adult's behaviour. Children are easily frightened by adults and for a long, long time believe what adults tell them, even when adults say irrational or destructive things in moments of anger. Your child does not necessarily know that you're on edge after a bad day. In fact, it is helpful after angry outbursts to tell children that, so they'll know you're not perfect. A child only sees that he displeases you (sometimes innocently).

Harsh disciplinary methods, because of their high intensity, leave their traces in episodic memory. So although a child may remember being punished for something he said or did, what he most remembers is where he was, how afraid he felt, and what his parent's face looked like contorted with anger or disgust. He is much less likely to internalize the intended lesson, especially when it is a general rule such as 'It is important to be nice to other people and not hit them.'

Smacking a four-year-old boy to quiet him will startle him and shame him into either tears or silence. Whatever the momentary gain for the disciplinarian, for the boy the lesson in shame and anger is lasting.


### *Dan with Chuck: Even at Forty, Never Good Enough*

Chuck sits in the same chair that he always takes, the brown one with the rush seat and straight wooden back – the least comfortable chair in my office.

He's talking to me about his past: 'I don't know. I guess my life was like a lot of people's. My dad worked all the time when I was growing up. He eventually became very successful. He started with this little garage – like with one bay. Now it's a chain, but they mostly do only oil changes. I think he has ten stores now. In fact, he just opened a new one. He drives himself pretty hard. He's got plenty of money but doesn't seem to want to slow down. My mum is convinced that he's gonna have a heart attack.'

'Did you ever think about working with him?'

'You mean *for* him. Sure, I thought about it. My sister and I used to work in the shop all the time. I'd sweep up, find parts for the mechanics, whatever. Once in a while one of the guys would let me drain the oil out of an engine or something. It was pretty cool for a kid. These guys were just filthy all the time. And when you'd hang around with them, you'd be covered in oil and dirt in about fifteen seconds. Boy's paradise. My sister would file or answer the phone. She still works for him, does all his purchasing, accounts receivable, everything. She's good at it.'

'Why was she able to do it and not you?'

'She gets along with him a lot better. With me, I was always fucking up, and he'd scream at me, sometimes in front of the guys who worked for him. I think he didn't want them thinking that I was too spoiled. And I realize now how hard it was for him to build his business. He grew up poor, risked everything he had to start the shop. It was like he was in a war or something, and he was always on red alert. Like if he slipped up even a little, some competitor would kill him. Maybe he was right. I don't know. In his mind I guess he figured that he was getting me ready to take over his business – that I had to have that same mentality. But, God, I was just a kid.'

'Do you remember any specific incident where he yelled at you at work?'

'Sure – like it was yesterday. It was the summer I was fifteen and he was letting me help do the stock check. He had two or three shops by then, and there was a lot of stuff to keep track of. And I guess he was always worried about whether he was keeping too much stock or not enough. But anyway, doing stock checking is incredibly boring. You just sit there and count how many cases of oil there are and how many of screen wash. And then maybe you'd count lightbulbs or something. I guess it was hard for me to concentrate. I was constantly losing my place and having to start over. It's a good thing I didn't decide to be an air traffic controller. Anyway, I had been doing this counting pretty much all day. And I kept sneaking off behind the shop to smoke cigarettes with one of the guys who worked for him. He was probably nineteen and had his motorcycle parked back there. I used to ask him a million questions about the engine and how things worked. There was nothing in the world I wanted more than to have a bike like that.

'Anyway, my dad comes around to see how I'm doing and finds me back there. I don't know if he saw me smoking, but he probably did. He had been double-checking my stock counts, and according to him, the ones that he checked were way off. So I started to get this lecture about how parts were money, that it was like there were five-dollar bills in these bins instead of lightbulbs. He got pretty worked up. Maybe business was bad. I don't know. Then he says something like, "You think you're a big man, but let me tell you something. What do you think you're gonna end up like if you can't even do a simple job like counting? Now get back there and do it again – and do it right this time." Then he swats me on the bottom with the clipboard he was carrying.'

The more we talk, the more I find out that this wasn't an isolated incident.

'If I got all Bs, they wanted As. If I got As, then they'd focus on some other thing I'd let slip. So what do I remember? I remember being worried lots of the time. You know, about what they'd do when they saw my report card. I remember trying to figure out ways to cover up or lie about stuff that I had done. In school the teachers used to send home notes or detention slips that parents had to sign. My dad had a weird signature that wasn't too hard to copy, so I worked on that till I had it down pretty well. I caught hell for it once, but I also got away with the forgery lots of times. But I spent a lot of time hiding. I was mostly scared, but I remember trying to straighten out, too. I would usually make a vow in September – you know, like "This year was going to be different – that I'd get good grades, and I would stay on the teacher's good side; that I'd try to follow the rules at home."

'It used to last about a month at most, then something would happen. I wouldn't turn in my homework or I'd smack some kid at break, and then it would be back in the doghouse, and I'd say, "Fuck it, it's not worth it. There is no way that I can do this thing right, no way I can 'do' school or please my parents." Maybe by Christmas I'd give it another shot, but it never worked very well. Sometimes in church I'd get really religious and make a deal with God and promise to do better; then I'd mess up again and figure it just didn't matter: I was going to hell anyway.

'I also remember how sweet it was to be away from there. If I would sleep over at a friend's house, I didn't have to worry about my dad or mum yelling at me about something. But this got me into trouble, too. I started drinking younger than most of the kids in my year too, and that was kind of a relief – until I got caught. It's not like my dad didn't hit the sauce lots of times, but the first time he caught me drinking, I had to clean out all this poison ivy in the back of our yard. It took me almost a week. By the time I was done, I was covered in the stuff. I hated him for it, but I felt like I deserved it, too. I was just too stirred up. I would just do stuff. Sometimes it was stupid – like the drinking; sometimes it was mean – like I'd pick on my younger brother and a geek at school. I guess I should have known better, but I didn't.'

Chuck had spent his childhood and adolescence getting verbally battered and belittled and sometimes hit. His father never missed a chance to tell him about his failings. There were probably some compliments along the way, but Chuck had a hard time remembering any. In some ways he did end up with his father's life-as-a-battlefield mentality. But the enemies weren't business rivals or shady suppliers. Chuck was watchful for the signs that he wasn't as good as everyone else. There was evidence everywhere because he had been whipped into seeing himself that way. He saw that his sister was good at things but that he was generally useless. As is often the case with people who are dissatisfied with themselves, he saw flaws in almost everyone and everything around him.

### What Boys Lose: Empathy, Conscience, and Connection

Paul was a very intelligent, highly educated, successful corporate executive with an equally accomplished wife and three gifted children
– a twelve-year-old boy and two younger daughters. They were a
family of visible high achievers, well known and respected in their
affluent community. Most of the time, Paul got along fine with his
son – a smart, thoughtful, eager-to-please boy – but sometimes,
when the boy became insolent in a particular way, Paul would slap
him full force across the face. It had a devastating impact on both
of them. Paul, shocked by his own violent outburst and feeling
remorseful, would typically go to his son's room to apologize within
a few minutes after the incident. His son – hurt, frightened, and
angry – would have none of it; unforgiving, he would refuse to
speak with Paul for several days, retreating behind a wall of silence
and acting cold and sullen in his father's presence.

In therapy Paul avoided talking about his own childhood and his
parents' disciplinary methods, saying simply that he hadn't been hit
much and that, even when he was, 'It didn't really have much of an
effect.' But the descriptions of his childhood that he shared over
time revealed quite a different picture.

Paul grew up in the 1950s, the middle boy of five brothers, in a
family that seemed fairly ordinary in most respects. His father was a
hardworking sales representative for a paint company. His mother
was a traditional, full-time homemaker, no easy task with five sons
and a daughter. Both parents were devout fundamentalist church-
goers and 'strict' disciplinarians, Paul said. In this family, discipline
was gender-specific. The mother would slap her daughter when the
girl misbehaved or was disrespectful. When the boys acted up, the
father whipped them with his belt. These disciplinary actions were
as likely to occur in public as in the privacy of home, and Paul
remembered one incident during a rowdy moment on a family road
trip when his father pulled off on a roadside and ordered the boys
out of the car for a whipping. Paul and his brothers – all but the
youngest, a five-year-old – climbed out of the dusty car to await
their punishment. The youngest refused to cooperate, however, and

he crawled frantically through the car's crowded boot as his father went after him, belt in hand. Finally, after great effort, the father trapped the squealing boy, whipped him soundly inside the car, then stepped out and did the same to the patiently waiting brothers. One by one, whipped by the roadside, they climbed back in the car, and when the family finally drove on, it was in silence, save for the wailing little boy in the back.

Recalling the incident during therapy, Paul laughed as he told the story as a television situation comedy, but he was reluctant to reflect any further on the harsh discipline he had endured and witnessed as a child.

Paul wasn't the type of violent man most of us are accustomed to seeing in the crime statistics or newspaper stories, but the reality was that, with every angry outburst, he was moving closer to joining their ranks. He'd had the training for it: a childhood of severe parenting and harsh discipline. Despite his determined effort to forget that element of the past, his own temper had been trained by it. Offensive as he found them, the lessons in harsh discipline that he had learned, literally, at his father's knee he now brought to his own son.

Other men share similar stories of growing up under a harsh hand of discipline, often by fathers, but many times by mothers, too, who struggled with anger or depression.

'I didn't get hit for bad grades, but any time either of my parents got really angry at me, they'd spank or smack me,' a fifty-year-old engineer told us. 'My dad would use his hand or sometimes a belt or a slipper. The belt hurt more, but the slipper stung, and the sound – I can still hear that loud *slap*! My mother used her hand, but she [also] did it with words that hurt just as much. I remember when I was about nine years old shouting at her one day: "All you ever do is tell me about all the things I do wrong! Why can't you ever say anything about the things I do right?" I never spanked my own kids much – I swore I'd never sink to that – but I know my own background made me short-tempered with them. I'd snap at them when I could just as easily say something less harshly. Whenever I did that, I'd feel like I was living out the anger my parents felt at me. I could feel them right there with me, angry and unthinking.'

One of the more robust research findings about the lives of men who went on to become violent criminals is that many of them had a history of being raised in a context of harsh, inconsistent discipline. The voices of delinquents ring with rage at this parental maltreatment. Arnold Goldstein, in his book *Delinquents on Delinquency*, a collection of interviews with criminals, quotes one young man as saying, 'Parents think that they can help a kid by [hitting,] and it makes them worse[;] . . . [the] anger just stays inside him[;] . . . the pain gets too much for him.'[10]

Research shows that this is true for 'normal' children as well. In one study that is representative of a body of work, the researchers found that children of kindergarten age who were spanked at home were more physically aggressive at school. They were much more apt to be bullies. Whether they were hit by their fathers or mothers, whether the spanking came in the context of physical abuse or was relatively mild and infrequent, it was reflected in the boys' own harsh behaviour towards others.[11]

After the playground shootings in Jonesboro, Arkansas, and Springfield, Oregon, in 1998, the public and the media engaged in a shocked debate about how this could have happened. How could American society have produced such boys? Although we were shocked by the loss of life, we were not shocked by the depth of the boy shooters' anger or their lack of empathy. We have seen such anger in potential Cains, boys whose anger could, under other circumstances, have turned murderous.

Of course, not all boys who grow up under a parent's iron fist turn shame into anger and anger into violence. Many turn their shame and anger inward, where it dims their outlook on life and darkens their experience of other, more loving relationships. The sadness reaches into every facet of their lives and tarnishes the emotional potential for even the most ordinary joys and pleasures.

## Discipline: The True Right Stuff

### *Sean: A Boy in Need of Limits*

Sean, at nine, had already made a name for himself, becoming an accomplished troublemaker, first at school and more recently in the community. He was a likeable boy, clever and conversational, but a bit wild. He had also recently been in trouble in his neighbourhood, engaging in some minor vandalism with a local juvenile delinquent named Bobby. He was sent to us when his teachers and his parents realized this was no phase: the pattern of troubling behaviour was growing more intense. Sean was a boy who had been dangerously ill as an infant and whose parents, especially his mother, were so happy that he was alive and well that they had a hard time making any demands on him.

At one therapy session, Sean shared the thought that, although he wasn't dissatisfied with the way things were, he didn't really like Bobby that much and he could sense that things were heading towards a bad end, but he couldn't figure out how to extricate himself from the relationship and routine. He knew he needed help. He sat thoughtfully for a moment, then asked if we could call his mother into the room because he needed to speak to her. When his mum came in, he sat her down, looked her straight in the eyes, and said, 'If you keep letting me get away with everything, I'm gonna turn out just like Bobby.'

Good discipline *contains* a boy and his energy, providing the sense of physical and emotional security he needs in order to learn the larger lessons of self-control and moral behaviour. Good discipline is consistent; it provides clear and well-reasoned expectations and firm, compassionate guidance by adults who model the same standards and behaviour in their daily interactions with a child and with others. Good discipline engages a child, encourages contact instead of isolation, draws him into discussion instead of sending him away. It involves the boy as a consultant. It may be with straightforward questions, such as, 'What is it you don't understand about this rule or don't agree with?' or 'What do you need in order to change this pattern of behaviour?' A parent may simply take into account a son's individual personality or temperament – consulting reality – to tailor a disciplinary response for the best fit.

In the process of consulting with a boy, we show respect for his experience and feelings. Through dialogue a boy can be made to understand the moral content of the expectation. We help him learn to look inward, identify emotions, and express them in a way that leads to improved connections with others instead of alienation. We strengthen our understanding of him and our relationship with him through conversation that carries no penalties.

There's an old comedy punch line that goes something like, 'If you're so smart, why aren't you rich?' Along those lines, if good discipline works so well, why don't we all just practise it? Because it's work. It takes a lot more time and effort to spend the hour with your son that he needs than it does to yell at him and then go do your own thing, whether it's work or a *Seinfeld* rerun on television. Parents often don't follow through with the commitment they make in therapy to change parenting habits that aren't working. The familiarity of old habits – even ineffective ones – works against change. Nobody's perfect; we all make mistakes, whether they're in our actions, our words, or our assumptions. When our disciplinary style encourages mutual understanding, it helps boys be better boys by leading us to better ways of teaching them.

# 4. The Culture of Cruelty

Cruelty and fear shake hands together.

Honoré de Balzac

Almost every man has boyhood memories of camaraderie and a coming-of-age story to tell. Maybe it's about a friend, or his gang of friends, and the memorable times they spent together – riding bikes, playing basketball, going to movies, or just 'hanging out'. Or maybe his story isn't about friends but about an event, a moment as vivid in memory as on the day it happened years ago. These are the stories men like to tell.

There are other coming-of-age stories that men don't tell so eagerly or won't tell at all, even years later, because the emotional pain of the experience remains as deeply disturbing as on the day it happened when they were ten or twelve or fourteen. These are stories of boy cruelty – of domination, humiliation, fear, and betrayal – that most women never hear and most men and boys are reluctant or unable to share even with one another.

Beginning around age ten, as a boy approaches puberty, normal cognitive development makes him more aware of himself and his place in the group and raises the stakes in the many diverse competitions that consume boy groups: who is stronger, who is more attractive to girls, who gets better grades, who is a better basketball player, who is richer and has better things, and who can get the upper hand in teasing verbal combat. A boy's eagerness for autonomy, the fact that he receives less teacher supervision, and his desire to cut loose from his parents' influence make him a willing recruit into this peer culture. At the same time, the group demands conformity and holds him up to ridicule for any failure to conform – whether it is in the TV shows he watches, the books he reads, the shoes he wears, the colour of his socks, the length of his shorts, the sound of his laugh, or the length of his stride. *Anything* a boy says or does can and will be used against him. Physical changes in his size, musculature, voice, and facial hair, for instance, only add to his self-consciousness. Almost all boys hide their hurt because to admit it appears weak. And they all look to make pre-emptive strikes when possible – to divert attention from themselves and on to others. In this psychological war no boys are truly protected, and there are no real 'winners'.

Boys are desperate for role models as they head into this uncertain age, and in most cases the dominant model for them is an image of masculinity that requires strength and stoicism. Among themselves boys engage in continuous psychological warfare. Younger boys see older boys picking on them – dominating them by virtue of their greater size – and they mimic this, creating an environment that pits the strong against the weak, the popular against the unpopular, the power brokers against the powerless, and the conformity-driven 'boy pack' against the boy who fails in any way to conform with pack expectations.

The headmistress of a boarding school wrote to us to share her concerns about cruel teasing that she felt was growing stronger and more damaging with the passage of time. It had become especially virulent among the boys at the school, going beyond the garden-variety insults and name-calling to more subtle psychological 'pranks' that showed a disturbing undercurrent of emotional cruelty.

One incident had occurred one afternoon in the common room of the dormitory, when a sixteen-year-old boy, flanked by sombre-faced friends, pretended to be distraught and in emotional shock about the death of his father. Another boy approached him to console him, sincerely believing the boy was in the saddest of circumstances. After stringing the caring boy along for several minutes, he confessed the ruse – his parents were alive and well – and with the joke splendidly revealed, he and his friends had a good laugh. The compassionate boy was made a laughing-stock and felt foolish and angry at the trick. And he learned his lesson: he wouldn't be so quick with compassion the next time around – perhaps never again.

Other troubling incidents by boys at this particular boarding school could have come from any school or neighbourhood in America where young adolescent boys gather:

On one unpopular boy's birthday, a number of boys gathered around him to sing 'Happy Birthday' but pretended to forget his name. When it was clear that he was embarrassed, they apologized, then brought out his cake – a block of ice covered with frosting.

In the school gym changing-room, some boys urinated on other boys' belongings or into their shampoo bottles. There were incidents of 'nipple twisting', painful and humiliating to the victim. Boys mooned one another or mooned and rubbed themselves against boys targeted for harassment. Boys left used condoms or trash on other boys' clothes or in their lockers.

Neither the victim nor his friends generally report these incidents to teachers, for the most part because they know the acts are so intimate and so obviously hurtful that any teacher or parent would disapprove and there would be penalties to pay; the repercussions could be worse than the original incident. To speak of the hurt also would be an admission of defeat and would only heighten a boy's vulnerability and invite new waves of scorn and attack. Every boy knows this. Why would a boy sit uncomfortably through an entire afternoon of classes rather than set foot in the boys toilets to relieve himself, as one of our students confided was his habit? Because an open row of urinals is an invitation to humiliation. All it takes is a quick push on the back, and a boy knocked off balance is left with wet trousers and endless ridicule. Not only the aggressor will tease; any other boys who see or hear of the incident will, too. They will taunt him with it and whisper and snicker about it until someone more humiliated is pushed to the forefront.

We consulted at a school where the members of the football team periodically would take two small fourteen-year-old boys out to a field and force them to fight each other. If they didn't fight, said the bigger boys, the rest of the team would beat them up anyway. And so these smaller boys would fight, and the older boys would videotape it and show it around school.

Despite collegial appearances, all boys live with fear in this culture of cruelty. They also adhere to the code, and they are loyal to its tenets even though they may not feel as if they fit it, because they view it as an inevitable test of their manliness. It is with this kind of power that the culture of cruelty corrupts friendships, dictates alliances, and depending on the moment, casts boys in the roles of perpetrator, potential victim, or uneasy silent witness.

With every lesson in dominance, fear, and betrayal, a boy is tutored away from trust, empathy, and relationships.[1] This is what boys lose to the culture of cruelty. What they learn instead is emotional guardedness, the wariness with which so many men approach relationships for the rest of their lives.

This is a culture that offers no security. Some boys are more frequently targeted than others, some more often lead the assaults, but all boys live with fear because they know they are vulnerable, each for his own reasons. As a self-possessed and popular boy confided: 'Everybody thinks you've got it so easy when you're on top, but being on top just means that you have to worry all the time about slipping or somebody gaining on you. All it takes is one mistake or a bad day, and all sorts of people are waiting to take you down.' For a boy not so high in the pecking order, life can be brutal – physically and psychologically – as the whim of the pack turns against him or, worse, turns a humiliated boy against himself, resulting in serious emotional problems, suicide, or violence. When boys are under constant pressure to assert power or be labelled a weakling, they are more likely to level cruelty at others with little recognition of, or regard for, its emotional impact. Boys are crueller, in part because they are afraid, and their need to defend against that fear is ironclad.

Colin, an insightful sixteen-year-old, reflects on his experiences when he was twelve: 'You get into a habit of saying stuff to people, and it gets to a point where you don't even think about what you're saying any more – like "You're a dork" – and then it happens so much, it gets worse and worse, and then it's just like another word, like "and" or "I", and you don't think of it as a word than can hurt somebody. I don't think you see the consequences of it. When you punch somebody in the eye, you see that they get a black eye, but when you and thirty other people call somebody a loser ten times a day, you don't see the kid having low self-esteem or being hurt by it. You might see it if he cried or something, but then that's only like pouring fuel on the fire: everybody goes after him for crying.'

We are realistic. To the extent that puberty and early adolescence is for all kids a time of radical change, self-definition, and emotional insecurity, it is to some degree inevitable that boys will become rivals, friends, enemies.[2] Powerful influences shape this culture of cruelty and perpetuate it. But just as one boy's careless taunt can inflict a lasting wound on another boy, so can even a few boys change the culture of cruelty dramatically with their decision to resist joining in the teasing or to stand up for a boy under attack. If the culture of cruelty thrives on boys' fears of vulnerability, then the challenge is to replace their fears with a greater understanding of their own emotional struggle and in so doing diminish their need for cruelty and their tolerance of it.

## Michael with a Group of Twelve-Year-Old Boys: Learning to Talk . . . But Not Too Much

The head of the middle school asks me to meet with the twelve-year-olds for an hour. She says there is a lot of teasing among the boys, and she's hoping that some conversation will make a difference.

The meeting takes place in a cellar classroom in the late afternoon. All the boys – about forty of them – are sitting at desks with their coats and ties on. Many of them have wet hair because they have just returned from athletics and their showers. It is always quite a sight, these boys with their fresh, open faces. They look so handsome, so adult-like, and yet they are not.

The boys arrange themselves in groups immediately upon entering the room, while some boys keep to themselves, and some hug the wall. There is always a centre group, very close together, that conveys a sense of power and popularity. 'You are going to hear from *us*,' their position tells me. I cannot exactly explain the underlying theory of power seating in a school, but I know it when I see it. Within seconds it's clear which boys want to be the centre of attention, which boys are going to compete for my time, which boys want to dominate the conversation, and which boys are going to be on the margins.

I begin by asking them why boys tease one another. To them it's a dumb question. Because it's funny, says one, everyone knows that. The joke is right there, the stupid behaviour is obvious; someone *has* to be pointed out. Then I ask them what the most painful moment – emotionally speaking – has been for them in school. There is an uncomfortable silence as the boys look at one another and shift in their chairs. A boy starts to describe an athletic injury, and I remind them that we are talking about hurt feelings. Someone describes having dropped a test tube filled with a smelly mixture in the science lab, and how everyone started to tease him about being a jerk. Another boy says he used to get teased a lot because he wore braces on his teeth.

Then Steven, one of the boys sitting alone and against the wall, begins to speak about being regularly tormented on the bus, having his books taken away from him, his papers scattered, and how all the kids laugh when he goes to pick them up. The tone of his voice signals to us all that his pain is recent and deep. The discomfort in the room is palpable. His tormentors are here, and he is telling their 'secret' to a 'stranger'.

What is most unnerving to the boys, however, is the emotion in his voice. He has taken the wraps off; this is real. Boys start to squirm or giggle; a few nudge one another. Little noises arise from around the room. I can tell that Steven knows he is breaking the code of silence but doesn't care; he has my attention, and he is going to tell his story.

I am torn, because, as a psychologist, I want to encourage this self-disclosure, but Steven has opened himself up for a whole new round of teasing. He is not reading the cues. If he goes on this way, exposing his vulnerabilities, the group will gang up on him. I want to help Steven speak his truth without having him become the victim, the 'Piggy' of the group, like the classic vulnerable boy in William Golding's *Lord of the Flies*.

In many schools this book is a standard part of the curriculum in English classes for twelve- to fourteen-year-olds. For the girls it is a powerful piece of fiction about the human potential for cruelty. For the boys the story is real: it's as close as the crowded hall between classes or the changing-room before gym period. It accurately captures their own, only slightly more civilized, world. It is a place every man has been. A boy lives that story, too, aware every day that the group could turn on him in a flash, that every moment holds the 'Piggy' potential, and that, if he is targeted, it will be almost impossible for anyone – even a friend – to stand up with him against the crowd. Except in the most violent communities, most boys don't face the potential of physical annihilation so much as they experience a marginalization – being made to feel worthless or virtually non-existent – that can be emotionally debilitating.

I stop Steven and thank him for his contribution. He starts to speak on two later occasions in the meeting. When I see the other boys becoming scornful, I close him down. I will seek him out, either directly or through the head of the middle school, and find some time to speak with him privately.

### Striving for Masculinity: In Search of the Big Impossible

Indeed, every child seeks the respect or appreciation of peers. Friendship provides you with affection, intimacy, and reliable alliance. From either a friend or the group, you can obtain practical assistance, nurturance, companionship, and enhancement of worth. What only a group can provide is a sense of inclusion, which all children crave.

For boys, this drive to fit in is supercharged by their developing sexual identity and the need to establish themselves as successful males within their peer culture. In the Eastern Highlands of Papua New Guinea, the Fox Indians call manhood the 'Big Impossible'.[3] What an appropriate name for manhood, which in so many cultures is recognized only after a rite of passage that tests the mettle of a boy against the fire of cultural expectations. Inherent in this thinking is the idea that to be a real man requires something more than simple anatomical maleness, that a boy must rise to a performance challenge that will earn him the rank of masculinity. When masculinity is defined as an achievement, then manhood becomes 'a prize to be won or wrested through struggle' and a 'precarious or artificial state', as David Gilmore notes in *Manhood in the Making*.

Performance-based masculine identity is virtually impossible to achieve in any lasting way. 'You're only as good as your last game,' they say in baseball. Boys understand this message on a personal level. In the boys' world, you can never, ever be satisfied with your performance. You have to prove yourself anew, continuously. This unending quest to fit in, to be cool, inevitably pits boys against one another – and against the men in their lives as well. In this psychologically competitive male environment, part of proving yourself is to belittle others.

A boy lives in a narrowly defined world of developing masculinity in which everything he does or thinks is judged on the basis of the strength or weakness it represents: you are either strong and worthwhile, or weak and worthless. He must also be willing to fight. Even if you have never fought, and never intend to fight, you have to pretend to yourself that you can and will. A respected boy is someone who can 'handle himself', as one non-violent fifteen-year-old put it, which he said meant mentally taking the measure of another boy and assessing whether you could beat him up if you had to.

A common debate in households is how to counsel a boy who is being harassed by bullies. Mothers take the position that 'violence doesn't solve anything'; fathers have no qualms about telling a ten-year-old son to 'punch out' the jerk, acknowledging that the punch might not get rid of the bully but feeling that that isn't the point. Walking away from tormentors is a sign of weakness, and the lasting feeling of cowardice is greater punishment than any blow.

Boys not only feel the pressure to appear masculine, but they feel that, in doing so, they must be clearly *not* feminine – perhaps even anti-feminine – and so they consciously and deliberately attack in others and in themselves things that might possibly be defined as feminine. This includes tenderness, empathy, compassion, and any show of emotional vulnerability. Whether pressures produce a street fighter or not, they impose a standard for masculinity that all boys accept and use to judge themselves.

Howard, a teacher from a family of teachers, confided a story from his own youth, when his parents sent him to a summer camp in Vermont famous for its manly traditions. Every Friday night there was an 'American Indian' ceremony by the campfire. All of the older boys, who had 'passed the test', dressed up as 'braves' and marched down to the campfire in single file. All of the younger boys were 'squaws', who marched down at the end of the line with blankets over their heads. A boy remained a squaw until he had passed the 'test', which involved singing a complicated 'Indian' song filled with unfamiliar words.

Howard could not learn the words to the song. Even so, each Friday night he stood up and tried to sing it, in front of the group, in front of all the 'braves', and each time he tried, he failed. For that entire first summer, every Friday night he had to wear the blanket again and be a 'squaw'.

To be labelled a girl – a 'squaw' – is the most humiliating thing that can happen to a boy. To have the 'honour' of manhood withheld from him because he could not memorize the words to a camp song added further insult to Howard's injury. In a life distinguished by a wealth of experience, subsequent accomplishment, and success, Howard nonetheless carries this memory as one of the most unremittingly cruel and humiliating experiences of his life.

## Vulnerabilities: How Masculinity and Sexuality Drive Defensive Behaviour

Between the ages of ten and thirteen, adolescent boys feel most vulnerable about their size, strength, performance, and developing sexuality. Naturally, then, those qualities in others are the targets of their most frequent and cruellest taunts.

Sexuality dominates adolescent boy humour and conversation, and penises are a source of extraordinary fascination as well as physical and emotional tension. A boy's recognition that he is developing sexually through wet dreams and the self-pleasuring of masturbation only adds to his confusion and fear surrounding his physical changes. An erection can present itself at any moment, and a boy worries about the potential for sudden and stunning embarrassment. Depending on the setting and the company, a maverick sexual response can be interpreted as a sign of homosexuality. And eleven-, twelve-, and thirteen-year-old boys fear homosexuality, literally, like the plague. They don't understand where it comes from, which makes it all the more frightening, but they do know it's not a 'cool' thing to be. Homosexuals are male, but they aren't *manly*.

The amount of teasing that goes on among early adolescent boys about possible homosexual leanings is staggering. 'Gay' or 'fag' is a constant taunt, whether a boy's 'crime' is his hairstyle, his accent, his clothes, a good grade, or a missed goal. Familiarity does nothing to lessen its power to hurt. The taunt is searing because a boy's fear of homosexuality runs that deep.

Although it is a minority of boys who actually engage in masturbation as a social activity, you'll probably never hear a boy or man acknowledge it. For most boys who do it, these 'circle jerks' – masturbating in the company of a number of friends – and other casual sex play are not necessarily a sign of homosexuality. If a boy feels embarrassment or shame associated with masturbation among friends, it is typically when just two or three boys are involved, raising fears that this may mean he is, or will become, gay.

So a boy struggles not only with the immediate physical and emotional discomfort of an ordinary sexual response or a non-sexual feeling of attraction but also with what those responses and feelings mean to others and to himself. Boys fear homosexuality because it defies the traditional norms of masculinity and invites terrifying pack retaliation.

The fear of homosexuality imposes a tough taboo that isolates boys physically from the comfort of touch and sexualizes any touching that does come their way. Especially at adolescence, boys feel they're too old to go to their parents for hugs and kisses, but the fact is that they still need the nurturing element that non-sexual touch provides. One reason masturbation is such a preoccupation for adolescent boys may well be because this physical isolation creates a profoundly lonely time for boys. For a boy whose sexual orientation will prove to be homosexual, this is a particularly desperate time of denial and fear, heightened by the generalized homophobic panic that grips the broader boy culture.[4] It's bad enough for a heterosexual boy to be called a 'faggot'; just think how bad it might be if one really did secretly have those thoughts. Author Michelangelo Signorile, in *Queer in America*, recalls how, as a teenager, he defended against his intuition that he was homosexual by joining a gang that routinely would seek out and beat up boys suspected of being gay.[5] The 1998 killing of Matthew Shepard, a gay college student in Wyoming, is brutal proof of the power of homophobia.

One of our clients told us how the appearance of Tom, a new boy at the school – a boy who also happened to have long blond hair and feminine features – upped the fear level of other boys in the class. One fourteen-year-old, Greg, was accused of being attracted to Tom. The tormentors chalked the boys' names together in a heart on the pavement in front of the school. They whispered 'faggot' quietly whenever they passed the targeted boy. One day they put a stick of butter in Greg's locker – butter being the preferred lubricant for anal intercourse in their world-view – and from that point on, they would just walk by him and whisper 'butter'. The ringleaders of this harassment were boys who were experimenting sexually themselves, engaging in group mutual masturbation activities. Their harassment of Greg was an effort to vigorously defend themselves against their own homosexual panic and the fact that they actually thought that the new boy was attractive – and what did that suggest about *them*?

## Size Matters: Bigger is Better

Size and sports are dominant themes in the male psychology. We are impressed by big football players, tall basketball players, and heavyweight boxers. Size fascinates us, and men discuss at length which athlete is bigger and who is tougher. Penis size is much more important to men as a measure of virility than for any functional difference in sexual activity. In all ways among men, size denotes power in a primitive sense, and in the boy culture, size alone buys you a major level of respect.

'Until I was about six, I got in lots of fights,' says a kid from South Boston, who laughs as he recalls being a punching bag for boys bigger than himself. 'When I got to be seven, I got all bigger, and everyone backed off. Everyone who knew me respected me.'

Men share similar recollections of boyhood brutality as often from the posh side of town as the impoverished one. Nigel described his days at an English boarding school when he was eleven, where, as one of the smallest boys there, he was continuously bullied by one of the thirteen-year-olds. One day he struck back, trying to retaliate.

A teacher intervened and proposed the traditional solution: a formal fight with boxing gloves at the end of the day. After classes all the boys trooped down to the playing fields, and Nigel and his much larger opponent were fitted with boxing gloves and encouraged to fight each other. They did so, but it was no contest. The bigger boy walloped him.

However, the unspoken social contract assured that the smaller boy got credit for his public display of courage; the larger boy was not supposed to, and did not, bully the younger boy again. Nigel's courage had earned him safe passage, and that helped. But what he really wanted that day was to beat the bully, and he had failed. Years later Nigel still remembered vividly how trapped he had felt by the situation, by the size of the bigger boy, and by the inevitability of his defeat.

Physical size becomes an issue of emotional importance in both sexual and non-sexual ways. Boys sense their differences and thus their vulnerability. A different kind of physical one-upmanship uses size as the determinant for respect; bigger boys tend to get more of it. Boys are completely aware of their physical stature and how, in that ranked order, they measure up. Boys who are small are made to *feel* small as well, with painful feelings of inadequacy disproportionate to any comparative physical shortcomings. Many small boys and men learn to compensate by overachieving; they act in ways that suggest that, from early in life, they have had to develop many psychological defences against the pain of being small and many compensatory mechanisms to make them feel bigger.

### Dan and Bobby: Losing the Struggle to Measure Up

Bobby was the smallest kid in his class in primary school. He was not athletically inclined but kept himself amused with more solitary pursuits such as books and video games, and he wasn't too interested in sports. But Bobby didn't seem particularly unhappy to his parents. They remembered thinking that he would eventually come into his own socially. And given that his grades were pretty good, there didn't seem to be much cause for concern.

When Bobby was twelve, he entered secondary school. Since

the other boys there were already in the midst of their physical development and growing taller at a rapid clip, Bobby's small stature and lack of development stood out more than ever before, and as a result the sharks began to circle. Much of the teasing was in the form of nicknames – 'Hairless' and 'Squeaky', among others. Bobby tells me now that he could count on a new name appearing almost every day. And at age twenty-five, he could remember almost every one.

Bobby endured the daily teasing. He wasn't beaten up. No one stole his lunch money. And on some days he was ignored; the boys had other targets. But the teasing took its toll, especially because Bobby had no friends, no sign from anyone that he actually belonged to the group.

Bobby eventually began to mature. His height went from four feet six inches to about five feet seven, and he was no longer the only boy in the shower without pubic hair. But at the age of fourteen he developed a fairly severe case of acne, and the names changed: 'Craters', 'Clearasil', and from the less clever boys, the inevitable 'Pizza Face'. A year later his tormentors started to lose interest in the teasing. Bobby still wasn't welcomed socially, but at least the teasing had stopped. For the rest of his time at school, he was pretty much left alone.

Today the social gap between Bobby and his peers is too wide for his parents to ignore. He shows no interest in dating – or more accurately, too great a fear of dating – and still has no one whom he could call a good friend. But he carries a scar from all those years of teasing. Like a girl who sees herself as fat when she is not and systematically starves herself, Bobby is obsessed by any perceived flaw in his appearance. He continually checks his face in the mirror for any signs of blemishes. When he sees something that he believes may develop into a pimple, he has an almost ritualistic approach to picking his skin and applying commercial remedies over and over to the affected spot. Most often, the blemishes can only be seen by Bobby, but his self-treatments have begun to disfigure his face. Though his height is normal, he wears shoes or boots with the highest heels that he can find. Terrified that a girl will make fun of the size of his penis, he assiduously avoids any sexual situations.

Bobby often believes that he hears people talking about his

appearance. This last symptom has perhaps the greatest impact on his life. He trusts almost no one and feels that in general people are out to get him. Because of this he has had great difficulty holding a job. His failures in this arena have only served to erode his self-esteem further. Bobby's condition has been worsening over the last few years, and I am concerned about his future.

No one guessed that Bobby was so fragile, that he was desperately shamed by his size – a genetic fact over which he had no control – and that every careless taunt inflicted lasting pain and further distorted his perception of himself and others.

### Sports: An Influence in Every Boy's Life, for Better or Worse

Every boy, regardless of whether he likes or is good at athletics, has a relationship to sports. Often participation in sports is mandatory, such as in gym classes, and so your peers know full well your athletic prowess or lack thereof. In the autumn, in towns in the north-east of America, a boy of nine or ten years old is defined by the fact that he either is or is not playing soccer. In other regions the sport might be basketball, but again, a boy either is or is not playing it. For many, playing sports is a joy, perhaps the greatest in their lives. For most others, athletics can be at best a mixed blessing. The sports culture that surrounds boys has as much potential to hurt their self-esteem as it does to promote it, because it rewards athletically gifted or above-average boys at the expense of other boys who may have other gifts less highly valued by their peers.

The incoming head of a public school told us, 'I'm inheriting a football coach who earns 50 per cent more than any other teacher on my faculty and a football programme that costs five times as much as any other sport and only a quarter of the boys in school play it.' It is that disproportionate allocation of resources, attention, and mental energy to sports that can be a tyranny in the lives of boys who are not athletic.

In schools the prestige associated with athletic excellence creates a 'caste system', in which boy-on-boy cruelty can be played out with adult sanction. In the mildest form it can mean that boys who are not athletic feel undervalued. In the crueller forms it can mean that the biggest, strongest boys make lower-status boys suffer. And not only do the less athletically skilled suffer, they often watch as the star athletes win the hearts of most of the girls at school.

Mike – a short, trim, handsome man, successful in business – for years had pushed his short thirteen-year-old son, Rick, to jog almost every morning and made him enrol in after-school sports despite Rick's clear lack of interest. 'Look, he's in training,' Mike explained to us. 'I'm preparing him for life. If he can excel in sports, he'll get respect, and he'll get a scholarship to a good college. Without that, he's just "the short kid", and they'll eat him alive. I know. I lived it. And I don't want my son to go through what I went through.' Rick put his other interests aside and continued to play organized sports as his father dictated, but his resentment towards his father grew, and by secondary school, he was a strong, fast, angry boy with a temper he employed on everyone around him. Nonetheless, Mike remained determined that his son stay active in sports and keep on 'winning'.

## Dan and Connor: The Ordinary and Important Inner Life of a Boy

Connor doesn't really look like a kid whom other boys would pick on. He isn't fat, unusual-looking, or too short. He is a round-faced, red-haired, thirteen-year-old whose average dress and appearance should make it easy for him to blend in. Connor's family is solidly middle class – his father is a salesman and his mother works part time in a grocery shop. But in the highly affluent Boston suburb where they live, when they drive into the school car park in their Ford and have to park between a Mercedes and a BMW, it's clear that they are in a somewhat different income bracket than their neighbours. Connor is one of the best basketball players in his class, which should afford him some protection against teasing.

Several of Connor's teachers have approached me, though, aware of a constant barrage of taunts aimed at Connor over the past weeks. When I finally have Connor captive in my office, it is only for twenty minutes. The school is on a shortened schedule today due to a last-period drug-awareness assembly, and before the bell rings, I manage to get out of him that he's used to being teased. 'It's no big deal,' he says.

I figure he probably *has* gotten used to it and that he isn't in any real 'danger' in the sense that we psychiatrists, psychologists, and social workers tend to think of these things. It's not as if he's wetting his pants or shoplifting or smoking pot. He's only learning to be on constant guard against the attacks of his classmates, only shutting down emotionally, only learning that he shouldn't trust anyone. There is no code in the diagnostic manual for these things.

As I watch Connor's red head bob down the hallway, I suddenly remember something, someone I haven't thought about in years – Mick, a red-haired boy I had gone to school with who used to get unmercifully teased. I was a fringe member of a popular clique and allowed to sit at their lunch table, and for a stretch of time one spring, they basically tortured Mick – another boy at the table, a friend, one of their own – every day at lunch. Mick was a low-key kind of guy, actually a nice kid, very sensitive, and he had very red, wiry hair. That was enough to make him a target. The leaders of this pack made it a point to give him a new derogatory nickname each day – 'Brillo' and 'Helmet' were two – making fun of his hair, of course. They all thought it was hilarious. Sometimes they'd start to chant – 'Don't let Mick eat!' – and it was like a rallying cry. They would blow snot on his sandwich or simply steal his food. One day they stole a bee from the biology lab and put it in his tuna sandwich. I didn't pick on him, but looking back on it, I can't believe I sat there and just let it happen around me.

This cruelty had become such a normal part of our world that we almost didn't think to question it. I don't know if Mick was ever the same after that. It's not as if he went nuts or became violent. Surely, though, it must have hurt – it hurt me now to think of it. And it must have hardened him.

But I wanted to find out more about what was going on with Connor. To get more information, I went to my informants in the same year as Connor, boys I had been seeing regularly since the beginning of term. Adam's father had died the year before at the start of the school year, and I'd been helping him talk through a lot of his feelings. Leon is an African-American boy whom I've sought out because he is the only student of colour in his class, and I am one of the faculty moderators of the students of colour 'club'; I help him manage what is always a very tough transition. Neither Leon nor Adam is having serious problems at school, but getting this special attention from me helps them feel more secure. An ounce of prevention is going a long way. I often have lunch with Adam and Leon, and today I take them out for hamburgers. We catch up on what is happening with each of them. Then I ask about Connor.

'What's going on in your class with Connor? What are kids teasing him about?'

'Are you seeing him?' Adam asks.

'Man, you know I can't divulge that information. Some of his teachers think he's really getting picked on.'

'I don't think he's getting teased that much,' says Adam. 'No more than anybody else.'

Leon has a different opinion: 'Are you serious? He's in my gym class, and they like torture him every day. They call him "Red Ranger".'

'Why?'

'Oh, yeah,' says Adam. 'I remember he had that old Power Ranger notebook in maths, and everybody started makin' fun of him for watching a baby show. Now everybody calls him Jason or Zordon. [Jason is the original Red Ranger, and Zordon is the master of the Power Rangers.] He gets so pissed off.'

Now I get it. To thirteen-year-old boys, the Power Rangers are completely passé. Connor has committed the sin of looking childish. In much the same way that an eight-year-old will make fun of younger siblings for liking Barney the purple dinosaur, thirteen-year-olds must disavow any lingering liking for the Power Rangers. My guess is that Connor doesn't like the Power Rangers either but that his parents couldn't justify wasting money by throwing away a perfectly good notebook. I also guess that Connor 'lost' that notebook pretty fast. One of the reasons the teasing must hurt him so much is that it is unfair. He knows he ought to be cool enough to fit in. I would agree, but I also know that few boys his age are spared.

The fact that he's new to the school makes him even more of a target.

Adam admits he's joined in sometimes, and he also tells what *he* gets teased about – his last name. 'Hohner – boner. Get it? Pretty hilarious, huh?' he says.

Leon has pretty much stayed out of it. Because he is black, he is sometimes on the receiving end of a kind of indirect cruelty – ignorant comments, even in class, about African-Americans that he usually endures silently. I find myself wondering whether Adam and Leon will mind some extra company at lunch, and whether Connor would agree to come. I decide the group is small enough, and if I'm there, the boys won't be tempted to go at one another.

The boys have been helpful. At least now I know what's going on with Connor. This is a too-familiar problem, probably the biggest problem faced by middle school boys and administrators who care enough to want help. This is also one of the hardest situations to change. There is no clear point of attack, and the target is always moving.

In our work as therapists, we comb for clues like detectives, reading between the lines of boys' stories, tracing events, interviewing participants and observers in a boy's life, and examining his feelings in pursuit of explanations instead of alibis. It is tempting for adults to take the easy route, to go along with the denial, the missed meetings, the vague answers, the assurances that everything is 'okay, I guess', when we know it isn't, to rationalize a boy's troubles as 'growing pains' and let it go at that. Instead, we must actively pursue the Connors of the world; we must take the time and make the effort to find out what they're feeling and track their troubles to a source. This is the legwork of parenting, teaching, counselling; there is no shortcut.

A boy's ability to survive in this environment has everything to do with his emotional resources – his ability to recognize and understand his feelings and those of others. Boys fortified by emotional awareness and empathy are less likely to inflict hurt on others and more resilient under the pressure of cruelty that comes their way.

## Friendship and Betrayal in the Culture of Cruelty

Lefty, Swifty, Red Rose, Popsy, and about a dozen other boys were barely teens when they forged a clubby friendship in 1937. Sixty years later they found themselves celebrities, featured in a *New York Times* news story, not for any of their accomplishments in war, work, or raising families but for this: they were still close friends.[6]

Two of these seventy-something men told the reporter how their friendship began when, as four-year-olds, one boy had knocked the other off his bicycle. One of the men recalled: 'Our mothers brought us upstairs, and they said, "You're going to be friends," and we took that literally.' Another added: 'There's nothing we wouldn't do for each other. We're friends. It's that simple, and it's that complicated.'

Maintaining any friendship through six decades would be complicated. But the fact that this particular group of friends had remained close was even more impressive – deemed newsworthy, in fact – because they were men, and it's no secret that men often find close, personal friendship an elusive thing. This is the cost of the eroding of trust; for many boys the story of youthful friendship can have a disappointing and bewildering end. The capacity for more loyal and deeper friendship grows alongside the capacity for greater teasing, cruelty, and exclusion. These parallel themes are present in the lives of boys from the age of seven, and even earlier in much tougher environments. The stakes become appreciably higher in early adolescence as the protection of parents and adults diminishes.

Real friendship means being able to be yourself, to let your guard down, and trust that your friend won't take advantage of what he knows and use it against you. Boys can be torn between the desire to be expressive in friendship and the gender-stereotyped expectation that they be assertive and forceful, or strong and silent. Sharing secrets with a friend doesn't fit the bill. And yet the need for emotional expression is very great in all children. Furthermore, as a boy begins to move further and further from his parents, and develops a life separate from them, a friend becomes even more important as a confidant. A boy who enjoys a close relationship with one or both of his parents typically still shares different information, and shares it in a different way, with a close friend.

Even boys who want to be friends have to struggle against the corrupting influence of the culture of cruelty, which demands that a boy place allegiance to the group above allegiance to a friend and be willing to prove it, and where friends betraying friends is a common theme. The betrayal can be obvious and dramatic: leaving a friend out of a planned activity; losing him 'accidentally on purpose' while on an outing, as a prank; or revealing confidences. Or it can be passive: failing to defend him against the group's taunts. For the friend betrayed, the loss of trust in that moment is profound. The betrayer learns the same lesson in a different way: he knows he could be next. Both come away less trusting and for ever wary of exposing their vulnerability in relationships. Because trusting childhood friendship offers a template for lifelong relationships, its sacrifice to the adolescent culture of cruelty has especially sad repercussions.

Gary looked back to the turning point in his own adolescence when first he turned away from a friendship with an unpopular boy because it was 'too risky' and subsequently found himself the object of the same retreat by a trusted friend: 'When I was ten, my best friend was a kid named Peter. We spent every day after school studying and talking together at his house or mine, and on weekends we played hunting and tracking games in the nearby woods. He was the closest friend I ever had. Peter was the shortest guy in the class. He was a good enough athlete, but the following year the other boys started to tease him about his size. At first Peter just ignored it. I defended him a few times, but after a while it started to seem like I was his mother or something. Then one day in the changing-room when we were all getting dressed, a ring of boys formed around Peter and started snapping their towels at his crotch and taunting him. Peter was holding his hands in front of his crotch and trying to get his pants on. I remember the moment when his eyes caught mine. He wasn't exactly pleading for help, but he was checking to see what I was going to do. What I did was finish getting dressed and walk out of the changing room. We never talked about it, but that was the end of our friendship. To be honest, he had become a liability for me, and I didn't have the guts to deal with it.'

Gary made a new 'best friend', Lee, who was a good athlete, a top student, a real leader. They wore the same size clothing and would trade neckties, sometimes even jackets, which was an important signal of friendship and allegiance. Just before he turned thirteen Gary prepared for his bar mitzvah, the Jewish coming-of-age ceremony in which a boy demonstrates that he is ready to accept the responsibilities of a religious adult. His Jewish identity had never been a matter of comment before, he said, but that year, at the small, predominantly non-Jewish school he attended, it became a red flag for ridicule.

'When the "Jew jokes" started up, I didn't know whether to ignore them or fight back,' Gary said. 'I remember looking to Lee for help, but he was laughing nervously along with the other kids. When I got bar mitzvahed that year, I invited about a half-dozen boys from my class, the ones I thought were my friends. Not one of them showed up – not even Lee. When I asked him about it later, he admitted that the other boys had talked about it and decided that none of them wanted to go to the synagogue because they would have to wear a "kyke cap". I guess he felt the same way. That's what becoming a man meant to me when I got bar mitzvahed: I realized I was on my own. I never had a best friend again.'

## The Silence

Throughout these losses – of friendship, of trust, and of self-esteem – and the emotional shutdown required to achieve the Big Impossible of manhood, the culture of cruelty imposes a code of silence on boys, requiring them to suffer without speaking of it and to remain silent witnesses to acts of cruelty to others. The power of this cruelty is so strong, and it is such a pervasive part of the masculine identity, that boys take it for granted, and men remain silent about it. Boys silence themselves for a variety of reasons. They fear being victimized again. They don't want to be responsible for disciplinary actions against other boys. They don't want to be ostracized from the peer group. They have learned their lessons in emotional silence well. To remain silent is strong and masculine, and to speak out is not.

Boys have their reasons for remaining silent; teachers and parents have their reasons, too.

For several months when he was twelve, Brian became the target of teasing and initially struggled alone with the hurt. The treatment included teasing about his height, his hair, and his clothes; being 'iced out' by the group in the canteen; having his schoolbooks and supplies stolen; being tripped as he returned to his seat in the classroom, and being 'accidentally' knocked down by boys in line. The more determinedly Brian refused to respond, the more intense the undercurrent of teasing became. One day in the playground the pack of boys snatched Brian's favourite ball from him and started a running keep-away game, ultimately gaining the amused attention of most of the other children in the playground. As the chase became more frenzied, one of the jeering boys dropped the ball to the ground and stomped on it. The other perpetrators joined in, and in seconds it was reduced to a small, shredded mass in the dirt. Humiliated and angry, Brian grabbed one of his tormentors by the shirt, and it ripped. For this the playground supervisor sent him to the headmaster, and in that discussion the fuller story came out.

When Brian's teacher was contacted about the boy's problems, this genial man said he had noticed nothing unusual in the classroom, but the school counsellor subsequently confirmed that the boys teased Brian about 'just about everything' – from his silent reading choices to his comments in class discussion.

In our experience, we find that most teachers who don't take a stand against this kind of harassment either believe that this 'typical boy behaviour' is normal and non-scarring for boys or see the cruelty but feel helpless to stop it. They haven't been trained to conduct this kind of emotional intervention, and the school hasn't defined it as part of their job. We also know male teachers who, scarred from their own middle school years, don't want to oppose the power-flexing boys who are doing the teasing for fear of being seen as uncool. Or they don't want to identify, or empathize, too strongly with the uncool kid because they were uncool in their own childhood and cannot go back to that painful place, even with adult authority and perspective.

Those same emotional barriers keep many parents from responding more actively to cruelty in a boy's life. Often mothers are unsure whether they should speak up about the problem or let it go, as the boy himself seems to prefer. A father may choose to ignore the problem because he knows too well from his own childhood the adverse consequences of trying to do anything about it. In instances of a father's treating his own son cruelly, it is often because the father hasn't worked through similar issues of social cruelty in his own life. He is humiliated to have a not-cool son, and so he disavows him. Because a boy's father is in a unique position to be a source of support during this harsh passage, this betrayal is a particularly sad legacy of the culture of cruelty.

Boys aren't looking to be rescued by the adults in their lives, but they take adults' lack of response as a sign that the culture of cruelty operates 'outside the law' and the ringleaders will not be held accountable. It is parents and educators who need to create a climate that clearly communicates a moral code in which cruelty is neither tolerated nor ignored. In a home or school environment that fosters emotional awareness and personal accountability, where adults give those values a voice, the silence of boys will be broken and, with it, the culture of cruelty's silent power in boys' lives.

## 5. Lost Fathers, Lost Sons: A Legacy of Desire and Distance

And so we beat on, boats against the current, borne back
ceaselessly into the past . . .

F. Scott Fitzgerald, *The Great Gatsby*

There is little that can move a man to tears. He can talk about a
failed marriage, disturbing children, career disappointments, ruinous
business decisions, and physical suffering with dry eyes. When a
grown man cries in therapy, it is almost always about his father. The
man may be hated or revered, alive or dead. The story may be one
of a father's absence, his painful presence, or his limitations of spirit
and feeling. The word *love* rarely comes up in the stories men tell,
but that is what these stories are all about. Fathers and sons are players
in a tale of unrequited love – a story told in yearning, anger, sadness,
and shame.

An emotional gulf separates most sons from their fathers, and it is
uniquely damaging to a boy because of the central role a father figure
plays in a boy's developing view of himself.

For too many sons, this emotional breach between them and their
fathers remains a lifelong source of sadness, anger, bitterness, or
shame. While this emotional distance keeps many good men from
being better fathers, it doesn't diminish a son's desire for connection.
No matter how impossible a father may be, at the deepest level of
his being, a boy wants to love his father and wants to be known and
loved by him.

In his autobiography, *Always the Young Stranger*, American poet
Carl Sandburg wrote of a moment when the emotional distance
between himself and his father filled the universe of his young boy
mind:

I remember walking on Christmas morning with my hand in my father's. I had been reading in the books about stars and I had this early morning been taking a look now and then up at a sky of clear stars. I turned my face up toward my father's and said, pointing with the loose hand, 'You know, some of those stars are millions of miles away.' And my father, without looking down toward me, gave a sniff, as though I were a funny little fellow, and said, 'We won't bodder about dat now . . .' For several blocks neither of us said a word and I felt, while still holding his hand, that there were millions of empty miles between us.

Despite the emotional light-years between him and his father, the poet expressed his enduring need for his father's love as 'a rich soft wanting'.

We are witness to this yearning that sons have to be loved and well regarded by their fathers, at any age. Men tell us they want to do 'a good job' raising their sons, a better job than their own fathers did, but also that their sons 'never listen'; they 'don't understand'; they are aggravating, disappointing, or worse. Boys describe their fathers in similar terms of discontent, as men who don't listen, don't understand, and demand respect without offering it. Mothers often tell us that they look for ways to bring their husbands and sons together but find themselves mostly relegated to the role of referee or nurse, soothing tempers or mending hurt feelings. Many women are angry with their husbands for not being more involved in their sons' lives.

Andrea describes the growing rift between her husband, Ron, and their son, David, echoing the sentiments we hear so often from other mothers. As his own father had done, Ron had worked long, late hours at the office when David was young. Andrea had put in the long, late hours at home with their son. The situation worked well enough until the year David turned nine and began to want to spend more time with his father. As he became increasingly insistent upon his father's attention, Ron felt unfairly pressured to 'perform' as a father and resisted David's suggestions for weekend activities, such as movies or bowling.

'David seems almost desperate to be pals with his dad, but every-thing he does rubs Ron the wrong way,' Andrea says. 'David will try to tell him about a video game he's excited about, and Ron complains that he is talking too loud. The only time Ron really pays attention to David is at report card time, and then he just lectures David about getting better grades. He's constantly on David's case about something. They both seem so oblivious to each other's feelings. Ron will yell at David for not taking out the rubbish, and the next minute David's asking him if they can go to a movie together.

'I worry that, if things don't change, when David gets a little older, he's going to decide he hates his dad, and they'll never have a chance to have a close, loving relationship.'

It is clear to us that the most emotionally resourceful and resilient boys are those whose fathers are part of the emotional fabric of the family, whose fathers care for them and show it in clear, comforting, and consistent ways. Sadly, it is a minority of fathers who share this kind of relationship with their sons.

Our culture's historical assignment of relationship work to women has turned emotions into a disregarded 'second language' for men. As a result, most men have limited awareness or understanding of their feelings or the feelings of others. Not having learned from their own fathers, they find it difficult to think in terms of 'love' or to express the love they do feel for a son. Instead, they tend to fall back on what they have been taught to do with other men – namely, compete, control, and criticize. When an adolescent son begins to challenge his father's authority, this is a father's common response – even within relationships that had been fairly strong in the years before. This hampers the father's relationship with his son and creates obstacles to understanding the emotional consequences of his own boyhood.

Most men are burdened by unresolved feelings about their own father, no matter how far removed they are from him by distance or death. And so the pattern of desire and disappointment is handed down from father to son, a sad inheritance.

## Sons under the Influence

Mark Twain once observed that, around the age of twelve, a boy picks a man to admire and imitates him for the rest of his life. Though he doesn't always know it, or may try his best to avoid it, that man is usually his father. No matter how far from his father's life a son purposefully directs his own, he eventually comes face to face with his 'old man'.

In a radio interview Buddy Guy, one of America's greatest living blues guitarists, told a story about the son he sired but didn't raise. As the boy grew into young manhood, Buddy sought him out, hoping they could become closer. His son had also become a guitarist, but he was so full of bitterness at Buddy's absence that he wanted nothing to do with him or his brand of music. He had his own, more contemporary rock star idols, most notably the singer formerly known as Prince. When the young man anonymously sought a teacher who could help him in his quest to emulate his idol, he was told that, if he wanted to sound like Prince, he needed to understand how to play guitar like Jimi Hendrix, the musician Prince had sought to emulate. And in order to understand Jimi Hendrix, the teacher said, he needed to learn about *Hendrix*'s biggest musical influence: the guitarist Buddy Guy.

Many men find that they have become like their fathers when it's not what they set out to do. Abandoned by his father, a government clerk and small-time gambler, at the age of six, Jack determinedly charted his own life course in the opposite direction. He was a straight-A student through school, won scholarships to college, put himself through medical school, and went on to become an emergency room physician at a major medical centre. His drive to succeed was all-consuming; he had little time for friendship and was ill at ease in social settings.

Eventually Jack married, and with two young sons he found that he preferred the controlled chaos of the emergency room to the familial chaos at home. Work was at least rewarding. He had the respect of his peers and the satisfaction of knowing he was saving lives. His talents were rewarded with a substantial six-figure salary.

At home he felt criticized and pressured by his wife to spend more time with his boys. A promotion led to additional work hours that consumed his weekends, and soon his schedule was so full that he rarely saw his wife and children except in passing. By making good in the world and providing materially for his family, Jack had overcome his father's legacy of financial failure. But with his older son about to turn six, Jack met his father's shadow as he walked out the door each day to his own more lucrative and socially acceptable escape from family.

## Daddy, Do You Matter?

In July of 1998, in an article entitled 'Daddy Dearest: Do You Really Matter?' the observation was made that, although you could fill a railway carriage with the research that has been done on the importance of the mother–child relationship, you could transport all the work done on the importance of fathers in the boot of your car.[1] But this situation is changing, fuelled in part by federal mandates to address the increased absence of fathers as 'the single biggest social problem' in the United States today. Because more than one-third of all children live apart from their fathers and half of all children experience the absence of their fathers at some point during their childhood, there has been a surge of interest and activity in father research.

Two important developments reflecting this new wave of father research were an October 1996 conference on father involvement sponsored by the American National Institutes of Health and the publication in May 1998 of a special issue of the journal *Demography* that was devoted to new research on fathers' influence on the lives of their children. These new research findings are compelling and show clearly that having a father in the picture, especially an involved one, is good for kids:[2] they tend to be smarter, have better psychological health, do better in school, and get better jobs. When presenting their findings, some of these researchers even depart from the normally arid language of science to use words such as *remarkable* and *astonishing* to describe the powerful influence they found fathers to have on their children's development.

In one of the largest of such studies, Greg Duncan of Northwestern University, along with colleagues at the University of Michigan, studied a group of more than a thousand intact families in the United States over the course of twenty-seven years, examining many aspects of these families' lives that were thought to be influential in determining the future occupations and incomes of their children, including the parents' occupations, incomes, education levels, and IQs. They also looked at what would normally be considered less influential factors, including how much the father helped with housework, whether he used his free time to go to bars or watch TV, how often the family ate dinner together, whether they attended church, and whether the father had any involvement in PTA meetings. What they found surprised them. Of the dozens of factors they considered, father attendance at PTA meetings was the most influential in terms of the child's income at age twenty-seven.[3]

In one of the studies published in *Demography*, researchers at the University of North Carolina and Pennsylvania State University studied 584 children in families that had remained together over the eleven years of the study as part of the National Survey of Children. These children ranged in age from seven to eleven years at the study's inception and were between seventeen and twenty-two at its end.[4]

These scientists were interested in the effects of a mother's and father's emotional closeness and involvement on the psychological and educational well-being of their children as they moved into young adulthood. Fathers who were both emotionally close and highly involved had children with greater educational attainment. Further, having an involved father made it less likely that the child would commit delinquent acts, such as vandalism or selling drugs. These influences were not seen for mothers' involvement. This is not so much because mothers aren't important but because mothers don't differ as much in their level of involvement, so when a father is highly involved, it is a big plus.

Perhaps the most impressive research with respect to the issues of emotional education and empathy are the results of a twenty-six-year study that followed a group of boys and girls from the time they were five years old until age thirty-one. The researchers examined

both maternal and paternal parental roles, looking at several attributes
of parenting, including how much the mother tried to inhibit her
children's aggression, how satisfied she was with her role in the
family, and how much the father was involved in child care. Although
these maternal characteristics were related to a higher level of empathy
at age thirty-one, the most influential factor – more important than
all the maternal factors combined – was whether the father was
involved in the child's care.[5]

Research also shows that fathers, when they are involved, tend to
devote more of their time and effort to boys, particularly during
adolescence.[6] Fathers can play a significant part in boys' emotional
development – especially in the areas where boys lag behind girls,
as in the capacity for empathy – and they protect against problems
in areas that disproportionately affect boys, such as delinquency.

Even though fathers in two-parent families today tend to be
slightly more involved in child care than they were twenty years ago
(a gain of about 15 per cent), their involvement doesn't always
translate into the kind of emotional connection that boys want.[7] We
find that boys feel shortchanged, not only in terms of time but also
in terms of affection, and this loss remains with them into adulthood.
This is illustrated in a finding from a survey of corporate men. In
this study three hundred male executives and mid-level managers
were asked what single thing they would have changed about their
childhood relationship with their father. The leading response,
expressed by a majority of the men, was the wish that they could
have been closer to their fathers and that their fathers had expressed
more emotion and feeling.[8]

### In the Beginning: The Lost Mandate of Fatherhood

In the 1950s, when we were kids, the image of the expectant father
was good for a laugh. In TV comedy skits and cartoons, he was
shown pacing the floor outside the delivery room, smoking cigarette
after cigarette, waiting for the matronly nurse to poke her head out
and proclaim, 'It's a boy!' He was clearly an outsider, a bystander at
his child's entrance into the world.

This image mirrored reality. As the child grew, the dad remained an outsider, for the most part. Child care was mother's work: the feeding, the physical and emotional tending. Dad was good for an occasional game of catch or a weekend fishing trip, but his most important role – and it was clearly defined and accepted – was that of the good provider and disciplinarian.

Expectations of the new father have changed. Today a man often takes childbirth-preparation classes with his wife – some hospitals even require it – and he is expected to be in the delivery room as a coach, holding his wife's hand, helping her breathe during contractions. Today a father is expected to be present for the pain of the delivery, and his are often the first hands that cradle the newborn.

But this intimate partnership often ends when the new father is confronted with the intensity of his infant's needs and his own inexperience as a caregiver. In many instances, a mother simply assumes the role of expert, either by choice or by default.

Even when a man willingly helps with changing nappies and two a.m. feeds, he still defers to his wife as the child-care expert. By turning to his wife whenever a boy is sick or upset, a man misses an opportunity to form a closer connection with his son. These nurturing 'tasks' establish a relationship of caring. This is an important way for a father to first establish a strong, loving presence in his son's life. Without that involvement, men easily slip into the role of 'disqualified dad' at home and withdraw further into work and the role of provider rather than that of participant in the emotional life of the family. This only perpetuates their inexperience in the relationship work of a family and adds to their own and sometimes others' misgivings about the value of their contribution.

'I was there when Ben was born, and I knew just what to do. Everybody thought it was great,' remembers Mark, forty-nine. 'But when we got home, I didn't know what to do, really, to help. Sandy was tired, but she seemed to know what Ben needed, when he needed it, and how to do it. I didn't see a logical way to fit in any more. When I did feed him or give him a bath or play with him, I felt as if I were being watched, like I was on probation. If he cried, Sandy came to settle him down, and if I did something differently, she would have something to say about it. I started finding other ways to stay busy. It was easier to do the laundry. At least I didn't hear any complaints.'

Many women we have talked with acknowledge feeling that they don't fully trust their husbands to care for their infants. One woman's husband left their three-month-old infant alone on the changing table to go answer the telephone. The baby rolled off, luckily sustaining only minor bruises. Another dad stood at the low end of a tall slide and let his toddler son climb the towering ladder to the top, not realizing that the child might topple over the high side of the slide before reaching the end, which, of course, he did.

Most men aren't trained for infant care and aren't eager to look foolish. So at a time when they could, through caring physical contact, be forging the earliest emotional bond with their sons, they instead begin to back away, or they are pushed aside. This is unfortunate because, even in their stereotypical role as the knee-bouncing, toss-the-baby-in-the-air dad, fathers can have a distinct and significant influence on a child's development. Studies indicate that an important contribution that many fathers make is as a play partner, especially in the active, stimulating style of play they most often engage in with sons. This type of active play is highly arousing for the child and is thought to be important to both cognitive and emotional development. When a mother 'protects' a son by routinely correcting his father's style to match her own, she diminishes the opportunity for a genuine and uniquely valuable quality of parenting.

## Middle Childhood: Being a Good Enough Father

In middle childhood, the way a father behaves during play or shared activities teaches his son how to manage his emotions. The problem-solving strategies that boys bring to adolescent and adult social situations are directly traceable to the lessons learned from dads on playing fields and in family dens. For instance, research shows that young boys who are aggressive and are low in 'prosocial' behaviours – meaning they don't share – have fathers who are more likely to engage in angry exchanges with them, such as yelling back at a son who yells at them.

A boy observes how his dad resolves conflicts, cooperates, and works as a partner in marriage and family, in the community, and at work. In all arenas of his life, a father's actions speak more loudly than his words, and a boy is listening carefully to both. If a father can be emotionally honest, candid, thoughtful, and flexible in his responses, then a son's respect will follow. A man who idealizes his strengths, his accomplishments, his confidence, or his relationships distances himself from the reality his son inhabits – a world of more varied emotions and experience.

For example, a father and son are playing tennis. What does the father do when he hits a bad shot? Does he swear and pout, or does he demonstrate for his son how to take it in his stride? When they're working side by side on a project or task and the son drops a tool or makes a mistake, does his dad shrug it off or make it a gentle 'teachable moment', or does he take a punishing stance? When he wrestles with his eight-year-old, does the father have to show the son that he is stronger? Is the tone aggressive or playful? What does a father do when his six-year-old is sad or angry? Does he respond in kind with angry words, does he pretend not to notice, or does he reach out to the son and try to address the underlying problem?

In their attempts to preserve peace and order, parents often forget that one purpose of play is to shake things up. When a boy wrestles, plays basketball, or engages in other play activities, emotions are bound to surface. He may fall down and get hurt, miss or make a crucial shot, experience temporary despair or elation. This recreational disorder seems to offer the developing brain a chance to practise problem solving, critical thinking, and emotional expression in a friendly setting – in short, to play at feelings. An active, playful father can help his son explore a broad emotional landscape, including showing him how to accept frustration, win and lose graciously, and control his temper.

Psychologist Erik Erikson aptly described boys in this middle age of childhood as 'purposeful, productive, and proud'.[9] Growing up is a challenging task, and boys need a sense of pride and confidence that they are up to the task. In their early years, when they are rank beginners at so much, their father's opinion of them carries enormous weight. Whether a boy plays soccer, drums in the band, or builds a model ship in front of his father, he is exquisitely sensitive to his father's reaction.

Raul tells of taking his non-athletic six-year-old son on a skiing holiday and asking afterwards what his son liked best about the experience. The boy replied, 'Watching you watch me ski!' What really mattered to the boy was not how well or poorly he skied but what his dad thought of him. So it is with most boys in middle childhood: their opinion about whether they are competent depends on how they think their father sees them.

A boy wants to look up to and admire his father; he needs to feel that his father is capable, because that helps him believe that he, too, will grow up to be competent. A boy wants a father who thinks he is fantastic – one who knows that he is still little and cannot do everything well but loves him anyway.

The lesson about emotional honesty that a father teaches by how he responds to his own shortcomings and failures is more important than his actually being an expert in every endeavour. Whether conscious or unconscious, a father's emotional façades don't fool his son past the age of about eight or nine years old. A man who acts as if he were better at some things than he really is, or who can't admit mistakes, teaches his son a defective model of manhood.

Contrary to some fathers' fears of creating a 'crybaby' by coddling an emotional son, a father who accepts and assists his son in distress helps him grow stronger emotionally. These are fathers who know that, as Mark Twain wrote: 'Courage is resistance to fear, mastery of fear – not absence of fear.' These are fathers who will gently help their sons with the hard tasks of growing up rather than try to harden or toughen the boys to match a tough world. In our work with boys, we find that the ones who are most prone to break down when the going gets tough are those who have been raised with the idea that to admit vulnerability, even to themselves, is to be weak.

### Michael and Will: Respecting the Child in the Boy

When my son, Will, was six years old, we were driving through the Green Mountains of Vermont to visit his sister at camp. We drove through a brief but very powerful thunderstorm with much lightning, thunder, and sheets of rain that made it very difficult to see the road or stay on it. Though I concentrated intently on the country roads and slowed down to stay safe, I did a couple of times look in the rearview mirror to see how Will was doing in the back seat. He was obviously frightened, but then again, my adrenaline was pumping, too.

When we had passed through the storm, I asked Will how he was. My brain presented me with a couple of culturally stereotyped ways of asking a boy about his fears, such as, 'You weren't scared, were you, buddy?' – an invitation to a boy to deny his feelings. Instead, I asked him, 'That was a little scary, wasn't it, Will?' and he replied, 'No, Dad, that was *very* scary.'

Asking a question this way gives a boy permission to express emotional vulnerability.

### Fathers and Their Adolescent Sons: Separate Realities

For the majority of boys, adolescence is a period of emotional ups and downs as they struggle for control – or the appearance of control – over their lives. The effort to keep vulnerabilities hidden puts a boy on the defensive everywhere he goes – including at home, and especially with his father. A teenager still needs his dad emotionally, but he doesn't want to admit it. To him, Dad is still an uncomfortable reminder of his dependence, of the fact that in some ways he is still a little boy, and of his present unallowable yearnings for Dad's love, attention, and approval. This is at odds with the boy's increasing loyalty to his peer group. This tension drives a wedge between fathers and sons, widening the gap of misunderstanding between them.

Adolescent boys' observations about life with their fathers confirm what research indicates as significant sources of conflict: competition, criticism, and a lack of understanding. Boys in one study reported that they sought their father's opinion or advice about practical issues, but they did not feel that their fathers reciprocated, showing any interest in *their* opinions. At times, it is as if fathers and their teenage sons don't share the same reality.

In a study of family experience often referred to as 'the beeper study', family members carried beepers and were 'buzzed' by researchers at random moments. They then recorded in a diary what they were doing and their feelings at the time. Family members' differing accounts of the same moment or event gave striking evidence of the gap of experience between fathers and sons. *In the study, about 50 per cent of the time, a father and son reported completely different experiences of the same shared moment.*[10]

Perhaps the discrepancy in the fathers' and sons' experiences is attributable to the fact that fathers always experienced themselves as being in control of the conversation. For example, a father who was working around the house with his son when the beeper went off might say that he was enjoying his time with his son and was teaching him a skill. The son, however, would describe that moment as boring or as one in which the father was 'yelling at me'. On the other hand, adolescent boys most enjoyed times when the control of the situation was shared, such as when they were able to teach their fathers something and the fathers were willing to learn.

The same study found that most teenagers felt that their fathers knew them less well as adolescents than they had earlier, and most fathers were unaware of their children's feeling of distance. 'Fathers appear to be the weak link in the emotional life of the family,' researchers Reed Larson and Mayse Richards concluded. They noted that fathers generally related to their sons in three ways: as a leader or teacher, as a promoter or booster, and as a disciplinarian. Fathers were reluctant to give up leadership and control to adolescents and, in general, used a narrower range of strategies for controlling their children's behaviour than mothers did.

Both mothers and fathers can feel affronted when a son begins to challenge them, and both can be wounded by negative or confrontational behaviour. However, we have seen that mothers most often try to keep repairing the bridge to their sons or find some way to build another bridge. Many fathers react with anger and a desire to regain control.

Fathers generally don't bring this same level of antagonism to their relationships with their daughters. Research describes a clear difference in the way fathers interact with sons and daughters from an early age. Typically, dads tend to treat their infant daughters more gently and speak more gently to them. As the children grow, dads mess around more with their sons but show less physical affection, correct them more often, and play more competitively with them. With each passing year, a father's attitude typically becomes more protective of his daughter and more competitive with his son.

Not surprisingly, then, teenage sons do not talk to their fathers about emotional issues. In fact, one large study found that, of all the people in a boy's life – including parents, sisters and brothers, and friends – sons most frequently identified their father as the person to whom they are *least likely* to confide their true feelings.[11] And for good reason: much of what teenage boys talk about is wild-eyed or unrealistic. A father has difficulty hearing a teenager's exaggerations for what they are – an experiment in thinking or a necessary calibration of an unfolding identity. When a father hears foolishness, he sees a fool. He fears a collapse of character and intelligence, or an unacceptably cavalier attitude about the future, and he's quick to try to set his son straight.

## When Father Doesn't Know Best: Competition, Criticism, and Withdrawal

One of television's early and beloved dads was the father, Jim Anderson, played by Robert Young on *Father Knows Best*. We laugh at those old shows now because of their idealized portrayal of family life, but in fact, the popularity of *Father Knows Best* reflected our yearning for a father figure who wore his role of good provider and fair arbitrator of family squabbles like a favourite comfortable sweater. In reality, a father's lack of experience in the emotional realm puts him at a distinct disadvantage as his son enters adolescence.

Under increasing pressure from another male in the household, vulnerable fathers turn to time-honoured defensive responses to maintain the fiction that 'father knows best': control, competition, and criticism.

## Control

Much of our work with fathers of teenage boys involves trying to keep them from reacting with knee-jerk over-control to their sons' normal behaviour. When a thirteen- or fourteen-year-old boy comes home and says that studying maths is useless, especially since he wants to become a professional skateboarding champ, a vision of his son's demise unfolds before a father's eyes: he'll blow his chances at college, a good job, success in the adult world; he'll make his parents look bad. The father feels he has to do something immediately, such as lecturing his son about the qualities a man must have to really be successful.

If, instead, a father can learn to listen to his son, asking questions and showing genuine interest, he will likely realize that skateboarding is merely the fantasy of the moment, but he will have validated his son's enthusiasm and established a pattern for sharing. But with no way for fathers and sons to talk about anything with strong emotional resonance, the typical father–son relationship at this age becomes a practical arrangement: fathers meet the material needs of their sons and in return expect obedience and respect. An adolescent boy struggling to establish his identity and be more independent needs to be taken seriously. If he's not, he'll tune out. A father may win the struggle for control of his son's life for a period of time, but he does so at the expense of their relationship.

### Dan with Larry: Taking the Fun out of Sports

'This kid has talent; he's probably got the best pure swing on the team,' Larry's golf coach told me, 'but it's like he shoots himself in the foot when he's out on the course. It's like he doesn't want to win.' His teachers told me the same thing in a faculty meeting: 'Larry isn't failing, but the effort just isn't there.'

Larry was a tall, thin fifteen-year-old with dark brown hair and bright blue eyes that never seemed to rest. When he talked, Larry continually looked around the room, sometimes making eye contact for an instant. But he wasn't like some boys who just want to get out of my office as fast as they can; rather, he seem relieved to be there and have the chance to talk. Whatever Larry was running from, it seemed to be something inside of him.

His parents had recently separated. Just a few minutes into our conversation, Larry started talking about his dad: 'When I was younger, he really pushed me to play golf. He thought it would help me get a college scholarship or that I would at least thank him someday when I got good. I tried to like it, but he took all the fun out of it.'

'Is he a good golfer?'

'I think he used to be pretty good. I can usually beat him now. But when I was a kid, I felt like that was all he could ever think about.'

'What did he do to take the fun out of it?'

'It was always, win, win, win. Practise, practise, practise. I didn't have a choice.'

'But you're a good golfer now, aren't you?'

'I'm all right, I guess. But I don't really enjoy playing all that much. I'd much rather play baseball, but he'd probably kill me.'

When Larry was around thirteen, he had begun to voice his opinions about golf and other matters, which led to heated arguments that sometimes threatened to erupt into physical violence.

The separation agreement between his parents required Larry to spend every other weekend with his dad. It wasn't long before he started to balk.

'I don't want to go there. I can't see my friends, and all I'm supposed to do is hang around with him and my sister. And he's always such a hard-ass. He won't admit that anything is his fault,' Larry said.

'With him, it's always the same conversation. He thinks that, just because he pays for everything, I should want to hang out with him and tell him I love him. It doesn't work that way. He just yells at me if I say I don't want to spend the weekend. Like that's really going to make me want to show up. He's says that I've got to show him respect. But actually, I don't respect him. He'll say, like, that he's going to change, but it lasts for about a day, and then he's back doing the same things.'

Larry's problem with his father was bigger than we were going to fix in forty minutes per week during the school year. I continued to see him and talk to him, but he also had started family counselling and even had some sessions alone with his dad. But much of the talk was the same. Larry's dad saw the sessions as a way to get Larry to spend time with him, not as a way to work on their relationship. Larry was not always easy to get along with – he was, after all, an angry teenager – but his father was unable to see any point of view other than his own. And this is what was distancing his son from him. By not listening to what Larry had to say, his father was denigrating Larry's thoughts, feelings, wishes. He might as well have been telling Larry he doesn't exist. So in order to feel as if he was alive, as if he had some control over his life, Larry had to resist his father, which included not living up to his potential on the golf course.

## Competition

Men's lives are filled with competition for dominance, status, and power, often just for fun. In adolescence a boy's competition with his father reaches a fever pitch, with predictably volatile results.

There is an inevitable conflict between the growing confidence and power of the adolescent and the increasingly defensive posture of the father. Fathers of adolescent boys are highly vulnerable. Typically well into their forties, men are beginning to see and feel the effects of ageing, not only physically but often in their work and recreational pursuits. It is a sobering realization that their youth is spent, and often there is denial and anger over the loss.

At the same time, their sons are going full throttle through puberty. They are growing rapidly in height, weight, and muscle mass. They are full of the joy of new capabilities. Every leap forward by the son accentuates the growing physical disparity between his father and himself. In a relationship defined by emotional distance, these developmental steps are not marked by conversation or celebration, but they are nonetheless milestones in a boy's emotional growth. Most men have a vivid recollection of the time when they first realized that they could 'take' their father:

Tom, who is nearly fifty, recalls: 'I remember it because it was the last time we ever wrestled. I was sixteen, and my brother was fourteen. We were going at it pretty hard, and Dad was starting to take it pretty seriously. Finally, he managed to pin us both down. Then he called it quits. We learned the next day that he had broken two ribs.'

Dave, in his early twenties, recalls a similar defining moment: 'I was almost seventeen. [My father and I] were arguing about whether I deserved to take the car out on Saturday. He was giving me all kinds of crap about my attitude and how I was irresponsible and why should he let me have the car if that's the way I was going to be. It was a bunch of bullshit; I was basically a decent kid. Pretty soon I couldn't stand it any more. I started to yell back at him. I had my finger right in his face. I guess that was too much for him, and he snapped. He slammed me up against the wall in the kitchen, and I shoved him back so hard he fell down. Then I stormed out of the house. We stayed out of each other's way after that. About two months later, he had a mild heart attack. I knew then – and I could tell that he knew, too – that I would never fear him in the same way again.'

Rick, who is forty, remembers: 'I think I was about sixteen. I was wrestling my dad in the living room. We were about the same height, although he outweighed me by quite a bit. We were on the floor. I had my arms around him and was working pretty successfully at not letting him up. Then he broke free with one arm and started punching me. He was only hitting me in the arm, but he was hitting me as hard as he could. I was kind of stunned. Clearly something was different. Wrestling around had always been fun. We would mostly laugh while we did it. But he was upset. Then I figured out that it wasn't easy for him any more. He could no longer physically dominate me. I remember feeling weird about it. I don't think we ever wrestled after that.'

★

Fathers need to celebrate the accomplishments of their sons, to honour them for who they are. Unless a father can avoid making a son his proxy – pushing the son to achieve in a particular sport or endeavour so that the father can vicariously claim the victory won – there will be little room for their relationship to develop.

A friend in his mid-forties tells of his local soccer team, composed mostly of fathers and sons. There are four men in their fifties and their seven sons, all in their late teens and early twenties. The older men have been playing together for more than twenty years. Many of the boys played for Sunday league teams, sometimes coached by one father or another, and then later for the same high school. Soccer has therefore had a central place in their lives. It is, in part, this shared interest that affords these fathers and sons the opportunity to celebrate each other.

Their season begins in April, when many of the sons are still away at school. At first it is the fathers, hampered by diminishing skills and chronic injuries, who must carry the load. As May rolls into June, the athletically gifted sons return and begin to play alongside their fathers, sometimes replacing them in the line-up.

A woman watching the games might not see the love between these men. It is peculiarly male. It is not expressed in hugs or very often even in words. But it is palpable. It can be seen in a father's quiet joy at his son's goal. It's evident in the son's trying to help his father fight the ageing process. One son worked persistently over two seasons to get his father to buy some glasses that would help him see the ball when he kicked. Another designed an off-season weight-training programme for his dad.

This team won the town championship last year, and this season you can hear the love between these men in the reminiscences of the glories of their shared triumph.

### Criticism

If a father feels he has to dominate or control his son, he'll use whatever power is at hand. Sometimes it's punitive restrictions on the use of the car, the phone, money, or the boy's own free time. Even when a son finds that he is physically stronger, he continues to experience his father as emotionally dominant. And a father's ultimate psychological weapon is criticism, because most sons remain acutely sensitive to a father's put-downs well into adulthood.

The war stories from this father–son front come to us from all sorts of survivors: angry, depressed young sons; men who remain bitter as adults over their father's determination to dominate them as youths; and women who wince at the memory of fathers and brothers, husbands and sons engaged in an uneven emotional duel.

Louis, a fifteen-year-old, says bluntly that he hates his father: 'He's totally clueless,' the boy says. 'He can't talk about anything with me. He finds something wrong with everything I do, and when he's not putting me down, he just talks about himself, like I'm supposed to be interested in this stuff that has nothing to do with me. Most of the time he doesn't listen to what I say, but it's worse when he does, because then he just starts in on me. Everything turns into an argument, and there's no way to win.'

Louis has learned to avoid his father whenever possible. When it was time to find an after-school job, he chose one with evening hours to keep himself out of the house three nights a week. Eventually, Louis will move on to a career and life of his own; the landscape of his life will change, but the emotional gulf between him and his father shows no sign of shrinking.

Joan had a hardworking, responsible father who worked two jobs to support his wife and four children. He was dutiful, even sweet to her sometimes, but he was not much of a one for talk unless it was criticism of her brother: 'My father rarely talked with any of us, but he criticized my brother over absolutely everything – his hair or his clothes, the look on his face. My brother was so creative, so smart, and had such a great sense of humour. As far as my sisters and I were concerned, he could do no wrong. It never occurred to me how hurtful it must have been for my brother until I had a son of my own. Now I see how much my son enjoys it when my husband is kind to him, even in the littlest ways, and I see how much it hurts when he is short-tempered or critical. I feel sad for my brother. The relationship never changed for him and my father, and once my brother left home, he pretty much avoided my father for the rest of his life. My father died last year, and my brother is on wife number three, with four children he's left behind with ex-wives. He has no relationship with any of them. I love my brother, but his life is a mess. I don't exactly blame my dad for that, but – as a mother of a boy, now – I can't help but think there's a connection.'

The consequences of withheld praise or unbridled criticism are deep and lasting. Well into middle age, men can vividly recall specific feelings of hurt, anger, or bewilderment. A fifty-two-year-old patient tells of the day he graduated at the head of his class at a respected university. He told his parents he planned to take his expertise and enthusiasm to the classroom: he wanted to be a teacher. His father's one and only reaction was angry dismay: 'You mean, after all that, you want to be a teacher? Why can't you get a *man's* job?'

A friend from a churchgoing family recalls his adolescence and the days filled with strife between his father and himself: 'I only wanted to hear him say, just once, what God said about Jesus: "This is my son in whom I am well pleased."'

More fathers need to communicate more often to their all-too-flawed sons the simple message that they are loved and valued.

## Fathers and Sons: Closing the Emotional Gulf

We have witnessed father–son relationships in which men and boys have thrived, in which the inevitable tension between fathers and sons has been converted into a bonding experience. Sometimes a family crisis – a mother's illness or death, for instance – has brought them together. But more often, they have created an emotional dialogue through shared activity and a receptive attitude – simply doing things together and listening and talking to each other with respect.

A strong father–son relationship may look and sound nothing like its counterpart between a mother and a son. Specifically, there may not be the level of talk or of physical contact that we often associate with emotional closeness between women. Between men the talk may be centred around action instead of reflection. A physical expression of affection may come in sharing a space – sitting side by side to assemble a model or standing at opposite ends of the field for a game of catch, the arc of the ball tracing the bond of affection that is clearly there.

One father says he and his thirteen-year-old son enjoy their closest moments when they are working on a fix-it job. He happily recalls helping his son with an adjustment on his in-line skates one day. He screwed the fitting down with a flourish, and his son clapped him on the back and said emphatically, 'You're *the man!*'

Another dad says that he and his son, now a teen, have played chess together since the boy was young. When they sit down to this largely silent and pleasantly competitive game, the tension of the day or the sting of a recent disagreement between them dissolves. Chess provides a safe, easy space for them to be together and enjoy each other's company.

Are these relationships less 'emotional' because they don't include much direct discussion about love or conflict? Not necessarily. We believe that in general it is better not to leave important feelings unexpressed and that words are often the clearest and most unequivocal way to do this. But is there an absolute quality-of-relationships scale that requires that you talk about things? We do know that talk isn't the only way to express love or resolve conflict. In fact, there are times when words get in the way.

Simple activities bring a father and son together in a way that allows them to experience sharing, even if it's on a modest scale. One man accompanies his young son on 'bug walks', ostensibly looking for insects to study; they routinely return home empty-handed and happy. Another father and son go together for haircuts once a month, while another takes his son to the shops every Saturday morning to buy cold cuts and rye bread for weekend sandwiches. These and other simple rituals of sharing can be the foundation for strong father–son relationships. Many fathers and sons have been able to reclaim shared activities that they had put aside years earlier, and they've recovered a lost sense of camaraderie along the way. Simplistic as it may sound, we've often observed that just having a ritual activity to share can boost the odds that a father–son relationship will survive the stormy waters of adolescence.

Patterns of emotional isolation can change. Fathers can change them. A man who wants a more satisfying relationship with his son can begin to build it in simple but meaningful ways: a bedtime story, a game of catch, a compliment, a smile. The willingness to try is, itself, the start of a new pattern that can replace the disappointment of emotional distance with a legacy of love.

# 6. Mothers and Sons: A Story of Connection and Change

*There is an enduring tenderness in the love of a mother to a son that transcends all other affections of the heart.*

Washington Irving

A mother, Jane, and her twenty-four-month-old son, Alexander, have made their daily trip to the park. She sits quietly reading. He surveys the landscape looking eagerly around for things to explore. Mustering his courage, he ventures a few feet away from her – investigating the grass, the twigs, the bugs, and the rocks around him – then he returns to his mother. He hugs her neck, climbs on her back, and then is off again. Each time he leaves her, he ventures a little farther, making a slightly wider orbit of exploration. She keeps her eye on him, and when she feels that he has gone far enough, she calls him back and goes out to meet him halfway.

This is the fundamental pattern of relationship between a boy and his mother. He is the explorer; she is his 'home base'. Emotionally, as well as physically, throughout his childhood, as a boy explores, he carries the safety and familiarity of his mother with him. As he grows, a boy must be able to leave his mother without losing her completely and return to her without losing himself. A mother's loving task is parallel: she must try to understand and respond to what her son needs at different stages of his life. When a relationship has this balance, we describe it as *synchronous*.

Mothering any child comes down to this delicate balance of closeness and distance, but between mothers and their sons, there are many ways in which the synchrony can be disrupted. If she doesn't recognize, in his changing behaviours and attitudes towards her, the necessary phases of her son's growth, she may fail to provide what he now needs, or she may continue trying to provide something he no longer needs or wants. For many women, mothering a boy is additionally challenging, in that they feel they don't understand boys, because they have never actually experienced the world as a boy or they have expectations about boys drawn from relationships with fathers or brothers, which colour the way they view their sons.

It is common to regard a mother's connection to her son as finite, an inevitable casualty of a boy's growth into manhood. Certainly, there comes a point in his young life when a boy must shift his central attachment from his mother to his father and begin to identify himself as a man-in-the-making. However, there is *no* point – not at age four, or nine, or thirteen, when a boy must 'give up' his mother, or when a mother must 'give up' her son. A synchronous mother–son relationship transforms itself – and each of them – over the course of his childhood. We believe that a boy who is cut off from his mother is at risk. Yet many boys begin to act as if everything a mother once represented – intimacy, warmth, love, nurturance – is now off limits, the closeness they shared irrevocably lost. Many women resist this. We see a great number of mothers who want to preserve the closeness, but they don't know how. Women who love their sons fear losing them, yet they feel impelled by cultural messages to 'cut the apron strings'. A mother who cares about her son and wants what's best for him can easily fall prey to the worry that, if she stays too close, he'll turn out to be a mummy's boy, or worse, a sissy.

For his part, a boy brings his need to feel competent and distinctly male. He looks to his mother for love and acceptance, but he will distance himself from her when he feels the need for autonomy or to assert his 'boyness'. That is natural and expectable, but a boy never loses his need to be understood and loved by his mother. This fluctuation between independence and deep need can confuse many mothers. Because a boy's task of growing and changing is quite different from his mother's task of guiding and nurturing him, their relationship plays out in two distinct versions: his and hers. The two don't always mesh.

### When a Mother and Her Son are out of Sync

Boys often complain, 'My mother just doesn't get it.' They don't need her to, actually; she's a parent, and there are some things parents just don't 'get'. But boys become frustrated with the relationship when they feel that their mothers misunderstand them more often than not or that their mothers – by being either appalled or naive – overreact to what is normal for boys their age.

Sam and his mother had always been especially close. When Sam's older brother was off playing basketball with his dad, she would take Sam, still a toddler, along to her sculptor's studio and give him his own pile of clay to work with. At night, when father and older son were poring over Civil War history books, Sam and his mother would snuggle together on the sofa, as she read him the poetry that she had loved as a child.

But when Sam turned twelve, he began to pull away from his mother. Almost overnight, he began to complain that poetry was for 'babies' and working in clay was 'boring'. He started to dodge her hugs and after dinner on most nights beat a quick retreat to the privacy of his room. His mother tried not to feel hurt, reminding herself that at this age Sam needed some room to grow, but his emotional withdrawal was difficult for her to accept. So every time he pulled away, she stepped in to close the gap.

In a reprise of their cherished bedtime routine when he was younger, she began knocking on his door at night, wanting to come in and talk. As she sat on the edge of his bed, trying to make conversation, he made no effort to conceal his impatience. When she tried to explain that she simply missed their conversations, he only said, 'Mum, I have to get back to my studying. Would you please just leave?'

'When I finally started locking my door, that was the final straw for her,' he says.

For the next week or so, each time she knocked, he called out through the door for her to leave him alone. Then one day, angry and frustrated, his mother pounded on the door, shouting, 'Open up! I'm your mother, dammit!'

A mother can experience her son's first moves towards independence as rejection and loss, but that isn't what they are. Sam's mother's intense effort to hold on to him only damaged their relationship. Thirty years later Sam still recalls the friction of that time.

When mothers tell us how difficult it can be to constantly adjust, to change their perspective or responses to accommodate a son's new place on the developmental curve, we often hear a version of the 'sweater story', in which a mother feels so deeply bonded with her child that, when the temperature drops and she feels cold, she runs to get *him* a sweater. But there comes a point when a mother must allow her son to make his own decisions – to make mistakes, even if it means blue lips and chattering teeth.

## Developmental Changes and Expectations

'The child, in the decisive first years of his life, has the experience of his mother, as an all-enveloping, protective nourishing power,' wrote philosopher/psychologist Erich Fromm. 'Mother is food; she is love; she is warmth; she is earth. To be loved by her means to be alive, to be at home.' When a mother reacts reliably and sensitively to her infant's needs, he will form an internal connection to her – what psychologists call 'a secure attachment' – that will provide a strong foundation of trust and love on which he can build other relationships.[1]

From this beginning of absolute closeness, certain developmental milestones in a boy's life mark shifts in the mother–son relationship. The key transitions are toddlerhood, when a boy becomes mobile and can explore his world; when he enters kindergarten and a new world of adult supervisers who will be influential in his life; puberty, when he becomes interested in girls, and when the influence of his peer group challenges his mother's influence; and after he graduates from school and often moves away from home. At each point a mother must adjust her connection, providing both the emotional grounding and the emotional freedom her son requires in order to grow. A boy needs to feel that his mother has confidence in his ability to manage new experiences.

The classic children's story 'The Runaway Bunny', by Margaret Wise Brown, celebrates this dance of separation and connection. A young bunny happily taunts his mother with the threat that he will run away from her and she will never find him. He will become something else entirely – a mountain, a flower, a sailboat, a bird, a trout. Each time, his mother meets his fanciful vision with her own image of reassuring presence. If he becomes a mountain, she will visit him as a mountain climber. If he is a trout, then she will be a fisherman. If he becomes 'a crocus in a hidden garden', she will become a gardener. 'If you become a bird and fly away from me,' she says, 'I will be a tree that you can come home to.'

'The Runaway Bunny' is pretty heady stuff for a three-year-old boy, who is thrilled by the image of adventure with the assurance of his mother's unwavering love and presence. Although a boy never outgrows the need for mothering or that emotional home base, his expectations of it change with age and maturity. To a fifteen-year-old boy, 'The Runaway Bunny' image of mother-at-every-turn is the 'smothering mothering' of boys' nightmares.

### Michael with Jason's Mother: Blue Hair and Self-Determination

Jason was his mother's dream son. He was a cheerful baby, an active, inquisitive toddler. By the time he was three, his mother, Anne, saw his daring shows of independence as amusing and acceptable; if he was defiant or threw a tantrum over something, usually she was able to distract his attention or charm him into compliance.

Jason was ten when his father began to travel extensively for work and was often gone, sometimes for weeks at a time. Jason pitched in, taking more responsibilities around the house. He was cooperative. If his mother said to be home by six o'clock for dinner, he was home. If she said he needed to practise clarinet before playing with the computer, he did that, too.

At fourteen, the dream son began to change. He challenged Anne on everything. He let his responsibilities slide; she felt she had to nag him constantly about homework and clarinet practice. He began to defy her: if she said to be home at six o'clock, he'd come in at seven; if she made it seven, he'd come at seven-thirty.

Then it was minor, but constant, skirmishes over the length of his hair.

She thought she'd won that battle, until the day Jason walked into the house with his hair dyed electric blue. She demanded he get rid of the blue, so he did – replacing it with Halloween black. Then, when she came home from work one evening, the black was gone, along with the rest of Jason's hair. He'd shaved it off.

'I don't know what's happened to him,' she said. 'He hardly talks to me at all, and it seems like everything he says or does is something he knows is going to bother me. We argue constantly. I don't know what to do.'

Anne wondered if her husband's extended absences were at the heart of her son's change in behaviour. Other couples were experiencing similar rebelliousness by their teenage sons. She thought his challenging academic load might be getting to him. But his teachers said he was doing fine.

'That only leaves one other source of the problem – me,' Anne said. 'And I'm sorry, but I resent the idea that somehow it's all my fault. I am not a bad mother.'

She wasn't a 'bad' mother, but with every move Jason made to exert his budding sense of independence, Anne clamped down, fearing she was 'losing control'.

Part of the issue for Anne was that she didn't recognize that an adolescent bid for autonomy is normal. Teenagers like to 'test limits', to see what they can get away with, to see whether they can drive their mum nuts. It's like a repeat of the terrible twos. In a group counselling session once with several teenage boys, one of them made a horribly sexist, misogynistic remark. I came down hard on him – but he disarmed me. 'Hey, look – I'm a teenager,' he said. 'I'm *supposed* to say provocative things.' When a mother's authority is being challenged, she has to do two things at once: recognize and support a boy's continued dependence without throwing that dependence in his face, and accept his small bids for independence without reacting to them as if they were threatening or scary.

You can tell how fragile a boy is by how ferociously he fights over autonomy. The more confident he is of his strength, the easier it is for him to acknowledge his dependence. Anne endured two years of this battle in part because she resisted this transition; with her husband gone, she felt she had to be more tenacious than ever about maintaining her authority. Jason felt he had to keep taking increasingly stronger stands in order to assert himself. And so they had to battle it out.

No matter how closely matched you and your son are in terms of temperament, interests, or outlook, you can never assume that your son will see eye to eye with you when the real issue is his quest for autonomy – the right to make his own decisions – and his need to distance himself from his history of dependence and the most prominent witness to it: his mother.

## Mothers as Teachers of Emotional Understanding

A mother has tremendous psychological power. The emotional bond a man has with his mother is the most deeply rooted connection in his life. For many boys she is the only person they can trust. If a boy doesn't have that kind of relationship with her, he can suffer a devastating loss.

Andrew, fourteen, arrived for family counselling one afternoon with his parents. From the moment he walked in, he'd been moving around the room, opening closets and doors, spinning in his chair, climbing under the desk. His mother asked him to sit down, and he began tapping his foot against her leg. Rather than embarrass him more by asking him to stop, she simply took his foot in her hand, holding it gently but firmly as she continued to talk. Within moments Andrew quietened down. His mother's nurturing gesture calmed him and enabled him to engage when it was his turn to talk.

When we asked two teenaged boys who we know enjoy good relationships with their mothers to describe that relationship, true to age neither used the word *love*. But both described a comfort level they felt with their mothers, and one finally defined what he meant: 'Well, she's pretty much right about everything.' By that, he explained, he meant that she usually understood him. For a mother, finding the 'right' answer often involves a struggle to distinguish her son's emotional considerations from her own.

### Dan with Doug's Mum: Balancing Fears and Needs

Carol came to see me shortly after her divorce from Rick, who had been physically and emotionally abusive for the last half of their eighteen-year marriage. What I didn't know then was that this was the beginning of a long struggle for Carol, in which she eventually would face one of the most difficult kinds of decisions: to let go of a son.

In the beginning Carol and I talked a lot about how she could extricate herself from her ex-husband, how she could avoid his cursing, raging phone calls. How she could stop feeling guilty wondering whether, if she had done something differently, things would have worked out better. And she talked a lot about her son, Doug, a fifteen-year-old who was underperforming at school and seemed to be angry and confused about the divorce. In fact, it was hard sometimes for her to stop talking about him and focus on herself and her own issues – whether to try to get a university degree; how much she really liked the new men she was meeting; and the status of her relationship with her mother, who she felt blamed her for the divorce and still maintained a close relationship with Rick.

'I worry about Doug,' Carol said one day. 'Sometimes I see flashes of Rick's temper in him, and I get scared. Not for me. I don't think he would ever hurt me. But I worry that, growing up in that house and seeing what he did – I don't know. I wish I could protect him from ending up like his father.'

'How about the custody situation? Is Rick continuing to fight for Doug to live with him?'

'They set a new court date, but my lawyer says he doesn't stand a chance. In fact, he tells me that Rick's lawyer keeps trying to convince him to drop it – that he's only wasting money.'

'Sounds like he's going to try to stay connected to you any way he can.'

'It's awful. But I won't give in. I think his having Doug every other weekend is more than enough. I don't want to take Doug away from his father, but it makes me crazy to think about him over there. I know Rick tells Doug terrible lies about me and expects him to be his spy, asking him about who I'm going out with – things like that. I wish he could see that it's bad to put Doug in the middle like that.'

Carol was faced with the painful prospect that confronts many single parents: being legally bound to send her son to live with someone she felt was harmful. It's like telling a mother of a four-year-old that she has to send him out on to a busy street to play.

But Rick was his father, after all, and Doug had to come to terms one day with what kind of man his father was. He would learn that when he was ready, but for now Carol knew that Doug needed to have as good a relationship as possible with his father. Although she knew that, she wanted so much to protect Doug from a man whose evil side she saw so clearly.

Over the next few years, Carol gradually picked up the pieces of her life. She went back to college, got seriously involved with Bob, a man she had met through her church, and came to an understanding of sorts with her mother. Rick had been less bothersome. He had even moved away for nearly a year. But he was back now and up to his old tricks – the harassing phone calls, the lies, and spiteful efforts to get Doug away from her. One day he succeeded.

'Doug wants to move in with Rick.'

'Why?'

Carol wiped tears from her eyes. 'I don't know. I think Rick has been telling him horrible things about me. Doug asked me the other day whether I had had an affair with the guy who lives next door to us. My God! Who does he think I am? Rick is so crazy. He thinks I slept with every man on the planet.'

'Do you think Doug will really leave?'

'Oh . . . this is so . . . hard. I think maybe he *has* to, you know? Rick is the only father he's got. Doug wants to believe in him. Maybe Doug and I have been too close. Sometimes I think I loved him too much.'

'What do you mean?'

'That I depended on him too much, that I cared about him so much that he's been afraid to hurt me by moving away.'

'But you've always been clear with him about that. I think you've showed him that you are strong and that you could handle it if he moved away.'

'I think he may be testing that theory now. The other day he said some very ugly things to me, and I told him, "If we're to share a home, then you have to treat me with respect. You can't live here and behave like that." '

Carol's first inclination was to hold on to Doug at all costs. She wanted to believe that she could hold on to him and help him deal with the pain that so clearly afflicted him. But she also saw the other side. He was almost eighteen; their relationship needed to change. He could still remain at the centre of her heart, but he couldn't – shouldn't – be at the centre of her day-to-day life. And he needed to understand his father. Despite the fact that Rick had been a horrible husband, she knew that Doug's relationship with his father was not as bad and it would be a mistake to undermine it. Finally, she knew that her son's behaviour was getting intolerable. And in the end that's what finally made her let him go. But it was not a planned or pleasant parting scene.

One night when Carol came home late from an evening with Bob, she found Doug drunk and in a rage. He threw a lamp through the window and loudly cursed at his mother. He repeatedly shouted, 'Aren't you gonna call the police? Aren't you gonna call the police?' – something his father had said at times when he would batter Carol. It took a neighbour's help, but Carol finally got Doug quietened. The next day, when he was sober, Carol told him he had to go. When she told me about it during our next meeting, she was clearly sad but no longer weepy. She knew she had done the right thing.

'I told him he couldn't do anything that would make me stop loving him. I know that he's got to have one solid place in his life, and that's me.'

He was only gone four months. 'He came back in trickles,' Carol said. 'At first he would sit out back on the picnic table and watch me as I hung out the laundry. He'd say about two words and then leave. Sometimes when he'd talk to me, I could see his lower lip quivering. It was very hard on him.'

A little over a year later, I attended Carol and Bob's wedding. One of the first things Carol did when I saw her there was pull me aside and say, 'Look at him – I'm so proud.' She wasn't talking about her new husband, Bob. She pointed to Doug. I realized I hadn't seen him in a long time. He was a young man now. He had his own flat and a pretty good job. He no longer had that angry, brooding look I remembered from before. He was smiling and poised.

After the ceremony he stood up and made a toast to the bride and groom. I don't remember his words, but I do remember that after he said them, he leaned over and gave his mother a kiss. For mother and son, it had been a difficult but determined passage, and now they had plenty to celebrate.

## Mothers and Sons at Odds: When Expectations Become Obstacles

The mother of a boy faces two gender-specific obstacles that may disrupt the synchrony of her relationship with her son: if she didn't grow up with brothers, she may not feel she knows very much about what boys are like. Or if she has had difficult experiences with boys or men, it may colour how she views her son. How successful a mother is in seeing her son only for who he is and in bridging that gender gap has a great deal to do with how successful she is going to be in reading, adapting to, and especially, enjoying her son.

Tom, six, had learning problems and difficulty controlling impulsive behaviour. His mother, Alice, was extremely worried about him and highly anxious, but at the same time almost fatalistic in her outlook, as if her young son were already beyond help. In therapy Alice described how her childhood was indelibly marked by her brother's death in the crash of his small airplane during a flight the family later learned involved drug running. He had had learning disabilities and behaviour problems similar to Tom's when he was young, and Alice had spent her childhood worrying about him. Now she carried the same consuming fear for her own son, amplified by her feeling that Tom was headed for a bad end and she was helpless to stop it.

After identifying the deeper source of her fears, and separating her experience of her brother's life from the facts of her son's life, Alice was able to see her son's needs more clearly and respond in a more direct and meaningful way. She arranged for a learning disabilities tutor to work with Tom and stayed on top of his needs as the school year progressed. In this way she was able to avoid the kind of denial – the emotional blinkers – her family had had about her brother's high-risk behaviour and thus protect her son in the best way: by responding to his needs instead of reacting to her fears.

A mother's attitude towards men also communicates to her son a message about her feelings towards him. If a woman is disappointed in her husband or ex-husband and communicates this to her son, she not only undermines her son's relationship with the only father he has but is implicitly criticizing him as well.

A mother who enjoyed having brothers growing up may be at ease living with that boy energy in the family again, and the message she communicates to her son is that his activity is understood and he is lovable. If her brother was her chief tormentor, she may feel especially angry or defensive about her son's casual way with feelings.

Every mother of a boy faces the task of trying to understand aspects of boy life and boy thought that she cannot experience: Why can't boys sit still? Why do they bite their toast into gun and dagger shapes? Why don't they think more often about the consequences of an action *before* they do it? Why don't they say more about their lives?

Anger, high activity, silence, and physical risk taking are characteristics of boys that women need to try to understand. Fran was distressed over her five-year-old son's angry tantrums. He would pull all the clothes out of his drawers and fling toys around his room. Whenever her young son had a tantrum, she shouted him down and ordered him to a corner of a quiet room in a distant upstairs corner of the house, but more often lately the time-outs seemed to be backfiring: he flagrantly disobeyed her order to stay in the corner and would come back more belligerent than before. What was wrong with him, she wanted to know, that he should be so ferocious, so reckless, so disobedient?

Fran was terrified of her son and didn't realize it. She thought she had a real 'wild man' on her hands and tended to use overly powerful disciplinary methods, which only made the boy fight harder to maintain the connection he needed to have with her. What she had was just a five-year-old boy who needed limits. She thought he was a monster. She had never spent much time around young boys, and she needed to remember that he was just five. But because this five-year-old came in a boy package, she couldn't figure it out.

Whatever a mother's fears or expectations about life with boys, whether they are voiced or only thought, they are nonetheless communicated and will affect her son's feelings about himself and the quality of the mother–son bond.

Rhonda, the mother of two fine college-age sons, recalled how different her two sons were as young children and how she responded so much more comfortably and readily to her older son, Jonathon, who was more like her – talkative and demonstrative. 'He used to come home and talk about everything that happened to him from the beginning of his day to the end – everybody he saw, everything he did.'

Mark, her younger boy, was quieter, seemed to understand the boundaries of good behaviour, and usually shared little about his day at school or his friends. He was more self-effacing and reflective, like his father. Two months into his first year at college, he broke up with his girlfriend from school but didn't tell his parents about it. Rhonda only found out when she ran into the girl's mother at the grocery store. Rhonda called Mark to ask why he hadn't shared the news himself. Mark told her that he was sorry but that he didn't think it was such a big deal. He said he would have told her eventually and tried to assuage her by saying, 'I promise I'll call if I run off and get married some weekend.' Rhonda felt hurt by Mark's failure to communicate the news of the break-up and tried to make him feel guilty about it for some time afterwards.

Mark hadn't kept silent on the matter in an effort to hurt his mother's feelings, and yet his silence did, indeed, hurt her feelings. When her unhappy response suggested that he had done something wrong, that he had come up short of her expectations, he couldn't understand it and felt unfairly criticized. When Rhonda judged his actions based on a feminine standard – in this instance, that it is reasonable to expect someone to immediately share something this important – she set herself up to be disappointed.

What any woman must do to bridge the gender gap is to understand that there really is a different way of thinking and being 'over there' and that her perspective as a woman will not always give her a clear picture of her son's motivations or meaning. It's a mistake to interpret a son's withdrawal the way you would the withdrawal of a woman friend. It helps to understand a boy's reactions first as a reflection of his perspective as a boy and then in terms of the unique mother–child relationship. When a mother misreads that cue as a lack of feeling and responds herself with hurt or anger, the misread cues are compounded and the synchrony of their relationship suffers.

## The Transition of Touch

Almost every mother notices, at some point, that her son shies away from overt displays of physical affection between them. And almost every mother reports that, at some point, she feels uncomfortable hugging, kissing, or caressing her son as she once did routinely when he was younger. Mothers and sons experience this transition quite differently.

In a parenting group discussion, Sandy, the mother of three, described her recent concerns about casual physical contact with her thirteen-year-old son: 'Ever since the children were little, they would come jump in bed with me to snuggle and chat. It's always been that way. Lately, when my two younger ones come on to my bed to chat, I don't mind, but now that Bryant is thirteen, it doesn't seem quite right. I'm not comfortable with it any more. It doesn't seem fair to him: he can't help it if he's thirteen. But it just makes me uncomfortable.'

Asked what she feared, she continued: 'I don't know. He's always been a cuddly kid, but now I'm thinking, "He's touching me. What kind of effect is that having on him?" I'm starting to think these things, and I just don't want to ruin our relationship; this is definitely interfering. I guess I'm worried that he might end up with thoughts that he might not know how to handle. I'm worried about him growing up normally, and I want our relationship to be appropriate. It's not that he's doing anything wrong, really. It's just me worrying. I don't know what I'm afraid of, except I just don't want to do the wrong thing.'

Some mothers fear that physically affectionate mothering may make a boy homosexual or a 'mummy's boy' or that their physical closeness will send 'the wrong message' or be misinterpreted, especially by an adolescent son whose sexuality is becoming a more prominent feature in his life. Many mothers tell us they simply don't want to embarrass their son in front of other boys in ways that might make him a target of teasing. All of these beliefs or fears have meaning in a boy's life, but the meaning is often quite different from what a mother presumes.

Nurturing touch plays a strong role in infant and child development, and research suggests that it continues to be important as a way of communicating love and caring between parents and their older children.[2] Most mothers continue to share some level of physical closeness with their daughters throughout the growing-up years. The picture is quite different for boys. Most mothers of boys find that this nurturing physical contact with a son grows more awkward and less frequent by around age eight or nine, but the shift is perhaps most dramatic as he moves into adolescence.

Maureen, the mother of a seventeen-year-old boy, remembered the day she no longer felt comfortable with casual physical shows of affection. 'It was the day I looked at him at fifteen and realized he was bigger than me and, with his hairy chest and fuzzy face, looked basically like a younger version of my husband. I felt awkward hugging him the same way after that.'

Sandy described how her ten-year-old son still kissed her hello and good-bye and simply to express affection at other moments in the day, and still liked a back rub at bedtime. But she was starting to pull back. 'I know the time is coming soon when I won't be doing this. It's just not appropriate to be hugging and handling your sixteen-year-old son the same way. I don't want to be weird. I don't think there's anything uncomfortable about it for him right now, but I'm trying to cut back on it because I don't want him to have to tell me to stop.'

Like many other aspects of mothering, physical closeness remains important throughout a boy's life. It may look different for a five-year-old than it will for a fifteen-year-old, but the message of a loving connection remains the same. There is no downside to this message. A mother's simple physical affection, when it respects a boy's comfort level, carries no hidden dangers. It doesn't determine a boy's sexual orientation. It doesn't promote incest or unwholesome sexuality, and it will not weaken a boy's sense of masculinity.

Aaron, thirteen, was an affectionate boy as a young child, and he and his mother, Hope, had always exchanged a quick hug and kiss when she dropped him off at school. By the time he was nine, Hope noticed that most of her son's classmates' mothers weren't doing that any more, but she continued to offer the hugs, and Aaron continued to reciprocate.

'When he was ten, on his first day of school in the autumn term, we pulled up in front of the building, and he gathered up his backpack and grabbed his clarinet case, and then there was this awkward pause – he didn't lean over for that hug – and we each looked at the other for a second, then we broke out laughing and I shooed him away. We shouted byes, and I figured this was it. This was the new "hug and kiss",' she said.

Their routine changed. Each school morning, they exchanged smiles and a few happy parting words, and that was that. After about a week, Aaron calibrated the closeness to his own liking. 'He came in after school, and later in the afternoon he wandered over and asked for an "energizer hug",' his mother said. In the years since, she said, the request for an 'energizer hug' has become shorthand, not only as an impromptu expression of affection but sometimes as a cue that her son's day has been particularly stressful and he needs that extra boost.

When boys shun overt displays of motherly affection, it's typically because they are reminded of 'little boy' days of dependency – something every boy is struggling to leave behind. 'It's kind of embarrassing to show affection, like if your mum kisses you in public,' explained Matt, nineteen. To even tell anyone that you love your mum 'would feel a little weird', he said. But he did like the back rubs his mum used to give him at bedtime. Those stopped when he was about fourteen when he began staying up later than she, and although he missed the closeness, he never said anything about it.

Boys won't usually say anything about it. That doesn't change the fact that, whether the physical expression between a boy and his mother continues with thoughtful hugs or playful wrestling, boys need and want the caring touch that mothers can provide. His mother is one of the few women who can give a boy the emotional comfort of physical warmth in a non-sexual context, and boys need to experience that physical tenderness if they are to speak the language later. Otherwise, we leave their touch training to football coaches, playground bullies, and casual sex partners.

## A Mix of Mothers, a Mix of Messages

We've spent a good deal of time at playgrounds with our respective children, and the diversity of mothering styles we see there reflects the same range of responses we see as boys grow older and their circles of activity shift to school, sports, and more independent pursuits. There are the anxious, hovering 'helicopter mums', who zoom in at the slightest sign of trouble, or mothers who simply never leave a son's side, even when he is old enough and able to be left. There are the mothers who never rush over, even when a son is clearly in distress or when he is clearly distressing others. There are the playful mums – involved, interacting, seeming to enjoy their boys enormously – and mothers who sit attentively watching from a distance, exchanging waves and comments with their sons, allowing them to move freely with the ebb and flow of their interests. Most of these mothers are motivated by the same desire to see their boys grow up to be happy, successful men. There is no one right way to be a mother, and there are mothers who enjoy wonderful synchrony with their infant sons but very little with their teenagers. In other cases the reverse is true. But as we sit in these playgrounds watching this variety of mothering styles, we cannot help thinking about the different lessons these boys are learning.

Lewis, sixteen, was top of his class, a member of the soccer team, and the debate team, and he was active in his church. He loved his girlfriend and her warm, caring family and spent most of his off-hours at their house. He did everything he could to avoid going home because he was angered and saddened by his mother's constant criticism. On the sidelines at the soccer games and in the local shops, his mother spoke proudly of his accomplishments to her friends, but when she was alone with Lewis, she constantly questioned his judgement and criticized his choices, whether the issue was clothing, food, academic planning, or homework.

As we talked one day, Lewis described his mother's chronic criticism and asked searchingly, 'She never has a kind word for me. Why would a mother do that to her son?'

It hurts a boy to believe that his mother views him as incompetent or unlovable. We see these hurting boys often in the school setting, where competition is fierce and a mother has become critical of her son's efforts or overly anxious about him.

### Dan with Jerry: When a Mother Sends a Message of No-Confidence

Jerry was fourteen and it was the spring before he was due to start at a new public school, where his parents had enrolled him following a disappointing few years spent at another public school. His mother, an attorney, had asked for a 'staffing' – a meeting with key teachers, the school's head of year, and myself – because she felt the teachers at his previous school had never asked enough of Jerry, never understood his special need for structure, and never provided the support he needed to bridge what they believed was a clear, though mild, learning disability that kept him from achieving his best.

Jerry, a lanky, neatly dressed boy, ambled in respectfully, though it was clear he resented the meeting and felt self-conscious there. His mother took a seat and, pulling out the chair next to her, instructed Jerry to do the same. He looked quickly around the table, as if searching for other options, and his glance rested on a chair at the other side, but there were obstacles, and he sat down next to his mother. The head of year introduced himself and each of us, and asked Jerry if he had had a chance to tour the building yet.

His mother answered, explaining that their schedule had been so tight that she had been unable to bring Jerry there earlier but that they hoped to have a look around after the meeting. Throughout this meeting, when a question was directed at Jerry, his mother either answered for him or finished his sentences for him when she felt he wasn't expressing himself clearly enough.

During the course of the year, and in subsequent counselling, this pattern persisted. In family therapy his mother would finish Jerry's sentences, and he would stop talking. She was making it clear to him that she didn't trust him to be a consultant on his feelings at all, and he became more and more withdrawn and passive and said less and less.

No matter how clearly excessive Jerry's mother was in her management of his life, the effect on Jerry – as it would be on most children – was confusion. He knew that she had always been this way and that, when he was younger, it had been helpful. If she had his best interests at heart all this time, how could she be wrong now? And yet, at fourteen, he felt capable of speaking for himself and felt the need to be more in control of his school situation. His mother's constant and overpowering involvement sent him a vote of 'no-confidence'. As a result, Jerry felt incompetent, hopeless – and angry at his mother.

It can be a fine line between constructive advocacy and destructive micromanagement of a boy's life. A boy needs the opportunity to learn about the world in non-lethal ways. Physical or learning disabilities add to the challenge, but eventually the learning issue remains essentially the same: he needs to learn to stand on his own and experience failure in a reasonably safe setting. In most ways, it's better to let a boy fall on his face as a thirteen- or fourteen-year-old and learn about consequences than to continue to arrange for success and leave him unprepared to be responsible for himself as he moves into adulthood.

Reclaiming Lost Boys: Strengthening Connections

In the tale of Peter Pan, Never-Never Land is home to the Lost Boys, a rowdy tribe of young orphan boys who delight in their capture of young Wendy, so desperate are they for a mother they imagine will sing them songs, tell them tales they 'long to hear', and be there for them in simple ways that speak of a mother's love, wisdom, and comfort. In literature and life, although this image is often dismissed as sentimental hype, the emotional presence of a mother that it describes is very real and exceedingly important in a boy's life. Without it, he is, indeed, a 'lost boy'.

As a boy moves through the emotional turbulence of adolescence and the culture of cruelty, a mother uses this connection wisely when she helps her son feel loved and respected and when she can expand his understanding – help him see farther, deeper, or in a new way – so that he can make more informed choices. We see mothers strengthen this connection with a son through direct conversation about an issue, reiterating certain moral values or expectations, for instance, or through simple expressions of caring – listening to him without judging or trying to solve his problem, making his favourite meal, playing his favourite game, chatting about a movie or a book, or surprising him with a gift that has special meaning for him. Just knowing that his emotional 'home base' is there for him can give a boy the boost of hope or energy he needs to solve a problem himself.

Darryl, twelve – a good student and a mellow, good-humoured boy – exploded angrily at his mother, Jan, one afternoon just after school, when she commented to him that he would need to make a commitment to practise piano more regularly if she were to continue to pay for private lessons.

'Nothing I do is right! I can't do anything to please anybody – nobody – I'm a total loser!' he shouted.

Jan was startled by this uncharacteristic response, but instead of reacting angrily to his outburst, she sat down next to him, suggested that he seemed troubled by something bigger than piano practice, and asked if there was something bothering him at school. 'No,' he said. Then Jan made fun of herself, mimicking her dictatorial pronouncement about piano practice, and after a good laugh, Darryl told her he was stressed out by the teasing he was enduring from 'the jerk pack of popular boys' at school.

'You're so wonderful – what could they possibly tease you about?' his mother exclaimed. Darryl recited the list: his hair, his T-shirts, his sweat pants, his socks, his shoes, his reading choices, his good grades – anything and everything about him. He wanted to put an end to the teasing, but he didn't want to fight, and he knew that any retort he made would be turned against him. He was at a loss to know how to make it stop, and he felt trapped because, if he retaliated against his tormentors, he felt certain he would get a detention.

His mother acknowledged the injustice of the situation and asked Darryl if he saw any option for taking action. He didn't – and no, he didn't want her to call his teacher. Jan thought hard the next day about whether to privately contact his teachers or leave the situation alone, as he had requested. That afternoon Darryl returned home and announced that the problem was solved. He had signed up himself and his major tormentor for a peer mediation session – the school's student court of last resort – to resolve the conflict. When the headmaster's office sent a note to the room notifying the two of their 'court date', the tormentor agreed simply to stop the behaviour, and he did. His followers moved on to new targets, too. In the telling, Darryl was clearly pleased that he had resolved the situation himself.

Mothers often underestimate the value of the emotional support they provide by simply listening, sharing the emotional burden a son carries, expressing confidence in him, and supporting him as he takes action to solve his own problems. This routine emotional connection, in whatever form it takes, allows a mother access to her son for more direct conversation about more serious issues when they arise, too.

Charlotte's son Ron was fifteen and head over heels in love with Pearl, a new girl at his school. Pearl was charismatic, beautiful, and returned his affections, and the two were constantly in each other's company. Charlotte wasn't keen on her son's total immersion in the relationship – he'd lost his appetite and seemed listless and more distanced than ever before – but she was even more troubled by aspects of Pearl's behaviour and appearance that suggested she was a drug user. Ron denied it and resisted any discussion of it.

One day the school headmaster called Charlotte to report that Pearl was being questioned by police regarding drug trafficking at the school and that the police also wanted to talk with Ron. Charlotte was frightened and livid at the same time. She and her husband drove Ron to the police station for questioning and heard the disappointing facts unfold from Pearl herself: she was an active heroin user and supplier. And Ron had lied. He knew of her drug use and had tried the heroin himself for a short period in the beginning of their relationship. He had stopped, however, and now was determined to rescue Pearl from her addiction, he said. Pearl was placed in a residential drug rehabilitation programme in another city, and Charlotte felt it was important to act immediately to help Ron rediscover his own interests and a vision of a more promising future.

Carefully avoiding the role of adversaries, Charlotte and her husband had a number of lengthy discussions with Ron in which they expressed clearly their love for him and their faith in him as a good and decent person. Ron had always been very close to his mother and his father, and his parents discussed the family's values, how the drugs and the lying had placed Ron in conflict with his own sense of right and wrong.

Charlotte avoided being critical of Pearl because she understood that Ron, in love, would feel compelled to defend his sweetheart and the brighter future he envisioned for them. Instead, in quiet conversation, Charlotte shared with Ron her perspective as a woman and a mother, explaining how a teenage girl might think in certain circumstances, helping Ron understand Pearl's trouble as well as the meaning behind some of her hurtful and self-destructive choices. And she elicited Ron's thoughts about these issues, providing him with the opportunity to explore his feelings and talk about them without having to defend either his love interest or his lapse in judgement.

As Ron explored those feelings over the next several weeks, he recovered a perspective on his life that had been skewed by the drugs, the drug-related circle of friends, and the love relationship. He began to renew previous friendships and resume his participation in activities he had previously enjoyed. And he began to focus on college and the need to improve his grades to get into the place of his choice.

Charlotte made a special effort to be available when Ron seemed to need company or conversation and to provide transportation or other practical support he needed to rebuild his life in school and the community. After several months, Ron eventually chose to end his relationship with Pearl. It was not an easy choice for him, but it was *his* choice. Instrumental in that was his mother's continued support and emotional grounding, which made it possible for Ron to explore his needs and aspirations more fully and make a wise decision for himself.

## Dan with Mum: Making Room for Other Relationships

The first time, it wasn't even a girl, only her picture. I was twelve. She sat next to me in the school band. And believe it or not, I carried her books home after school. We went to the same dancing school, and I think we liked the fact that we were always sure of a partner when it came to ladies' or gentlemen's choice. We never kissed. And I never introduced her to my mum, but I did show my mother her picture once in our yearbook. I don't recall it being a great picture, and although she was pretty, she was not one of the three girls in the class who were the acknowledged beauties.

'What do you think?' I asked my mother.

'She's very photogenic.'

'What does that mean?'

'That means that she photographs well, that she looks good in pictures.'

'Does that mean that she's pretty?'

'No . . . it only means that pictures of her will tend to look good.'

'Do you think she's pretty?'

'Well, yes.'

I don't think I knew at the time what I wanted my mother to say, what I was hoping to hear from her as she looked at this tiny picture of a girl I thought was special. Perhaps I was looking for a word of approval, a vote of confidence. I recall being a little surprised, though not offended, by her fairly reserved reaction.

She maintained this respectful demeanour through my high school experimentations with romantic relationships, and she maintained this poise even well into my college days, even though I knew she had strong negative reactions to some of my more politically strident left-wing, counterculture girlfriends. This one was a little more earthy than my mother could embrace. That one gave her a lot of grief for employing a cleaning woman. Another one's infidelity went strongly against the grain of my mother's values and made her want to protect me from the emotional hurt of a wandering partner. I never knew about those feelings until much later, long after the girls and I had parted ways. Just as I never knew that one woman I'd almost married was someone my mother had (at last!) liked very much, but when I ended the relationship, she never questioned my decision. She responded in a similar way to girls and women who moved through my two brothers' lives.

When I asked her about all of this recently, when I told her that I appreciated how she had handled my relationships with my girlfriends, I was again a little surprised by what she had to say: 'When I realized that all I would ever have was sons, I figured that I needed to get along with whomever you married or I could lose you. You know the old saying: "A daughter's a daughter for all of her life, but a son is a son 'til he marries a wife",' she said. 'I didn't want that to happen.'

And so she had maintained her calm through the years and the girlfriends, offering a reliably non-judgemental response with only slight variations – never a cheering section, never a harsh judgement. She made it clear, though never in words, that the girlfriends I had were my choices – not hers – and that if she was biased in her sentiments, she was simply in favour of me.

When we see a mother and son in a synchronous relationship, we see a mother willing to look upon child rearing as a practice – like meditation or yoga – and willing to try to view the world through her son's eyes in order to understand his needs. That willingness to learn from a child is the single strongest trait in a parent, and it is so important for the mother of a boy because she has so much to learn about boy life. Her practice of this mothering Zen makes it possible for her to strengthen her relationship with her son even as the physical distance between them increases.

## Michael with Ethan, Tyler, and Susan: Lessons in Letting Go

I had the extraordinary privilege of being Susan's therapist in the last year of her life. She died of pancreatic and liver cancer at the age of forty-seven. About eighteen months before she died, she called me up and said she wanted to come back into therapy and wanted to stay until the end of her life. Though we talked about many things, one of the things we discussed was how she helped her sons – Ethan, twenty-three, and Tyler, nineteen – prepare for her death. Because Susan was divorced, she had to do a lot of that job on her own, though she asked her friends to participate in training her sons to pay bills and manage a household.

She had been very close to her sons, and Ethan had spent much of the spring with her, sleeping at her house three nights a week during his final year in college. Tyler had been away for his first year in college. The three of them had been living together during this summer break, and Ethan had decided to live with his mum in the house until her death; Tyler had planned to return to college in the autumn.

By late July Tyler, usually the more temperate one, was slamming around the house, getting angry at curtain rods and cabinet doors and anything else in his way. Finally, Ethan and his mother discussed what might be bothering the younger brother, and Ethan subsequently suggested to Tyler that he take the next year off from college and stay at the house, too. Within an hour Tyler had settled down, and later his mother approached him.

'Tyler,' she said, 'Ethan tells me that you're thinking about taking a year off and not going back to college this autumn.'

Tyler nodded yes, then added: 'Mum, when are you going to die?'

'Well, I don't know for sure,' she said. 'Why?'

'Because I told everyone at school that you were going to die this summer and I would be back in the autumn. And you haven't died this summer.'

'No, apparently not.'

'Well,' Tyler continued, 'if you don't die this summer, you have to wait until next summer.'

'Tyler, I'm not sure I can wait that long.'

'Then you have to die during my holidays,' Tyler said, '– except not on Christmas holiday, because if that happened, we'd be so sad every Christmas because we would remember you and that you died then.'

Accepting the limitations of his insight at nineteen, Susan countered, 'I don't think I can plan on dying during a holiday from college. Do you want to take the next year off and live here with me and Ethan?'

Tyler exclaimed, with great relief, 'Oh, yes, I'd like to do that.'

Tyler's concern about the calendar timing of his mother's death was just one of many ways in which the brothers sought that year to exert control over a situation that, in reality, was a frightening emotional free fall. Each time Susan used these opportunities to explore their underlying feelings, she helped calm their fears and fortify them for the painful days ahead. By asking Tyler what he wanted to do, using him as a consultant, Susan had made it possible for him to express a feeling that, until that moment, had been the emotional engine driving his stormy anger.

In the weeks following the CAT scan in March, when it was clear that the cancer had spread to Susan's liver and that her death was inevitable, it was Ethan who became irritable and angry around the house. One day he told his mother he was focused now on planning 'a trip to Tibet or something' after she died.

She asked, 'Do you think that's wise?'

'Well, that's what I want to do,' he said.

'Why?'

'I don't want your dying to scar me for the rest of my life,' he replied.

'Oh, I see. Ethan, I'm afraid it is going to scar you in some way. I don't think there's any way around it.'

'Does it have to be that way?'

'Your mother is dying when you are young,' Susan said. 'That's going to be part of your life for the rest of your life.'

'Oh,' Ethan replied.

His angry countenance became calmer in the days that followed, and he dropped the subject of travel. Instead of focusing on his escape from emotional pain, he took from his mother a better understanding of the emotional turmoil he felt. It was a fortuitous trade. In the months after her death, a travel itinerary would have been worthless against Ethan's grief, but her lessons in the emotional language of the heart stayed with him to become a source of comfort and a feeling like love.

When I asked what was the most significant conversation the boys had had with Susan before she died, Ethan reflected on the way he had wished for more talk at a time when his mother's capacity for conversation was steadily diminishing. Even so, he said, he had understood from some past source that 'what you really need to know is that your mum loves you unconditionally – that it doesn't matter if you win an Academy Award or you're sitting, divorced, drinking in a bar at two in the afternoon, and you're fifty-five. She loves you either way. And I just brought this up with her, and she said, "I love you absolutely, unconditionally."'

They watched the full moon rise together. Her sons recall carrying Susan, from the car to the house after visits to the doctor, and from this place to that place in the house, as needed.

One of the last nights she was in the house, Ethan said, he sang to her. 'I knew I wanted to sing "You are my sunshine, my only sunshine . . ." to her,' he said, singing the first few lines of the song to me. 'And I got that far before I couldn't, basically, you know, do anything more. And she, you know, she sang the rest of it to me, which is what I guess I really wanted to hear. I wanted to have her be able to hold me or be tender with me. And then, when we were done, she said, "That really helped." And it did.'

Susan's expression of love for her sons took many shapes in her last year, synchronous with her sons' needs: she included them on medical appointments so they would know what they could know. She recognized their emotional struggle to deal with the rest and helped them understand the feelings beneath the feelings of anger or agitation. She guided them through the process of talking about feelings and in these and other ways modelled an emotional courage that would be her lasting gift to her sons.

This emotional imprint, this internalization, is, after all, how any of us hold on to those we love even as we let them go. It is how we keep our children's love 'with us' when we cannot be with them, and it is how a boy keeps his mother emotionally 'close at hand' even when she isn't.

We enjoy the mother you never see in the popular children's book *Where the Wild Things Are*, by Maurice Sendak. In the story a little boy named Max gets into mischief 'of one kind and another' all afternoon, but when he talks back to his mother, threatening to eat her up, she sends him to his room for some quiet time. Banished to his bedroom 'without eating anything', he sails away on a dream voyage, cavorting in an angry reverie with fearsome monsters who celebrate his wildness and beg him to stay among them as 'king of all wild things'. This land of unbridled wildness is an exciting place to visit, but Max doesn't want to live there. He grows lonely, and his response to the invitation to remain among the wild things is unambiguous – a simple, emphatic 'no!' – and so saying, he chooses to return to the comforts of home, a place where people 'love him best of all'. He wakes up in his room to the warm smells and comfort of a hot dinner, clearly left – we like to believe – by a mother who had faith that her 'little monster' simply needed a little room and a little time to find his better self.

Frightful little 'Max' reminds us of boys at every age who venture into new emotional territory, face a struggle of one kind and another, and often cover up their emotional confusion with an elaborate masquerade of anger or aggression. As a boy moves farther and farther from his mother's protective physical presence, and especially as he enters adolescence and the culture of cruelty that awaits him there, he needs to be able to carry her in his heart, in the security that her love provides him and the emotional education she has given him. He needs to know that, between his mother and himself, however they maintain their connection, he can always find the place where he is loved 'best of all'.

# 7.  Inside the Fortress of Solitude

I am a rock, I am an island.

> Simon and Garfunkel, 'I am a Rock'

Emotional isolation has become virtually a reflex by the time a boy reaches adolescence. He has learned to deny his emotional neediness and routinely disguise his feelings. Intimidated by the constant threat of humiliation presented by the culture of cruelty and the ensuing erosion of trust, boys strike a psychological bargain – a bad one – namely, that they'd rather hide out than take any more hits. The more pressure a boy feels, the more deeply he withdraws.

Adolescent girls in therapy commonly struggle with too much feeling. They focus too much on their own and others' emotional responses. It is just the opposite with adolescent boys. The girls tend to be comfortable discussing emotional ups and downs with friends; boys typically avoid discussing their feelings with anybody. They struggle alone, often with tragic consequences. A romanticized image of isolation so often defines boys and men. In film young boys see Superman's icy Arctic retreat – his remote, towering crystal Fortress of Solitude. When the pressures of life among mortals become too much – the never-ending struggles between good and evil and the romantic complications – Superman fades out to his fortress to be alone with his thoughts. Batman, haunted by the loss of his parents at an early age, turns to an unending fight against evil, retreating between rounds to the stark, dark 'Bat Cave', an underground den full of gadgets, computer technology, and a set of hot wheels but bereft of any emotional comforts.

These comic book heroes come and go easily from their fortresses. When a boy is cut off from meaningful connections – from parents, friends, and peers – he must face the social pressures of adolescence on his own. With no help from the outside and ill-equipped to find their own way out of hiding, many boys become stranded, digging themselves deeper and deeper into emotional isolation, building stronger and higher walls around their emotions until there's no sign of them at all. Withdrawal is one of the most common signs of emotional distress among boys in their early and mid-teens and may presage a further descent into depression and possibly self-destructive behaviour such as substance abuse or reckless sex.

A boy distanced from genuine emotional interaction misses the opportunity for genuine emotional growth. For all of us, psychological and personal growth comes when we can face what it is that bothers us, gain an understanding of it, and figure out what to do about it. An emotionally isolated boy, when troubled, is more likely to look for a scapegoat, blaming other people or circumstances for his problems. What neither a boy nor his parents realize is that this effort to cut himself off from his family, his emotions, and any reflection on his state of mind is exhausting. When boys succeed at it, they only add to their own misery.

### Martin: Hiding from Emotional Hurt – and Growth

Martin, a bespectacled video production technician, recalled life as the son of a corporate executive – a man of high intellect and short temper – and a mother he experienced as dutiful but emotionally distant. School was more of a struggle for Martin than his father could accept, and his criticism was relentless. Martin could not recall ever having had a conversation with his father that had started and ended on a pleased note.

Middle school began one of the worst periods of his life. Martin's grades were just average, even though he worked pretty hard. He wasn't at all athletic and was made to feel self-conscious when he was forced to do sports in gym class. At home his mother was too busy with three-year-old twin sisters to offer much support, and he preferred to avoid his father and the predictable criticism altogether.

He considered a couple of boys in his class 'school friends': they sat together at lunch, but they never socialized outside of school. It seemed to Martin that nothing in his life was working right; his grades, his social life, and his father's criticism were continual reminders of his status as 'a loser'.

'I'd come home every day and go upstairs to my room to "study", but it wouldn't last long. I couldn't track on the material. So I'd sit there and hate myself — *really* hate myself — and think about how many ways I was a loser. I'd think about how my father would blow up when he heard about the latest bad test grade.'

When his feelings of self-loathing became intolerable, Martin's response was to retreat — literally — to a corner of the attic, where he used his pocket knife to carve into the rafter a countdown of the days left in the school year. He would sit for hours by the tiny attic window, staring down at the people and the world below him that he felt was passing him by. Then he discovered a box with his father's old collection of *Playboy* magazines, and sexual fantasy gave him some relief from his painful feelings.

'I'd spend entire afternoons up there, lost in these X-rated fantasies for hours,' Martin said. 'At first it was great, but after a while, even as a teenager, I thought it was pretty pitiful that I sat there "doing it" with these magazines. It was probably the loneliest time of my life; the fantasies gave me some kind of crutch, and I was desperate for that. I don't know if anyone ever noticed I wasn't around. Nobody ever asked any questions or said anything about it. Even though my father was still a powder keg about my grades, I just remember it being like background noise. I blocked out all of it with my afternoons in the attic.'

At one point in Martin's final year, on the advice of his academic adviser, his parents arranged for him to see the school counsellor, who encouraged him to follow through with some vocational interests that eventually led him to a video technician's job at a local cable TV station. However, his continued reliance on sexual fantasy for emotional comfort, aided now by a library of pornographic videotapes, kept his relationships with women stuck at a superficial level. When Martin was twenty-eight, it was a girlfriend who recognized the emotional pain still crippling his life and urged him back to therapy.

It is often someone else — a teacher, parent, or friend — who identifies a boy's symptoms as problematic and encourages outside help. But even those caring others may hesitate to intrude on a boy's fortress of solitude, since many normal teenagers seek more privacy at this age. Parents are often at a loss to figure out whether a boy's withdrawal is a sign that he's normal or a sign that he's troubled.

Sadly, the image of the disaffected teenage boy is so common that it is considered 'normal'. Thus, the grandmother of a sixteen-year-old boy who killed five family members can say to a newspaper reporter that her grandson was 'just like any other boy his age[;] . . . he was quiet; he stayed in his room most of the time. He played music.' The teacher of a fifteen-year-old boy who killed himself is haunted by the memory of a youngster who 'kept to himself and seemed troubled, but not any more so than a lot of other kids his age'.

It can be hard for parents to know when to worry that a son's increasing preference for time alone indicates a worrisome level of isolation. Normal adolescence includes moodiness and a preference to spend free time with friends. Bedroom doors that a boy once left open now stay closed; he may answer questions in a tone that shows he can barely tolerate his parents' hopelessly clueless understanding of life. A wise parent sees these signs as a necessary part of his growth. There are, however, some 'red flags' that should cause a parent to worry that a boy is drifting deeper into emotional isolation: a persistent dark mood; withdrawal from most social interaction, even with friends; declining grades; a big change in weight; or taking little interest or joy in activities. When these signs won't go away, parents shouldn't hesitate to talk with a physician or mental health professional about their concerns.

Red flags don't always appear. The withdrawal doesn't always transform itself into depression or substance abuse. Some boys can live in their cave for a lifetime, suffering only stunted psychological growth. With a boy like this, caring adults must perform the subtle task of both supporting autonomy and frustrating withdrawal, trying to coax the boy out of his cave. But this is difficult when a boy doesn't have the words to explain what it is he is hiding from, when he won't or can't talk about it.

### Dan with Tony: The Words Don't Tell the Story

Tony has just turned sixteen. He is at a school known for both academic excellence and a strong sports curriculum. Tony has always shown superior verbal abilities and is also an outstanding soccer player. He is tall, with dirty blond hair that is long in the front and often hangs over his right eye. When he talks, his gaze is usually directed towards his Nike sneakers. His voice is soft, and sometimes he mumbles his words. When he is more animated, which is not often, he may look up and make eye contact. Tony is like a traveller standing outside a door, uncomfortable in the cold, but tentative about coming in.

It is April and Tony has been sent for counselling because his grades are slipping. His parents and guidance counsellor don't know why and wonder whether I can figure it out. In looking through Tony's school file, I see that his teachers' comments show a pattern of concern over the gap between his ability and his performance as a student.

'Some of your teachers thought I should talk with you.'

'Yeah. I figured. My dad told me I'd have to see you.'

'Tell me what's going on.'

'I'm doing really badly in English.'

'Tell me.'

'Well, I'm kind of flunking.'

'Why?'

'Well, there was this big paper I was supposed to do, and I couldn't get it done, and now my grade for the term is ruined.'

His failure might not have been a cause for concern in some cases, but Tony's test scores have always been quite high. Reading comprehension has been a particular strength, with scores that place him among the top 2 per cent of students in the country. But it's not just that he didn't complete the one paper. Tony has been pretty much of a no-show all year – more so in English than in other subjects, but more or less across the board. Underachievement of this sort tends to set teachers off: they take it personally. From their comments, it's clear that they like Tony but are frustrated. One end-of-year comment from his previous English teacher reads: 'In class I don't hear as much from Tony as I used to. It hasn't been hurting his writing, but more participation ought to help him extend his ideas even further.' His adviser sums up the year this way: 'I am concerned that, although Tony is making an effort, the work is slipping away from him and that he may be sensing some real frustration.'

'Do you like English? Is Mr Roberts a good teacher?'

'Yeah, I like English and all, but his class is kind of boring. The books we have to read are pretty stupid. It's like all the books are about like how we screwed the Indians, or they're by some woman or black guy that was oppressed. They're not very good.'

'What kind of books do you like?'

'Stephen King is pretty cool.'

Tony's father is especially worried, since the following year is pivotal in terms of getting into college. He talks about the situation in the context of soccer playing. Tony had made the team the year before, and his father thinks he has enough talent to get a soccer scholarship to a good college.

'But with those grades, he'll screw himself,' says Tony's father. 'The good schools won't even want to look at him. I could have bought a Cadillac with all the money I've spent on soccer camps, and now it's going down the toilet.'

He says all this as if Tony weren't even in the room.

His disregard for Tony's feelings is startling. Tony's father had somehow come to view him as a commodity.

As part of my evaluation of Tony, I give him a picture from a stack on the desk – an illustration of a casually dressed man standing alone leaning against a wall – and ask him to write about it. His story is well written, with few spelling or grammatical errors, but its content is unnerving:

He had been a guest of the state penitentiary for six years. He wasn't what one would normally expect a prisoner to be. He wasn't crazy. He was quiet, and (I don't know how) got along quite well with all of the inmates and most of the guards . . . He had a friend, but one day the guards killed his friend. He didn't know why. He only knew he had to escape or he would die, too.

It's clear that Tony feels locked away and desperate. When I look at him, I see a boy who ought to be mad as hell at his father for being so callous and emotionally absent, or at least sad – and I see a boy who could be talking about all of this to his friends to relieve some of the pressure that's building up. Instead, he is just confused. He doesn't know what's going on with himself.

'Why do you think your grades are so bad?'

'I don't know. I just have to work harder, I guess. I can be pretty disorganized. I was really trying at the beginning of the term, but that paper really screwed me. I guess the Ivy League's not in the cards.'

'How have you been feeling about all of this?'

'I don't know. I'm usually pretty tired. I stay up late trying to get my work done, not that it helps much. So I'm pretty tired in school. That doesn't help my enthusiasm much.'

'Does any of it bother you?'

'I don't know. I'd like to get better grades, I guess.'

A boy's lack of energy for this kind of discussion often frustrates parents and teachers who feel that he must be stonewalling – refusing to share what he feels. Often, boys like Tony simply don't recognize their feelings. A boy can be suffering through a death, his parents' painful divorce, physical or sexual abuse, and rather than talk about how bad that makes him feel, he'll look for a problem he can fix. When there is a problem, a boy tends to look outward for the reasons. As far as Tony was concerned, his grades were dropping because he wasn't working hard enough. He couldn't recognize that there might be a connection between his not finishing assignments and his anger at his dad.

Boys may become disengaged from schoolwork for any of a number of reasons. If, like Tony, a boy has diverted all his energy to creating emotional shields to protect himself, such as maintaining a wall of denial or repressing strong emotions he is afraid to vent, he doesn't have much energy left for homework. Or he may not want to grow up. Another facet of retreat into the fortress of solitude can be expressed by a boy as a desire to not move from where he is, to remain a child for ever. Good grades are usually accompanied by other expectations and a look towards the future, something about which a boy may be fearful or anxious. And flunking out of school is certainly one way to avoid 'getting older'.


## Stoicism

Pride and stoicism knot together in many boys, reinforcing each other. Not only is it difficult for these boys to express themselves; they take a certain pride in not doing so, in keeping their mouths shut. In psychological distress, they are like the captain of the *Titanic*, standing on the bridge gallantly going down with their ship. They want to look strong. The difference is, of course, that most boys aren't on a sinking ship. They're just struggling with being young, with having high expectations of themselves, with wanting to please their parents, and with not knowing themselves very well.


### *Michael with Danny: Strong, Silent – and Suffering*

After years of athletic success, Danny, at age fifteen, found his hockey game falling apart, and no one could figure out why. His coach could tell he was struggling but couldn't seem to help him out of his slump. Danny blamed himself for his decline. At the same time, his grades, which had always been mostly Bs, were also slipping. Danny's father encouraged him to see me in the hope that I could help turn Danny around. Danny showed an air of casual confidence as we sat down to talk. Based on what he told me about how he was feeling, it was apparent by the end of our first session that Danny was not clinically depressed; he had too much 'bounce'. However, he was very frustrated and bewildered by the decline of the past year and talked about it as he might analyse another player's game from the sidelines. 'I know I'm a better goalie than the way I'm playing,' he said. 'It's like I'm distracted when I'm out there, and then when I don't play as well as I should, I get really mad, and then I play even worse.'

The anger that welled up around his sports performance spilled over into his efforts to study and pay attention in class. His parents' high expectations added to the pressure, but he was positive about their relationship: 'It's like we're on the same team,' he said. 'I can talk to them.' He had discussed with his father his growing sense of discouragement, and his father had assured him that setbacks were normal but that it was a test of character – and one that Danny was 'good enough to beat'. But the encouragement hadn't helped. In fact, Danny felt doubly bad to be failing parents who were so clearly supportive. He kept promising them that this game or this report card would be better, but the turnaround wasn't coming.

'I just want to put the past behind me and focus on the future and doing my best again,' Danny told me.

But instead of talking about the future, Danny and I revisited the past to search for the source of his distraction. It wasn't hard to find. It stemmed from two seemingly minor events of the past year.

During the autumn, Danny had been fooling around in the gym with friends and had torn a calf muscle trying to dunk a basketball by leaping off a chair. This injury had kept him out of three critical games at the start of the season that his team lost but could have won had Danny been playing. The injury had healed well, but he felt foolish and angry and had been hard on himself ever since.

The second disappointment was a non-event that nonetheless became a source of shame and self-contempt. Danny had tried out for the school football team the previous autumn. Though he had a great deal of athletic ability and had played on the football team the previous year, during the first practice he had been intimidated by the size and power of many of the other boys, and for one of the first times in his life, he felt unsure of himself. He performed passably, but not as well as he could have. In the end, Danny told the coach that he had decided not to play.

But in his own mind he had run away from the challenge. That evening, when his parents asked how the practice had gone, Danny tried to shrug it off and told them the partial truth – that he'd taken one look at the bruisers going out for the team and had just decided to specialize in hockey in the spring. What he didn't tell them was what he couldn't, at that moment, articulate: that he felt like a coward and loathed himself for it. In his own mind, when he hung up his football pads that day, Danny was taking them off for good. Football – the sport that he had been playing since he was eight, all the way through middle school and until he was fifteen, which had been a sustaining source of joy for him – was now a reminder of humiliation instead.

In the year that followed, Danny had kept all that anger and self-contempt to himself, picking away at himself, beating up on himself, but not telling anyone, because talking about how bad he felt would just be another sign of weakness, and he couldn't afford any more. The more stoic he became, the greater his burden grew. And when he finally came for help, it wasn't to relieve his anger or self-contempt; it was to improve his grades and his soccer game. As we talked about these incidents, Danny eventually came to recognize how his stoicism had only hidden the pain and kept him from doing something constructive about it.

What Danny needed more than anything was to air his feelings of cowardice and his constant self-reproach in a climate of trust. It had taken him almost a year to talk to someone because he had chosen isolation over conversation. He and I had only four conversations, but they opened the door for him. The psychological burden that had trapped him for a year was lifted; his concentration on the field and in the classroom improved.

Danny was motivated by his desire to revive his characteristic optimism and energy, and he was able to use his new insights to come to terms with the disappointments of the past. But for many boys and men, stoicism remains at the heart of their emotional isolation from friends and family and the self-contempt they cultivate from within.

### The Other Face of Emotional Isolation: Offence as Defence

Emotional isolation wears many faces. Sometimes it comes in the guise of anger, sarcasm, or hostility – boys who see almost everyone and everything as unworthy of respect when, really, it's *they* who feel worthless. Feeling vulnerable because of parental criticism or unreasonable expectations, or because they feel the power of their peers to humiliate them, these boys don't slip off quietly but instead adopt a confrontational 'I-couldn't-care-less' attitude. These boys can be the most difficult to reach. Their behaviour is so off-putting that they don't win much sympathy.

### Dan with Ken and Ascher: Dropping the Shield

Ascher was by any measure a social outcast. Physically awkward, emotionally immature, and lacking in the social graces, he had never been close to being popular. From his earliest days in school, his classmates had considered him an oddity, and he not only never outgrew the label, but by the time he was twelve, he wore it like a badge of honour. He had one saving grace: he was smart and did well in school – but he boasted of it until his classmates despised him. He had a vicious tongue and was an expert at finding anyone's vulnerability – be it a lack of acumen in maths, a homely sister, or the wrong residential address – and he wielded his skill like a sharp sword against his peers.

By the time he was fifteen, he was increasingly adopting the personality of a hate-radio host – brutally direct and critical of almost anything that didn't coincide with what he believed. It was as if he had given up, reasoning that, if the culture was to be cruel to him, then he would be cruel to the culture. In terms of social status, he certainly had nothing to lose. His teachers wondered out loud how he escaped being beaten up.

For reasons that I still do not wholly comprehend, I liked Ascher quite a bit. In part it was because I could see that he wasn't as mean as he was made out to be. Despite his tough-as-nails exterior, he was bothered by his lack of acceptance. I had even more sympathy for him when I learned about his volatile household.

Both his parents were unpredictable. Misbehaviour that would make them explode one day was laughed off the next. They both had been heavy drinkers until the time Ascher turned ten, and the house had been filled with angry shouting and, at times, neglect. Without safety at home or at school, Ascher grew up as a suburban feral child.

By secondary school Ascher had perfected his act. No matter how much people disliked him, no matter how much they teased him, he wouldn't back down. Ascher trusted no one among his peers, nor did he even have the support of the small group of teachers who didn't actively dislike him.

When his behaviour became even more outrageous, the school administration sent him to me, not so much because they wanted to help him but because they no longer knew how to handle him.

And not only did I like Ascher, but he liked me. I was predictable and trustworthy. I always kept my word. I gave him tangible signs of affection. Our sessions usually took place over lunch, and I bought him large pizzas when he asked for them, even though I knew it was far more than he could eat. I let him borrow my Walkman. I gave him a gift on his birthday. His childhood had been so full of rejection, I figured he needed these things in order to believe that I really did like him, that I was someone he could trust. He was very knowledgeable about politics, and we often talked about what was going on in Washington. He would sometimes challenge my liberal sensibilities with his right-wing rhetoric, but I wouldn't take the bait. I didn't pretend to agree with him, but I listened, without the shock or outrage that many of his teachers displayed when similarly confronted.

For the first two years of our work together, Ascher's behaviour didn't change much. Although I often found myself still defending him in faculty meetings, his good grades tended to protect him from harsh disciplinary action. But he still had no friends. He was still alone.

One day he asked me if he could bring someone along to one of our lunches: 'His name is Ken. He needs you more than I do. His parents are really nuts.'

The next time we met for lunch, Ken came along.

Ken greeted me by saying, 'Ascher told me that if I told you I was crazy, you'd buy me pizza.'

'I'll tell you what,' I responded. 'How about you don't act crazy and I'll buy you pizza anyway.'

Ken's parents were, by his description, a little off. They had huge, explosive fights, after which Ken's mother would take the kids away. He had a brother with severe, medication-resistant ADD that ran the family close to the frazzled edge. His father had stayed in the military reserves after serving in Vietnam and sometimes forgot that he was raising a family, not training a regiment. After that first meeting it was rare for me to see Ken without Ascher and vice versa.

Each had found his match in the other – and a friendship, too, for better or for worse. Their bond provided a kind of bunker from which they could launch their attacks on the world. Unless I stopped it, they could fill a whole hour with creative, erudite, yet venomous dialogue about the shortcomings of their classmates, teachers, and groups who did not share their political beliefs.

But from each of them I also learned about the other's soft side. Ken told me about Ascher's devotion to his mother and his cat, and Ascher told me how Ken would often care for his brother for long, difficult stretches without complaint. As time went by, this bond of friendship enabled each boy to admit to some of his fears. They joked about renting dates or setting each other up with a cousin. Sometimes I would ask them to analyse each other. They were so similar. By talking about his friend, each learned about himself.

'So, Ken, you be the shrink. How come Ascher has to blast Pedro [a Latino classmate] all the time?'

'Well, Dr K., I think Ascher's insecure. He attacks others in order to cover up his own perceived inadequacies. Minority group members have long played the role of scapegoat in our society, you know.'

'Thank you for that trenchant analysis, Ken. Ascher, what do you think about what he has to say?'

'He may be right about me, but that doesn't mean that Pedro isn't a moron. And it doesn't mean that Ken doesn't do the same thing. Ask him why he has to torture the younger kids.'

Eventually both boys were able to drop their defensive posturing. They became more conscious of the insecurity behind their behaviour, and this started to take the fun out of it. They could no longer be as righteous in their indignation. And they felt less and less as if they needed the confrontations with teachers and peers. Their political views didn't change, but they put them to more constructive use by getting involved with the debate team. The debate coach developed a genuine appreciation for their verbal skills, and they earned the respect of others on the team, especially the younger members. They even talked with, and nearly dated, some debaters from an all-girls school.

Ascher's and Ken's cases were extreme, but these same dynamics show up in many boys. Boys use shields of various forms to keep others away: irritability, sarcasm, nonchalance, stoicism, and others. Whether they use offensive intellectualism and humour or muscle and meanness, boys like Ascher and Ken seek to camouflage their fears with an exaggerated image of strength.

### Michael with Foster: Into the Fortress and Out Again

'This is totally my mum's idea,' says Foster, taking a seat. 'I don't really have anything to talk about. I don't have, like, any issues or anything.'

Foster is a short, chubby thirteen-year-old. He is the oldest child of four, and he has recently withdrawn from the affectionate, teasing relationship he had always enjoyed with his siblings. He spends less time with his mum than he used to. 'We used to be a lot closer,' she says. 'I wish I knew what was going on with him, and I wonder if he's okay.'

Foster's mother had a chronic kidney disorder that was being successfully managed, but despite her good check-ups, her children's anxiety about her health continued on a low simmer. Foster's father was an entrepreneur whose business was failing, and the stress level at home was on the rise. Just at the time when his mother had thought that father and teenage son would begin to enjoy each other's company more, the tension made for strained conversations punctuated with angry outbursts and stubborn silences.

Now, sitting in my office tapping his pencil nervously against his knee, it is clear that Foster is, in effect, battening down the hatches to keep himself, and his life, to himself. He needs to relax if we are to make any progress in therapy. With his parents' prior approval, we embark on a brief field trip to the neighbourhood's favourite corner store, the pink-and-brown Art Deco Store 24 across the street, where I tell Foster he can choose two items for a snack, something I often do with boys, in order to get them to let their guard down and to give us something non-threatening to talk about. It has to be something reasonable, like a drink and some chips or cookies. But that leaves a lot of room for uncertainty and creativity. Foster considers carefully, browsing thoroughly among the packets, and then picks a can of Pepsi and a box of Atomic Fire Balls. On the way back to the office, we discuss the relative merits of different junk foods, with a true gourmet-style analysis of Ruffles potato chips versus Pringles, Twinkies versus Ring Dings, Gummi Bears versus Gummi Worms.

I know that Foster is too nervous to talk about what's going on inside of him. The part he knows about scares him, and the part he only dimly senses but hasn't explored scares him even more. So in the beginning I am content with junk food and superficial conversation. Only after several weeks of talking junk food with Foster (and wondering to myself what my accountant will say about Twinkies as a business expense) do we turn to the 'work' of therapy, which involves questions about his family. We talk about the lie of the land at home, who's who, and then we turn to his feelings:

'I understand from your mum and your dad that he has had a very tough time at work. Do you know about that?'

'Yeah.'

'Does it worry you?'

'Yeah, sometimes.'

'Do you think he's depressed?'

'Yeah . . . maybe . . . I don't know, probably.'

'That's pretty scary, isn't it?'

'Yeah, but he's better now.'

'That's good. Do you think when he was at his low point you got a little bit scared and depressed yourself?'

'Yeah, probably. Actually, I was more worried.'

'Did you ever think about whether he might kill himself?'

He looks up in amazement.

'Yeah, I thought that, but then I thought, "He's not going to do that."'

This was great, I was breaking through. After this first, Foster did what so many boys do in this situation: they clam up again for a week or two, sometimes more, depending on how much the talking scared them and how much they trust you.

But within two weeks, more of the story began to come out, and it became clear that Foster was very concerned about his father's moodiness and felt saddened by his parents' troubles. As we talked these things through, Foster came to recognize that although there wasn't much he could do about the serious challenges facing his family – and they were unnerving – if he could learn to confront his fears and share them, their grip on his life was lessened.

After about four months of therapy, Foster was no longer in hiding. The change was visible: the hangdog demeanour was gone, replaced by a more buoyant expression and enthusiasm. He looked forward to our sessions, with our Store 24 ritual and 'Twinkie' conversations. In contrast to his first visits, I no longer had to 'do all the work' of our conversations about feelings. The therapy setting had done what it was designed to do: provide a safe environment for talking about difficult things.

Foster began to hang out with a friend who liked skateboarding, and they began skateboarding together. Foster became surprisingly proficient, despite his lack of coordination. Over the next year, we continued to work through Foster's feelings about his parents' marriage as well as his worries for his father and for his mother's health. Meanwhile, he spent more and more time with his friend. They built a skateboard ramp, and their skilful risky tricks attracted an admiring audience of other boys. Soon Foster had a group of boys around him.

Foster's mother saw him revive his interest in friends and activities that gave him pleasure; his performance at school improved. He still didn't talk with her as much or with the same urgency he had brought to it as a younger boy, but she worried less about him.

Sadly, Foster's family difficulties continued. His father's business went under, and the family struggled financially as he looked for work. Foster's mother stepped in and took over as the main breadwinner of the family. But ultimately his parents divorced. Even so, Foster had a pretty good school career, doing well socially and academically, and went on to continued success in college. He was not immune to disappointment or discouragement, but he was better able to cope with emotional challenge and work through it without withdrawing from life.

Clearly, Foster had learned to read himself, and others, too, to some degree, establishing and maintaining some vital emotional connections. Despite the difficulty of their collective family life, Foster had been able to separate himself out from his family's troubles and make something of an independent life for himself while still staying connected, in different ways, to both parents.

Foster's newly emerging emotional literacy couldn't save his father's job or his parents' marriage. But it did save *him*.

The difference between a boy who is emotionally withdrawn and a boy who is depressed is not always clear-cut, as we explain in the following chapter. But it is heartening to know that in many instances a boy who is withdrawn needs only to be persuaded that it is safe to come out. That isn't always easy or quick. It requires that a boy overcome years of emotional miseducation and the layers of attitude and behaviour that spring from it. He has to rediscover trust. He may have to be lured out of the fortress with wise, patient parenting or more directly gotten out through compassionate psychotherapy. Boys do want out, though; no boy wants to feel alone, or be alone, against the world.

# 8. Boys' Struggle with Depression and Suicide

> In a real dark night of the soul it is always three o'clock in the morning, day after day.
>
> F. Scott Fitzgerald, *The Great Gatsby*

Loren was about as engaging as a hornets' nest – an unpleasant, irritable fourteen-year-old. He worked well in class but was a snarly student, critical of teachers as 'stupid' and of fellow students as 'morons'. His teachers had pretty much written him off as 'a case' – meaning he was a boy 'with issues' – and they wondered at faculty meetings whether the school should even try to keep him. His attitude wasn't any better at home. He smashed things when he got angry, which was often. His parents blamed each other for their son's difficulties, creating tension at home. With him they alternated between appeasement and support to encourage him, and anger and punishment when he screwed up.

Loren was depressed, and as it does in many children, his depression presented itself, not as a sad, down mood, but as irritability. He didn't like himself very much, didn't really believe that anyone else did either, and didn't have much hope that things would change. Once he was properly diagnosed, he was treated with antidepressants and individual and family therapy over the summer. By the start of the next school year, Loren was recovered. Loren's was not a hopeless case; this was no miracle cure. He was a boy whose illness had been made worse when the people around him became so caught up in reacting to the symptoms that they couldn't see what was behind them.

Symptoms of depression in boys may be hard to read or be missed because the boys often don't *look* sad or 'depressed'. They look edgy or angry, hostile or defiant. A boy's depression is often ignored because he is meeting cultural expectations of masculinity. Stoicism, emotional reserve, or even a withdrawal into his fortress of solitude are accepted and sometimes admired male behaviours. Depressive behaviour in boys often only comes to our attention when it finally costs them performance points in school or on the playing field, or when it gets them into trouble with the law.

Nobody wants to think of boys as depressed or emotionally needy. We feel embarrassed or uncomfortable with the shame it will bring them, and we feel more secure with the idea that these idealized 'strong' fathers-in-training can protect us with their strength.

There isn't a parent or teacher who would suggest that clinical depression is character-building for boys, and yet boys are expected to 'get over it' on their own. Many boys struggle alone with their distress because they think they have to or because they think they can 'fix it' by themselves – even though it is very difficult, if not impossible, to get over clinical depression without help.

If a boy believes that, in order to be manly, he must be 'on top' of his feelings, he lives in psychological conflict all the time because he's trying to control feelings that may be too powerful and complex to be controlled. When the conflict can no longer be suppressed, then depression becomes the psyche's way of surrendering.

The results can be deadly. Combine depression and its shame, emotional illiteracy, and the impulsivity so common among boys; mix in access to weapons and a familiarity with violence, real or through the media – and you have a recipe for suicide. Statistics indicate that, compared with generations past, more boys are committing suicide, and they're doing it at younger ages.[1] In the United States suicide rates for teenagers have more than quadrupled since 1950. And most of those who die are boys. Boys account for 86 per cent of suicides among older adolescents and 80 per cent among younger teens.

Not every boy who confronts emotional hardships develops severe depression. But whether a depression is biological or situational in origin, the recovery from it is more difficult for a boy who has been trained away from emotional interaction and steered instead towards emotional silence and stoicism.

## Moody Blues: Emotions and the Shell Game of Adolescence

'I don't know what's going on with him,' said Fran, talking about her fourteen-year-old son, Jason. 'I think he's probably just going through a phase, but he's not calling his friends much any more, and he seems so gloomy about everything. He doesn't even care about baseball, and that used to be his life. He snaps at me when I ask him about these things. My husband says to leave him alone – that he's just got an attitude and he'll get over it – but I don't know what "it" is. I don't know what to think.'

It can be difficult at times to distinguish between the ordinary 'down days' of adolescence and depression. The rapid changes of adolescence can happen almost overnight, and a boy can suddenly find that he doesn't have much in common with his old friends. He outgrows a previous interest, or decides that it is no longer cool, and drops it. For many boys – *most boys* – the emotional ups and downs of adolescence are transient. Most teenagers muddle through their mood swings without doing too much damage to themselves or others. No matter how unpleasant it may be, negative attitude alone doesn't equal depression. But with the rates of adolescent depression rising, we must start paying attention.

Today boys are meeting the perennial challenges of adolescence at ever younger ages. The biological changes of puberty, which began at about age sixteen in 1850, begin today at about age twelve, or sometimes younger. But there is no evidence that suggests that young people are maturing emotionally any sooner. The increasing gap between biological and psychological development makes adolescence all the more stressful and risky, with kids being exposed earlier to the temptations of drugs, alcohol, casual sex, and for too many boys, more money and longer periods of unsupervised after-school time than in generations past.

## Depression: The Real Thing

In casual conversation, the word *depressed* has become synonymous with *unhappy*. Medically speaking, however, depression is a distinct diagnosis, an illness of varying degrees, with identifiable symptoms and a variety of treatment options, from various forms of psycho-therapy to prescription medications – usually some combination of both. Periods of depression can go on for weeks, months, or even years. And depression's theft of an individual's energy, enthusiasm, pleasure, and hope can be nearly absolute.

Depression can look and feel a lot like grief: days lived in an unrelenting colourlessness. And the precipitants may be similar: a loss or disappointment. But depression involves additional symptoms: it is often accompanied by anxiety, a kind of dull dread that something bad lurks around the corner. And a depressed person often feels alone and unloved. Depression is often accompanied by guilt, shame, or a sense of unworthiness – that you are somehow to blame for the situation because of an unremediable lack of personal merit. This 'depressive thinking style' makes it hard to recover and easy to relapse. Success is no guarantee against depression. Depressed boys often have a lot going for them – intelligence, creativity, and academic and social success. Under the influence of depression, these boys, who would seem to have it all, get down on themselves for perceived weaknesses or failures, or they dwell on losses they have suffered. The heavy burdens of depression exact their toll, and since the surface manifestation of depression may be irritability, these boys can begin acting towards the whole world like stereotypical 'cranky old men'.

While it's usually triggered by a specific loss, disappointment, or trauma, depression seems to appear on its own in some sufferers and transforms the emotional landscape into a vast, flat desert and life into a numbing journey punctuated by an occasional dip in elevation but only rare rises.

A distinction is made between the more severe form – major depressive disorder – and the less extreme, but chronic form known as dysthymia. Both types are less frequently seen in children, where the prevalence is about 2 per cent for each condition.[2] Approximately 7 per cent of teenagers suffer with each disorder.

Major depression is a condition that involves persistent feelings of sadness, emptiness, or irritability every day for at least two weeks, often longer. The average episode lasts about eight months. Victims of major depression typically lose interest in all or almost all activities and/or no longer take pleasure in those activities. They feel inappropriately worthless, guilty, or despairing and without hope. They commonly have trouble concentrating and sleeping and may experience large weight shifts up or down. Episodes of major depression can be unremitting if not treated and may become more severe over time.

Dysthymic disorder is also called 'low-level' chronic depression because the symptoms are less pronounced and the depressed feelings, while chronic and persistent (the average dysthymic period is four years long), are not necessarily experienced all day or every day. Sufferers are capable of other moods and reactions, but their 'highs' are infrequent, shorter, and less lofty. They suffer from similar, though less intense, feelings of low self-esteem, being unloved, and sometimes anger, anxiety, or irritation. Dysthymia often remains unrecognized for several years before its effects become so problematic that they demand attention. Parents of boys diagnosed with dysthymia often remark that they didn't seek help for their son sooner because they thought the laziness, negativity, and gloominess were his temperament or were 'normal for a boy'.

Thankfully, many boys can get relief from depression if it is recognized. Psychotherapy – especially 'cognitive behavioural therapy', which is designed to change the depressive thinking style – is often helpful. So is medication, most notably the new wave of serotinergic drugs: Prozac and its progeny, including Zoloft, Serzone, Wellbutrin, and others. Parents or others who suspect depression in a child or teenager should not hesitate to consult a mental health professional, especially if there is any family history of depression or alcoholism.

Depression isn't the only explanation for boys' emotional troubles, but it must always be considered when a boy is showing signs of emotional or behavioural difficulties. We ask a simple question: 'Are you feeling bad about anything?' 'Has something bad happened in your life?' Often enough, the answer is yes, and the recognition of that 'bad' thing can lead us to a discussion of the feeling associated with it – sadness. Often a boy's depression is clearly based in loss. It may be the loss of a parent or a friendship. Or it may be the loss of a role by which the boy defined himself, as in sports or academic activity, or even the loss of aspects of childhood that accompany growing up, such as the delirious excitement of opening Christmas presents. Or it may be the loss of respect a boy feels in a struggle with his parents. Sometimes the cause isn't so simple or clear, but when we hear from a boy that he is experiencing persistent feelings of sadness, emptiness, bewilderment, and confusion, or reacting extremely to a loss experience in his life, depression is a strong possibility. When a boy appears isolated or lost, it is essential to take a closer look at what is going on.

### Dan with Werther: Emotional Isolation

Everyone agrees that something is wrong with Werther. Through middle school he was an A student; now he's barely maintaining a C average. He's listless in class. Some of his teachers think he may be taking drugs, but no one has been able to figure him out or get through to him. His parents are worried. They know that he is jeopardizing his chances to get into a good college, and in his upwardly mobile suburban community, this is a great sin.

Werther enters my office quietly and smiles weakly. He is tall and thin. His longish dirty blond hair is unkempt, but not spiked or in some wild style. We exchange handshakes, but his is limp, and he withdraws his hand quickly, as if even this interaction is a great effort. Our first few sessions are trials of patience for both of us. With some reluctant boys, a therapist can use the therapy hour to build rapport with talk of sports or disliked teachers, but Werther resists. He seems interested in very little. He likes music, but although I make an effort to keep up with the trends in music, his favourite rock band is one that is too obscure for me. He is polite, however, and appears to feel a little sorry for me in my incompetent attempts to establish connection. We keep trying. It takes about a month of weekly sessions for Werther to open up. He acknowledges that he's not sleeping at night and is having a hard time getting out of bed in the morning. He's eager to get out of school but isn't planning to go to college.

'Have you thought about what you'll do after school?'

'I'd like to get into the Peace Corps and go to Africa or somewhere. But they'd never take me; I think you actually have to be good at something for them to want you.'

Nothing in the background he shares with me, and nothing in his school records or in interviews with his teachers or parents, suggests a striking reason for Werther to feel so down. This is, however, typical of a pattern of depressive behaviour for many boys. The discrepancy between how you'd think they would feel about themselves (fairly comfortable and confident) and how they actually see themselves (as failures who should apologize for consuming oxygen) is the classic shadow of depression. Werther is clearly an intelligent, caring young man with great potential. Yet he is almost inert.

In a faculty meeting where he is discussed as a 'student of concern', the theories about Werther differ. Some of his teachers consider him 'lazy'; others think he's learning disabled. Some wonder about marijuana use; someone else suggests chronic fatigue syndrome. Nobody mentions the possibility of depression.

Although I can't find a clear good reason for Werther's depression – and thus assume that there is, as with many cases of depression, at least some biological underpinning to it – his emotional miseducation had made it worse than it had to be. Through our work together, Werther began to develop an emotional vocabulary – an ability to identify his feelings and be able to talk about them – and a comfort level with the 'softer' emotions of sadness and fear that relieved the sense of shame and self-hate that had fuelled the depression. That, along with treatment with antidepressants that improved his outlook and made therapy work more productive, helped Werther gain new insights and turn his life around.

Some boys are so distanced from their emotions that, like Werther, they face a slow journey inward to understand their depression and pull through it. Girls work hard to keep their lives together, too, but they're more likely to be able to talk about what they are feeling and doing, and why. Dialogue and reflection provide opportunities for growth that boys so often miss in the stoic world of men. Boys are reminiscent of the cart-horse in George Orwell's *Animal Farm*: the worse things got once the tyrant pigs took over the farm, the more the cart-horse just ploughed and ploughed and ploughed.

We see many boys with a lot of pain and a lot of dignity; they're bearing it the best they can, doing the best they can to be good soldiers, just digging in until the battle's won. They know that their dad is overworked or that he's moody or hostile or an alcoholic. Or they know that their mother is oppressively anxious. And if someone died or some other bad thing happened, sure, it's depressing. But boys try to minimize their feelings. Like a Clint Eastwood character, every boy imagines himself to be willing to take the bullet – take the emotional pain – and act as if it doesn't matter. They believe that, if they're brave and strong enough, they can steel themselves and go on.

## Telltale Losses Mark the Trail

By the time boys come to us in our practice, it's usually because their parents are worried about the emotional ramifications of a major traumatic event – often parental divorce or a loved one's death. Their instincts are accurate: a divorce, a death or other loss, a change in the living situation can be the precipitating event for a depressive disorder. Most boys we see with depression have something like this in their recent history. Many depressed men experienced such events in childhood or adolescence, and the depression has never been resolved or treated. Boys whose parents send them for help are the lucky ones.

### *Michael with Jody: A Son Grieving for a Loved Father*

Jody first came to me when he was twelve, four years after his father had died of cancer. He was a small, slender boy with dark, neatly groomed hair, but sad, tired eyes. He walked as if he were carrying a heavy pack on his back. Jody had loved his father passionately, and his father had loved him. They closely identified with each other and shared a lot of interests. After his dad died, Jody fell into a deep depression, but at first it went unnoticed beside his mother's and his sister's more outward expressions of grief.

In therapy it became clear that Jody had a huge emotional hunger for a father, but he resisted developing a closer relationship with any of the older men in his life – his teachers, his uncles, a few family friends. Jody gave clear signals to me, too, that he did not want anything reminiscent of a father–son relationship. To become connected to any father figure would have put him into an intense loyalty conflict, because it would have felt to him like a betrayal and denial of his great love for his father. Jody was being loyal to his father by withdrawing from such contacts. He was carrying a torch for his dad.

I can still remember the pain in his eyes. But his sadness about his father was just half of what was doing Jody in. The other half was his isolation and his loneliness: the depression was like a force field separating him from other people. And here I am – I'm a 'feelings junkie', a psychologist who knows what this is and is trained to sit with it and work with it – and even I wanted to run out of the room. Now, if the intensity of this boy's pain can make *me* want to turn and run, imagine what *other* people in Jody's life felt.

Freud described many of his patients as suffering from 'strangulated grief' – grief that has not found full expression and progressed through all its stages. This occurs in both men and women, but culturally men – and boys, as well – are at risk for an incomplete grieving process. Why? Because grieving doesn't look strong or masculine. It looks weak and vulnerable and dependent. Grieving involves giving yourself over to your love and the sadness of missing the deceased person. But many men cannot stand to feel that level of helplessness, and that training begins as boys. Trapped by the 'Big Impossible' that denies a boy the freedom of emotional expression to grieve and be comforted, boys like Jody can become isolated with their sorrow, and when they fall into a depression, no one wants to be around it.

*Michael with Daryl: A Boy Distracted, Angry, and Fearful*

Daryl was a handsome and strong boy. Nothing about him 'looked' depressed. One would have thought that he was just a naturally quiet person, not a big talker, and indeed, he was not. At fourteen he was a studious and hardworking student at a very competitive state school, earning mostly As and Bs. He was known – until recently – as a good boy, one of the nicest in his class. But his history of academic and social success didn't square with his growing number of offences reported to the headmaster. In the past four months, Daryl had earned a number of detentions and one suspension for swearing at a teacher. He was caught copying another student's answers on a science test, he'd intimidated a classmate, and he'd made crude and devaluing comments to two girls in his class. One recent morning at home, when his mother complained that he wasn't taking his schoolwork seriously, he yelled at her, swearing. That's when his father made the appointment to see me.

I knew this about Daryl's home life: he was the youngest of three children, and both his older brother and sister were in college, away from home. The family lived in a modest home in a quiet suburban neighbourhood. Though the surroundings were comfortable, inside the house there had been almost constant turmoil. His fifty-two-year-old father was the owner of a small business, a limousine service. His mother was a frail woman, with deteriorating health due to years of struggle with anorexia. Daryl's mother didn't come to the therapy sessions, only his dad. I was puzzled by this unusual absence; mothers normally come to family therapy sessions.

A tall, thin, angular boy, Daryl seemed to fold in on himself as he sat down beside his father. He looked tired and acknowledged that his recent disciplinary scrapes gave him a sinking feeling about himself and about life, but he ascribed them to 'bad judgement'; he saw them as aberrations from his normal behaviour.

'I'm fine most of the time, but sometimes I just lose it and do something stupid.'

For his term research project in science, Daryl was preparing a presentation on anorexia and the effects of malnutrition on organ systems. Clearly, his mother's health was on his mind.

'Are you worried about your mother's health?'

'Not really. Well, sometimes. When she has to go to the hospital, times like that.'

'What worries you?'

'I don't know. Just that she's always sick.'

'Do you feel sad about her situation?'

'Yeah, sort of, I guess. Sometimes, anyway.'

'Sometimes sad and sometimes . . . ?'

'Sometimes she makes me mad. It's like she's too sick to do anything, but she's not too sick to complain about stuff and criticize me.'

'Do you ever talk with your mother about her sickness or your concerns?'

'No,' he said, shrugging. 'There's nothing to say, really.'

There was, of course, plenty that needed saying and hearing. Daryl had questions he needed to ask, feelings he needed to share, but he didn't have a history of being able to talk about feelings, and this was a hard time to start on his own. It was clear that he did worry about his mother's health, all the time – every day he thought about her dying – and it made him profoundly sad. If his mother and father argued over anything of substance, if they knew he was around, they usually excused themselves from the house 'for a drive', Daryl explained. But he knew they argued in the car, and he worried about their having an accident. He would often wait by the living room window until he saw the car's headlights safely in the driveway. Daryl knew that his parents often argued over his school performance, and while he expressed his fear for them in terms of a car crash, at a deeper level it was his fear of a marital crash – and his role in their marital conflict – that worried him more.

Despite his intellectual understanding of the suffering of anorexics, Daryl felt angry that his mother continued to starve herself, and then he felt guilty about feeling angry towards her. Much like a child of an alcoholic, he felt a sense of personal failure because he wasn't able to change her pattern of self-destruction, and he blamed his father for the same failure in larger terms.

But Daryl couldn't talk about his sense of hopelessness or his longing for the 'normal' life he believed other people had. He was determined to be 'strong' – which to him meant not admitting his sadness – for his mother, for his father, and for himself. This much he could do. He could work harder to distract himself from the sadness. He could keep up a good front of academic success, even if it meant stealing answers to get them right. And he could focus on his mother's illness surreptitiously – by using it as a research topic for a school project. When the internal emotional tension grew too great, he vented it in angry, aggressive behaviour towards teachers and fellow students, and desperate acts like cheating to maintain his grades.

I pulled out a piece of paper and a pencil, wrote 'Dear Mum,' and asked Daryl what he would tell his mother if he could share what was on his mind. Initially he balked, protesting that he wouldn't know what to say. But then he began to speak. First, he apologized for screaming and swearing at her. He said he was sorry. I wrote it down. And that he would try to be more respectful. He also hoped she would be more respectful of him. I continued to write his thoughts down, dictation style.

In the past, when it was quite common for a person to be illiterate, if you needed a letter written, you went to someone who could read and write; you'd tell him or her what you wanted to say, and that person wrote the letter for you. That's what we did. Here was a boy who had no idea how to lay out his feelings, and he needed some help walking through the process – he needed a translator to identify his feelings and articulate them so he could begin to understand them. He didn't have to send the letter to his mother. But he needed to 'write it' in order to spell out his thoughts and feelings so they could become available to him. What was important about the letter was that he'd said it all. So many boys are like Daryl, overwhelmed by their emotions but without the emotional literacy that lets them understand or make use of the feelings. They need help with the most basic task of identifying what they feel before they can begin to understand what to do about it.

## From Depression to Suicide: A Lonely, Angry, Sad Descent

As a culture, we treat adolescent suicide as a singular surprise, each one a startling, sad end to one troubled life. But we see disturbing patterns in statistics that suggest there is more to be learned about why kids kill themselves. About boys, in particular, the numbers make an urgent statement. One of the most challenging statistics about teenagers and depression is that teenage girls attempt suicide more often, by a ratio of about two to one, but many more teenage boys actually end up dead by their own hand. In the United States each year there are, on average, 1,890 suicides among fifteen- to nineteen-year-olds, 1,625 of them committed by boys. The most recent figures indicate a yearly rate of 330 suicides for ten- to fourteen-year-old children, of whom 253 are male. At every point of childhood and adolescence, the number of boy suicides far outweighs the number of girl suicides.[3] That any children are moved to kill themselves is a tragedy, but that the great majority of them are boys is a warning that something about boys' emotional resilience – or lack of it – places them at greater risk.

  Some experts maintain that the gender difference in attempts may be only a statistical artifact – that women are simply less likely to lie about it when interviewed and that, in reality, males and females attempt suicide with the same frequency. Other experts point to the fact that boys use more lethal methods (around 60 per cent of male suicides are with firearms, compared to around 40 per cent of female suicides), and because of their greater intent and lethality, more males die and thus are not counted among the attempt or repeated-attempt statistics. Because girls are more likely to take pills, a method that allows time for intervention, another explanation is that, for girls, an attempt at suicide is more often a call for help – that at some level they do not want to die. Boys are more likely to be shamed by their feelings of emotional vulnerability and more likely to choose a method that won't require them to ask for help or dwell too long in the unfamiliar territory of powerful emotion. That is one of the reasons why even hints at suicide – from anyone, but especially from a teenage boy – need to be taken seriously.

### *Michael with Keith: Suicide Notes were No Joke*

Towards the end of the school year, Keith, fifteen, circulated a note to his friends saying that he was going to throw himself off a bridge at the end of the day. The note also contained some extraordinarily vitriolic attacks on his parents and a lot of swear words. Two friends who were very concerned brought the note to me. I immediately went and pulled Keith out of his history class to talk with him about it.

Here was a sight – a boy who, if you'd scrubbed him up, would have been a ruggedly handsome young man. But Keith had a different statement to make. He wore the button-down shirt required by the school, but he had cut the sleeves off with pinking shears. His hair was short and neat but dyed a deep, artificial red colour. And his eyebrow was pierced. Piercing in and of itself is not a danger sign in a boy; for many adolescents it has the same meaning as long hair did in the sixties. However, in Keith it was one of several signs that defiance was his full-time job.

He was furious that the note had been brought to me and, of course, wanted to know which of his friends had 'narked' on him. He tried to back me off, insisting that it was meant to be a joke. Though he was articulate and at moments persuasive, I took the note absolutely seriously and called his parents.

When I finally reached Keith's mother, a busy corporate attorney, her irritation was obvious. She assured me that it was just her son's dark sense of humour, nothing more. She told me not to overreact in a way that would bring him to the attention of the school authorities. Stunned by her reaction, I explained to her that any suicide threat has to be taken seriously and that I was not going to let her son leave school until she and her husband came in to talk to me and their son. Very grudgingly, she agreed to meet with Keith's head of year and myself. During the meeting, Keith's mother demanded to see the note, took one quick look at it, and crumpled it up.

Keith's father was hostile, too. When I asked them if there was a history of depression in the family, the father acknowledged that he suffered from chronic low-level depression, for which he took medication, but insisted that his problem was his own and 'it's got nothing to do with Keith's stupid practical jokes'. Maybe not, but the fact is that depression does have genetic links and tends to run in families. The father was also an attorney, and the head of year told me that he had heard that Keith's father was in some 'serious trouble with the IRS' and was under investigation. His career was in serious jeopardy.

Without a doubt, the seething anger I was witnessing in the mother and the denial in the father had roots in the family's troubles. Preoccupied with their own careers, they simply couldn't face the idea that Keith was having trouble of his own.

The parents said 'yes, yes' to our recommendations for therapy and took Keith home, but they never followed up on those recommendations. They moved him to another school the following year. There, Keith made a very serious suicide attempt.

He was hospitalized and finally, in therapy long overdue, revealed that he had been abused between the ages of eight and ten by an uncle, who had threatened Keith, should he think about telling, and thus the fearful boy had kept this painful secret for four years. His parents, shocked at last into recognition of their son's unhappiness, recalled this time when Keith had changed from a good-humoured, rambunctious boy to a gloomier, more cynical version of himself. They had thought it was 'normal for boys', but as his attitude grew uglier, they didn't like it and over the years had come down increasingly hard on him.

Keith's note to his friends that day was a cry for help, and when his emotional pain was ignored, he lived with it until the day he felt he couldn't live with it any more. It took a suicide attempt for him to get his parents' attention, to bring into the open the painful secret that had ravaged him emotionally for some of the most formative years of his adolescence.

Even boys who survive a suicide attempt can remain inarticulate about the emotions that spurred them to favour death over life, notes Jay Callahan, a suicidologist who worked with suicide survivors for nearly a decade in emergency psychiatric services. Adolescent boys, particularly, are likely to describe the attempt as a symptom of 'a very bad time' and be willing to leave it at that.

'It would be nice to think there were some positive lessons that could come out of a suicide attempt,' he says, 'but for the most part they're just relieved that they didn't succeed at it – like a kid shouting to get a fight started, but relieved when his friends hold him back.'

Therapists have a pretty standard approach for assessing suicidal risk. It's not complicated. When someone reports a boy's offhand comment about ending it all, a note like Keith's, an essay in English class – anything that suggests a child is having suicidal thoughts – we first talk with the boy about it. We look for any danger signs, substance abuse, a recent disappointment or change, things like breaking up with a girlfriend or a parental divorce or whether a boy may be questioning his sexual identity. Although accurate statistics are hard to come by, the burden of coming to terms with a gay orientation in a hostile environment is a significant risk factor for suicide.[4] Just as a boy is eventually willing to talk about his sadness when asked about it, a direct question about suicide typically brings an honest response. We ask him directly about any thoughts or plans for suicide: 'Are you thinking about killing yourself?' It is vital to understand that the more precise a boy's thoughts and plans for suicide, the more likely he is to try it.

### Dan with Jihan: A Boy with a Plan

I'd known Jihan from his first tearful day at school, aged twelve, until he was eighteen. He had struggled through some very low periods along this route and at one point was quite suicidal. Jihan was a very handsome bi-racial boy who had a great sense of humour. His classmates knew him for that humour, not for the pain behind it. Both parents had very high academic expectations for him. The school he attended was quite competitive and required him to do lots of homework. Though he was bright, Jihan had never been a fast reader or swift worker, and this, combined with his hour-long commute, functioned to keep him playing catch-up for most of the school year. When Jihan would do poorly on a test, his parents' remedy was, like a jockey driving his horse down the home stretch, to figuratively 'go to the whip'. They would berate him, force him to spend nearly all of his free time on schoolwork, and to drive home their point of how important this educational opportunity was for him, they would tour the poorest areas of Boston to demonstrate to him how lucky he was to be able to attend such a good school. Jihan would work hard, at least in spurts, but in some subjects, especially maths and science, he had trouble getting Cs.

And he suffered socially. Being a bi-racial scholarship student in a predominantly white school made Jihan a mark for cruel comments from those in the majority. For the white students, his brown skin made him 'black'; to the African-American students, he was neither. He also did not fit the affluent profile of the school population. He attended the school on a scholarship designed to attract promising low-income minorities, and provisions included buses from his inner-city neighbourhood to this community of stately homes and wealth. In the Easter holidays, when many of these boys would head to Aspen or a tropical Club Med, Jihan would remain in the city.

When he was fifteen, the various threads of difficulty finally became so tangled that Jihan's life basically became one big knot. His grades were horrendous. He was in danger of losing his transport privilege and scholarship to attend the school. His parents' marriage was beginning to collapse, and Jihan could feel the tension between them. Jihan looked bad, and I was worried. It is hard to deconstruct this worry into its component parts. It might be a boy's posture, tone of voice, or lack of energy. I once took a seminar with a clinician who was a very experienced suicide specialist. When we kept pressing her for the formula for how she could tell the dangerously suicidal teenager from the one who wouldn't make an attempt, she said to 'trust your gut'. Looking at Jihan at that low point in his life was making my intestines pretty jumpy. But still, I was taken by surprise at his answer to my question of whether he had a suicide plan.

'How would you do it?'

'I'd just walk right out into the street and run out in front of the first truck I saw.'

'Are you serious?'

'Damn right I'm serious.'

Research suggests that, on any given day, if a fifteen-year-old boy is asked 'Do you think about killing yourself?' 14 per cent will answer yes.[5] The follow-up question – 'Do you have a plan?' or

'How would you do it?' – tells you just how much they've been thinking about it. While Jihan had not picked a date, chosen a time, or told me about a hidden gun or a bottle of lethal pills, the truck plan seemed real enough for me to contact his parents.

Fortunately, Jihan's parents took the threat seriously and stepped up their efforts to help him find social supports within the school and his home community. His father tried to be more communicative, more emotionally accessible, and less critical. And we continued to meet periodically, which gave Jihan a safe haven within the school, a place where he could talk freely about his situation and begin to develop some emotional strategies for survival. You can never know whether a boy *would have* killed himself or not, but I felt Jihan had been on the edge waiting for a slight push from a bad day.

## Untreated Depression: A Path to Delinquent Diversions

If left untreated, depression tends to get worse and places a boy at much higher risk for suicide. It also very commonly leads to substance abuse: nearly one-third of depressed teens have a coexisting substance abuse problem, involving alcohol or drugs. And substance abuse and delinquency go hand in hand. It is not uncommon for a depressed boy to get into trouble at school or out on the street. When a boy has walled himself off from supportive parents and friends, he is far more likely to seek solace in a bottle, joint, pill, or the oblivion of self-inflicted death. Needless to say, lack of support makes recovery from depression and its related behaviours that much more difficult.

Untreated, an episode of depression can last from three to six years – a boy's entire adolescence – and that carries heavy 'side effects'. If the boy isn't interacting with other children and the world, or he's interacting in a negative way, then he's missing out on important emotional and social growth. The long-term effect is not only the greater risk of deeper depressions but also the lasting memory of childhood as a sad time and a view of life as a discouraging prospect.

It's not uncommon to hear male depression referred to as 'hidden depression', but the image is misleading. In our experience, most adolescent boys don't purposefully hide their depression; if anything, their depression hides *them* – behind sadness, anger, destructiveness, or drugs. A boy suffering from depression may seem intentionally abrasive, hostile, or sullen, but the truth is, he is ill – he is depressed – and can't simply choose to be some other way. The package he wraps it in is simply his best effort to make a clinical mood disorder look like 'normal' boy behaviour. It's as close as he can get.

## 9. Drinking and Drugs: Filling the Emotional Void

[W]e accepted the folklore that being a man meant being able to 'hold your liquor' and we became fascinated with getting high.

Geoffrey Canada, *Reaching Up for Manhood*

In a drug-awareness class, thirteen-year-old students were asked to write down a half-dozen goals or dreams they held for their lives. There were the predictable career answers – sports star, teacher, political leader, scientist – and there were the poignant personal ones, such as helping a sick parent get better. The teachers directed the class discussion to the threat that alcohol and drugs pose to accomplishing those life dreams, a topic that adults find compelling but that is purely abstract to most teenagers. Asked why, with such great hopes for the future, a young person might choose to drink or do drugs, one boy responded with a laugh: 'Because that's *later*, and this is *now*.'

The present does loom large in adolescence, and the 'now' is filled with reasons to drink and do drugs. If you ask an eight-year-old boy if he is going to drink a lot when he gets to secondary school, he'll say no. If you ask ten- and eleven-year-olds the same question, only about one in ten will say that he will drink beer when he is a teenager, and that only for experimentation. But when boys actually get to the age of thirteen and fourteen, their attitudes begin to change. In a subtle psychological *pas de deux*, the emerging adolescent boy becomes attracted to the previously hidden satisfactions that alcohol and drugs can give him. At the same time, he begins to view these substances as less and less harmful. Just as the sentiment is nearly unanimous among eight-year-olds that they won't drink, it is almost inevitable that an older boy eventually will.[1]

By the time a boy reaches the age of fifteen, there is a good chance that he will have been drunk. The use of marijuana is on an upswing again – among thirteen- and fourteen-year-old boys it has tripled in the past five years – so the odds are also fairly good that he will have smoked pot, and the more educated his parents are, the more likely he is to have done so. More than 30 per cent of fifteen-year-old boys report having smoked marijuana during the past year. By the final year of school the odds of alcohol or marijuana use are even greater. Nearly four out of every ten males in their last year of school have smoked pot. Two-thirds of all males the same age have been drunk. Almost 40 per cent have been drunk within the past month. Seven per cent of boys this age smoke pot every day. Many have tried both alcohol and pot, often in combination.[2]

And that's just the light stuff. What about other, 'harder' drugs?

To an even greater degree than with marijuana and alcohol, males are more likely than females to use other illicit drugs. Although the rates of use for these 'harder' drugs – such as heroin, cocaine, crack, inhalants, and LSD – are lower overall (for example, 81 per cent of males in their last year of school have tried alcohol, compared with 14 per cent who have tried LSD and 7 per cent who have tried cocaine), they are much higher for boys than for girls. Drug use rates in the last year of school tend to be at least 1.5 to 2.5 times as high among boys as among girls. Teenage boys account for an even greater share of the frequent or heavy users of these drugs.


## The Seduction


Caught up in the world of 'This is now', twelve- to fourteen-year-old boys-who-would-be-men look to the men and older boys around them for signs of what to do. They see other boys, maybe a 'precocious' friend or sometimes an older brother or cousin, or men represented in the media, in movies, or on TV drinking or doing drugs and apparently enjoying it. They do not often see the degradation they have been led to expect by the drug-awareness preachers or ads run on TV or in drug-awareness classes. They see someone they want to be like drinking and using drugs and they are likely to try to emulate that person.

Boys interested in sports are more likely to try alcohol first, since alcohol is generally the 'drug' of choice for this group. Recent studies of college students show, for example, that athletes tend to drink far more than non-athletes.[3] This is not too surprising, given that every sports-crazy boy sees tens of thousands of beer commercials as he grows up watching his favourite teams on American TV. The repeated association between sports and beer that a boy sees causes them to become almost synonymous in his mind. The advertisement goals: to imbue beer with the prestige that comes with professional sports, to make drinking beer as safe as a languid baseball game, and to establish brand loyalty as an extension of home team loyalty. Some athletes also smoke pot and do other drugs, but it's boys more on the social fringe – a skater or snowboarder rather than a football player – who seem to be drawn to use less mainstream drugs like pot, mushrooms, or LSD. Although there are exceptions, it has been our experience that a high school boy who has long hair and likes the bands Phish or the Grateful Dead is very likely to have said yes to drugs.

### Dan with Secondary School Users: Getting Started

Randy, Devin, and Tan, sixteen-year-olds, sit together in an empty classroom talking about drinking and pot smoking. It is after school hours, and a classmate is interviewing them for an assignment on the subject; they've been promised anonymity.

'When did you start smoking weed?'

'Actually, the first time I smoked weed was with my brother and his friend when they were fifteen and we were thirteen,' says Randy. 'I smoked like two bowls, but I didn't even get high. I smoked a couple more times during the next summer, but I really started smoking like the middle of the next school year.'

'How often do you smoke now?'

'At least two or three times a week,' Randy says.

'Why do you smoke pot?'

'It helps me just chill, like at parties or whatever,' Randy says. 'Just sit around.'

'When did you start drinking?'

'During the summer I was fifteen,' Randy says, 'but I would only drink like every three weeks. But in the middle of the following year, I started drinking every weekend.'

'So you drink once a week?'

'I don't know. Some weekends I'll drink Friday and Saturday nights, and the next week I won't drink at all, but I guess it's about once a week.'

'How much do you drink at one time?'

'About six or eight beers,' Randy says.

'What do you like about it?'

'It's fun.'

'What do you mean?'

'I don't know,' Randy says. 'I can't really explain it, I guess.'

Devin says he began drinking when he was fifteen and now drinks every weekend.

'What about drinking do you like?'

'It's just fun,' Devin says. 'There's nothing else to do.'

Tan explains that he used to drink more – like every Friday and Saturday night, a whole six-pack each time – but now he doesn't drink 'that much' any more. Why?

'I guess I realized I was kind of being stupid about shit. So I calmed down a lot. I only drink like once a month, if that.'

'What do you like about it?'

'It's just fun, just a release from all the bullshit,' Tan says.

'You mean like a way to escape from problems?'

'No! Hell, no! I would just be with friends and get crazy,' Tan says, with great emphasis but little clarity. 'At first I liked drinking so much just because it was new. Now I just drink at parties. I guess I don't really know why I like it. One of the last times I drank, before I calmed down, I was with some friends, and we couldn't find anyone to buy us beer, so we went "garage hopping" – checking out garages in the neighbourhood for beer and then stealing it – and we almost got caught by some crazy mum with a shovel. We went in the woods behind the 7-Eleven, and I drank till I could barely stand.'

Like Randy, most boys are introduced to drinking by an older boy, and they find the experience to their liking.

Hank, an engineer in his mid-forties, recalls the thrill that so many boys feel, but can't articulate, about their early drinking experiences: 'I was about twelve or thirteen, and I was going to camp on the beach overnight with my friend and his dad. I bought a quart bottle of Bacardi rum from another guy in my class and stowed it away in my rucksack. After my friend's father went to sleep in the trailer, we snuck down to the beach with the rum and a six-pack of 7-Up. Neither of us had ever drunk before, not even beer, so we were sort of winging it. We kept passing the bottle back and forth, slugging down large mouthfuls of this terrible-tasting rum and chasing it with 7-Up. We drank half the bottle before we realized we were drunk. I remember – even though I eventually blacked out that night – feeling like I'd discovered some big secret. It was like, "Now I get it! This is why grown-ups are always drinking before dinner. It feels *great*!" And it really did.

'We staggered down the beach, hanging all over each other, to where some older teenagers were having a party around a fire. Even though we were several years younger, we immediately sat down next to two girls and began chatting them up, even rubbing up against them. They could see we were drunk and shooed us away, but we didn't care. We were on top of the world.'

For many teenage boys, these first tastes of drunkenness or being high cast the world in a different light. Drowning his fear with liquid courage, a boy is released. 'It's a feeling of power, of being kind of indestructible,' a recovering teenage alcoholic told us. 'You can be anything, do things you could never do otherwise, and you don't have to think about the consequences.'

Alcohol affects several brain systems involved in the way emotions are expressed and felt. One known effect of alcohol is that it reduces anxiety. Ethanol, in alcohol, possesses a pharmacological profile similar to the benzodiazepines, drugs such as Valium that help to reduce anxiety problems.[4] So much of adolescent boy life is anxiety-producing – the struggle to be stoic, to measure up to the impossible standards of manhood, to avoid the ridicule of the cruel peer culture. It is a rare boy who can withstand the pressure, who is confident that he does measure up. Contrary to the cocky or calm exterior he projects, an adolescent boy is in continual pitched battle with fear and anxiety. For boys faced with these challenges of growing up, alcohol can be a balm, bringing prompt and soothing relief. It can be, as Tan put it so succinctly, 'a release from all the bullshit'.


## Drinking and Drugs: A Male Rite of Passage . . . to Nowhere

By drinking, a boy is also released from the shame and anxiety of seeing himself as 'little'. The adolescent culture of cruelty has it in for any boy who slackens his pace in the race to prove masculinity, and drinking puts him up front with the *real men*. For boys, getting high, but especially drinking, is imbued with meaning that goes way beyond 'just having fun'. A boy's first experience with being drunk is a rite of passage. Like losing one's virginity or passing a driver's test, being able to 'drink like a man' gives a boy a certain kind of gender pride. The pressure to drink – and drink capably – is tremendous. We knew a young Asian college student who was a rugby player and participated in the almost ritualistic heavy drinking that followed games. He did this despite knowing that, like many Asians, he lacked an enzyme that helps metabolize alcohol. The result was that he got drunk faster and suffered far more the next day than his teammates. But it was important for him to keep pace, and he did.

'It's not like somebody shoves a joint into your hand and says you've got to smoke it,' another boy said. 'It's your own choice – but when the guys are passing stuff around, you want to be part of what's happening.' Girls have their own flawed reasons for drinking, but measuring up as women isn't one of them. Being 'too chicken' to drink just doesn't carry the same psychological weight for a girl.

In hunting societies a boy might prove his worth to society as a provider or a protector; he might show that he was a real contributor to the tribe by killing a buffalo or a lion. The Jewish bar mitzvah, the Catholic confirmation, and other religions' coming-of-age life-cycle rituals celebrate a boy's religious study and his acceptance as a responsible 'adult' member of the religious community. Unfortunately, this achievement doesn't affect his status in the broader culture and certainly not in the secular subculture of boys. Short of going to war, there is a void of meaningful contemporary rites of manhood.

For a boy today, high-risk drinking or drug use may seem the only options available to gain acceptance and join other boys in a test of 'courage' or endurance.

The stories boys tell about their high-potency intoxications are their 'war stories', replacing moments of high adventure and drama that have you floating near the edge, testing the limits of strength and endurance, figuring out who is strongest and most daring. And each time these drinking boys 'go into battle', it seems to call for greater bravado and daring.

Boys learn from their earliest days in the playground, jumping at dares, that the willingness to take risks is part of what it means to be a man. For adolescent boys, alcohol and drug use is the next step in the natural progression of risk taking. As Geoffrey Canada writes in *Reaching Up for Manhood*: 'Growing up my friends and I took risks all the time. We jumped off rooftops, climbed over barbed-wire fences, had rock fights. Later we accepted the folklore that being a man meant being able to "hold your liquor" and we became fascinated with getting high. We knew that to reach some of these highs you had to take risks, but for us risk taking had already become a way of life.'[5]

When a twenty-two-year-old 'college boy' in New York drowned on a riverbank during a drunken party, the college launched an aggressive alcohol education campaign. But at the end of it all, the tradition of alcohol abuse at the school remained alive and well. A first year boy told a *New York Times* reporter that, on his second night on campus, a dormitory neighbour announced proudly that he had drunk five shots of tequila and two beers.[6]

'Then they brag about how much they were vomiting,' he said, 'to show how much they were drinking and that they're still standing and they didn't die.'

## Risky Business

Peter, now nineteen, was drinking at a deserted beach with friends who decided to have a little fun at his expense.

'We were drunk out of our minds,' he recalls. Taking an old

aluminium beach chair from the boot of their car, his friends tied him to the chair with some rope they'd found and gagged him with a T-shirt. Laughing at the hilarity of their prank, three of them carried Peter and the chair, leaving him just at the water's edge, then turned back towards the car, as Peter's muffled yells echoed behind them. After about fifteen minutes, a wave knocked Peter's chair over, leaving him upside down in the water.

'If my friend hadn't turned around and noticed that I was missing, I'd be dead,' he says. 'By the time they ran down to where I was, I'd been under so long I couldn't have held out for more than a few more seconds.'

One of the most dangerous aspects of alcohol's effect on the brain is to destroy sensible judgement. Simply put, the more a boy drinks, the stupider he gets. Boys who drink may feel invincible, immortal, and beyond the reach of the law. A frequent comment we hear in Monday-morning sessions with boys is, 'I can't believe I did that.'

For adolescent boys any drinking is almost always 'problem' drinking.[7] When boys drink, they almost always drink to excess. In fact, because they must be able to respond to the challenges of their drunk peers to 'have another beer', typically, any time teenage boys use alcohol, they abuse it. It's not that adults don't misuse alcohol; indeed, many boys learn their drinking patterns from their parents or other adults. But while many adults can drink a glass of wine or a beer with dinner and never go beyond that, the characteristic pattern for a teenage boy is periodic bouts of all-out high-risk drinking rather than a steady rate of consumption.

With heavy drinking comes high-risk behaviour. Statistics indicate that, at some point during their last year in school, four out of ten boys will drive a car under the influence of alcohol. Three out of ten will pass out because they've had too much to drink. Males under the age of eighteen are ten times more likely than females to be arrested for an alcohol or drug offence. One of the reasons public health officials are concerned about teenage drinking is that it is routinely and directly responsible for adolescent injury and death resulting from car crashes, accidental drowning, cigarette smoking, illicit drug use, sexually transmitted diseases, violence, and suicide. Use of alcohol at younger ages is associated with a double risk of

HIV infection: these boys have more sexual partners and are less likely to use condoms.[8]

We hear many, many stories from boys in schools about alcohol use and near fatalities, like Peter's beach party incident. Ted, seventeen, fell asleep at the wheel driving home from a party. He was awakened abruptly when his car went off the road and rolled over on its side. He boasted that, through it all, he had not spilled the can of beer he was holding. And another boy, sixteen, reported nearly slipping into an alcoholic coma after 'funnelling' vodka. 'Funnelling', as the name implies, means having someone pour vodka through a funnel directly into the user's stomach, bypassing all that time-consuming swallowing. Fortunately, one of his friends was sufficiently aware to see that this was no typical passing-out and called for an ambulance.

For boys such exploits are bonding experiences, remembered fondly years later. For many men they never lose their appeal. Those who live through such behaviour don't necessarily outgrow it, either. A group of college friends who are now in their late thirties, and all very successful businessmen, get together once a year, rent a limousine, and get falling-down drunk. Like World War II soldiers who once clung to one another as German bombs fell around them, these men cling to one another as they struggle to walk down the street. Their odyssey might include a visit to a brothel or a strip club. Last year it included a trip back to their old college to break windows. Each year they relive their previous adventures in a drunken night of storytelling – their 'war stories'.

## Reach Out and Touch Someone: When the Only Buddies are Drinking Buddies

In American high school yearbooks where students are allowed to include their favourite photos of good times, it is not unusual to see this classic picture: a gregarious group of six or eight boys, smiling broadly with their arms around one another's shoulders. They are, of course, drunk, maybe stoned as well. In the adolescent boy culture, boys use alcohol and drugs as the basis for a good time and to break down some of the emotional barriers they've built. But even though emotions may come to the surface while drinking, this is a manly activity, so the absence of stoicism can be excused. You are not culpable: almost any action performed while drunk can be dismissed the next day, so it is safe and allows them to feel close to someone for a little while. It temporarily dulls the pain of isolation and loneliness.

Alcohol is an analgesic – a killer of all kinds of pain – through its effects on the brain's endogenous opiate system, responsible for producing that morphine-like substance that relieves our pain.[9] Most people know of its effects through heavy aerobic exercise, which releases endorphins. Less well known is the fact that the opiate system also partially governs emotional attachment by its connection to the sense of touch.

In a very real way, this tactile sense not only protects us from pain – we withdraw our hand when we feel the heat of a flame – but it also allows us to be comforted, whether it is being cradled by a parent in infancy, caressed by a lover, or touched by a friendly hand on the shoulder when in grief. All kinds of touch result in the release of these natural painkilling opiates. When a child with a skinned knee runs to his mother, her touch not only brings psychological reassurance and the promise of safety, but it also literally helps relieve the pain.

Boys who don't experience affectionate, comforting touch – boys who avoid physical contact out of fear, shame, or anger – can get relief from a bottle but no real healing. They learn how to take it like a man and go it alone. Rather than working up enough emotional courage and trust to admit that they would like to talk through a problem or to just connect with someone, they reach instead for a drink, then another and another until the pain of emotional isolation is dulled.

Boys are human: they want to connect with one another and, most, with girls. Drinking allows them to be more emotionally expressive and socially at ease. However, it is an artificial comfort because alcohol precludes meaningful communication and any genuine sense of security or competence. Alcohol and drugs reduce anxiety and inhibition and offer the warmth of an opiate hug, but the effect is temporary and leads a boy to substance dependence.

Drinking and drugs offer boys an escape from emotional complexity by diverting attention to the activity of drinking or doing drugs. It's easier to think all week about where you're going to buy beer and where you and your friends are going to drink it than it is to think about a self-evaluation of your level of emotional maturity. But the lost emotional lessons only exacerbate boys' difficulty understanding and responding effectively to life events and other people. Simply put, if you're drunk or stoned and your main task is staying conscious, nobody expects much complex thinking of you. For a boy who feels uncomfortable socially, emotionally, or sexually, the mind-numbing task of peeling the labels off your bottles of beer starts looking pretty good. To sit with the emotional ambiguities of an evening with girls or friends is to invite social uncertainty, and experiencing your own reactions to that uncertainty, which might be sad or alienated or rejected, is a hefty assignment.

The demand that a boy be *in control*, be on top of his emotional life, often leaves him feeling he's got a job that's too big for him. If you're a boy in that position, alcohol simplifies your emotional life a lot because you can't be very complex when you're stoned. On the other hand, the struggle to maintain physical control *under the influence* suggests physical prowess, an acceptable manly accomplishment. If you drink too much, then all you can pay attention to is *that*. No one expects any more of you.

Just as a tree's age and growth episodes are evident in a pattern of rings in the trunk wood, you can often trace the narrowing of a boy's emotional growth to the period when he started using alcohol or drugs. The restricted emotional development that can be seen in many men is the hidden cost of substance abuse, and it's one that most boys can't fathom, precisely because they lack the emotional experience and maturity to do so.

## Paying the Cost to be the Boss

Rather than do the hard work of facing his fears and trying to master them, a boy who habitually uses drugs or alcohol can find a safe niche, usually with a group of boys who are a lot like him, where he can avoid any challenge to his drug or alcohol use. So while boys come to drinking and drugs from many directions, with many expectations, as users they all travel the same road of emotional detours and high-risk dead ends. In the same way that it's difficult for many parents to accept sadness and depression in boys, many have difficulty facing the fact that boys are initially attracted to alcohol and drugs for the same reason adults are: the effects feel good, and they take the mind off the worrisome details of life.

Whatever the perceived benefits of alcohol and drugs, the innate grandiosity of adolescence, combined with the judgement-impairing nature of these substances, blind boys to the real risks. Boys who use or abuse drugs and alcohol are dancing on the edge of a cliff, but they experience only the exhilaration of the height and none of the anxiety over a fall.

### *Michael with Ted: A Young Alcoholic Looks Back*

Ted is eighteen, the son of a college professor and a school guidance counsellor who did not recognize his drinking problem for more than five years. After three arrests and several frightening episodes in which he ended up in a hospital emergency room, Ted's parents gave him an ultimatum: he could give up drinking and continue to live at home, or he could move out.

As part of the work of recovery, Ted has grown more at ease talking about his problem. When boys are involved with alcohol or drugs, they typically aren't able to reflect on their problem with much insight. But Ted is recovering, he wants to share where he's been, and he wants to help other boys make better choices. The first striking thing about Ted is how handsome he is. He's a very appealing guy, very articulate, very popular with girls. He speaks thoughtfully, is full of energy and a desire to help. Of course, there is something of the confessional Alcoholics Anonymous meeting about what he tells me. Why wouldn't there be? He's been to a lot of AA meetings by now.

I had meant to spend an hour with Ted; it ended up being two and a half hours. He was riveting, and his story was harrowing. I was grateful to him for telling it to me.

Ted had his first drink at the age of thirteen and began smoking marijuana later the same year. By the age of sixteen, he was an alcoholic. Ted described his journey into alcoholism as one that began with idle curiosity and enjoyment and grew with the support of his pack of male friends. They drank together and typically cared for one another when one among them passed out or became ill. It was the nurturing and bonding that would never have taken place without alcohol as the 'glue' that held the relationships together. 'Under the influence', these boys could talk with one another about feelings – however blunted by the alcohol or drugs – and they could share a physical camaraderie that, if they were sober, would be ridiculed.

Like most boys at thirteen, Ted wasn't thinking about his reasons for marijuana and alcohol abuse.

'I just drank to get drunk. It's difficult to say why. I guess I was drinking to forget, but not to forget anything special. I've never really thought about why I got drunk beyond the fact that I actually liked the sensation. Yeah, I drank because I loved the feeling of getting drunk. I remember sitting there and saying to myself, "Try and worry about something, try and worry about something. Actually think about something, and try and make it worry you." And I just couldn't, because I would live in the moment, and I would just do whatever, and that made me incredibly happy. It was this indestructible feeling where you could kind of do anything and be anything and it wouldn't matter, even if you had to wake up the next morning and think, "Oh, Jesus, what did I do last night?" or whatever, you know. At least in the moment you could kind of do and feel and say what you really thought. I was, like, being crazy; it was fun; I was doing things I wouldn't ordinarily have done if I were not intoxicated – you know, living a little more freely.

'Drinking is like an escape, almost. You can be what you want to be and wake up and feel the consequences, but not in the same way, you know. Like, my friends will come up to me and say they fooled around with a girl who I didn't think was so attractive and say, "I was so smashed," and I can say, "Yeah, yeah, yeah," and as much as I think it was just an excuse, if they were sober, it would be something different to me. Just because I would like it not to be an excuse, I understand that, when you do get drunk, you legitimately do stupider things.

'One of the reasons why I drank, and a lot of people drink, I think, is that it almost gives you an excuse to act without thinking. It's like socially acceptable to drink and be stupid. People can just go out and fool around and say, "I was just drunk," and that's okay. So it works for everybody.'

Ted understood clearly how alcohol worked as a convenient – and socially accepted – excuse to avoid responsibility for his actions. He might get into a fight or be cruel to a girl or be a real jerk in all the many ways boys can be jerks, and he wasn't forced to be accountable; he wasn't motivated to either examine his behaviour or try to be more mature the next time. He had an excuse for perpetual adolescence.

Sidetracked by the drugs and alcohol for five years, it was as if, like Rip van Winkle, Ted had fallen into a deep sleep and missed those years of his life, including all the emotional learning experiences that come with friendships, love relationships, and the practice of work and personal values. That's a lot of emotional education to cover, and there's no way to cram for the exam or cheat to get a passing grade.

Boys are reaching for an emotional connection when they turn to alcohol or drugs, but drinking and drug use only distance them from their own emotional responses and any insight into the emotions of others. And the danger is not just from becoming addicted. For every attraction that alcohol and drugs hold for boys, there is a cost they cannot see, in missed opportunities to develop emotional maturity.

### Dan with Eric: A Boy Hiding Out

During the summer he turned fifteen Eric smoked pot with his friends just about every day. He was at that fairly awkward age – too young to find meaningful work, unable to drive yet, but feeling too old for summer camp. He did the occasional odd job, such as cutting a neighbour's lawn, which earned him some money on top of an allowance that was fairly substantial. One of his friends usually had money, too, so as long as the cash supply held out, they had the means to buy dope.

His parents knew Eric had tried marijuana, but they were not sure how often he smoked it. Since they had both smoked marijuana when they were in college, they accepted his experimentation to a degree. It seemed hypocritical not to. At the same time, having come of age in the sixties, they knew what drug use could do. They felt unsure of how tolerant to be. His mother found it easy to believe Eric's story – that he had tried pot for the first time when someone showed up with some at a party and tried it once or twice after that, until he decided it didn't do much for him. It was a half-truth that Eric himself wanted to believe. But then Eric started hanging around with a different group of kids. When his hair got longer and he went and bought huge baggy jeans, and when he dropped out of basketball practice before the first team selections were made, his parents started to worry about how much he really might be using. That's when they sent him to me. Eric could have just been going through a phase, but they weren't taking any chances.

From our first meeting, Eric and I hit it off pretty well. We both had a connoisseur's appreciation of the basketball skills of Larry Bird and Michael Jordan, and as is often the case with many men and boys, sports served as an easy bridge between us. We soon moved beyond basketball, and Eric was willing to reveal a little about his drug habits.

'So what did you do Saturday night?'

'I went out with John and Toby.'

'What did you do?'

'We just hung out.'

'Did you get high?'

'Yeah, we went to this party that Tim [another classmate] was having, and we smoked with this guy who always shows up with this unbelievable weed.'

'Who was there?'

'There were mostly just some kids from my school.'

'Anybody else?'

'Yeah, after we smoked, these really hot girls from Concord came by. I had never seen them before.'

'Did you talk to them?'

'No, we just chilled and listened to music.'

Over the next month Eric started going out with a girl he had met at another party. She was three years younger than he was. Much of our conversation was now centred on this relationship. He thought she was really beautiful, and they had started having sex. He told me proudly that she had been a virgin. But it was apparent to me that one of the reasons Eric liked her so much was that he was not threatened by her. He was in control of the relationship. She was starstruck to be going out with someone his age and was in awe of the world he was introducing her to – a world that, of course, included getting high.

So I challenged him a little on this: 'Do you think you would like Elissa more if she were your age?'

'Maybe. My friends do give me shit about being a paedophile. And she's pretty hard to take when she's with her friends. They are ridiculously silly. They just sit around and laugh at the dumbest stuff.'

'Do you care as much about it when you're high?'

'I don't care about much when I'm high. That's what's nice about it. Nothing matters. It's like you might be worried about some stupid thing, then you smoke, and like, all of a sudden, you either forget about it or think it's funny. Like at a party you can just sit there and get into the music and not worry about all the bullshit.'

Over the course of the next few months, we continued to talk – about his friends who smoked pot all the time compared to other kids at school, about Elissa and why he was attracted to someone so young. Eric was really working hard at thinking about these things. I watched him debate himself. He would take one position on an issue and then rebut himself. He would, for example, say that he knew pot was hurting his schoolwork, but then he'd say that he thought it made him more creative. Back and forth. An honest look at himself, then a retreat. Then back for more truth. This went on for a while; I could see that he was becoming more aware of his motivations for making these choices. Then one day Eric walked into my office and told me that he had decided to quit smoking and that he had broken up with Elissa.

'What happened?'

'I don't know. I just kind of freaked out.'

'About what?'

'I don't know. It was kind of weird. It was like, I'm looking at all these girls being idiots, and I'm thinking, "What am I doing here?" You know, I was kind of scared, like there was something wrong with me or something. It's hard to explain. I kind of freaked, like my brain was moving too fast and I couldn't keep up with my thoughts. But it was like, I gotta get outta here. So I made up some excuse, and when I left, I kind of calmed down after a while.'

'And you decided to quit smoking then?'

'No. It wasn't until the next night, when Toby wanted to go out and get high and I just thought, "This is stupid. I don't have to do this."'

'So how is it working out?'

'Okay. School is certainly easier. I don't miss smoking that much. I think I'll probably smoke again, but I'm gonna cool off for a while, maybe at least until school's out.'

Eric did stay pretty straight for the rest of the year and in the spring started going out with a girl closer to his own age from another school. Staying straighter didn't solve all of Eric's problems. For example, because of some inadvisable wilfulness on his part, he had a run-in with a teacher in his final year that almost kept him from graduating. But he was growing from his mistakes. He was trying to face his problems instead of hiding from them. If Eric had continued along the path he was on, he wouldn't have looked all that different on his graduation day. Maybe he would have been accepted into his second-choice college instead of his first-choice one. Maybe his prom date would have been a girl he just wanted to hook up with rather than someone he was 'serious' about. The differences wouldn't have been that obvious, but they would have become more obvious over time. The cost of alcohol and drug use builds up slowly and insidiously. It's like mounting credit-card debt. Each month's spending doesn't seem that unreasonable. Then one day you wake up to the fact that it will take you years and years to get the balance down to zero, that much of your salary is going to pay off that high-interest loan, and you've got nothing good to show for it.

As long as our culture protects and promotes the male tradition of emotional isolation, it creates a greater demand in the teenage alcohol and drug markets. Without the basic emotional education they need to make more promising choices, that demand will be perpetual. For all of these boys, getting introduced to that world of emotional escape is fairly simple; for those without the emotional resources to anchor them, finding their way back can be hard.

## 10. Romancing the Stone: From Heartfelt to Heartless Relations with Girls

Maybe I'm amazed at the way I really need you.
> Paul McCartney, 'Maybe I'm Amazed'

Romeo, come forth; come forth, thou fearful man:
Affliction is enamoured of thy parts,
And thou art wedded to calamity.
> William Shakespeare, *Romeo and Juliet*, act 3, scene 3

Every boy is potentially a romantic and thoughtful lover. But first he is a boy, and the story of boy sexuality, and an adolescent boy's sexual awakening, begins well before girls enter the picture. Boys have a sexual nature that is biologically driven, without any doubt, but it does not preclude emotional intimacy and committed love relationships. It does, however, require that a boy make the journey from the simplicity of sex to the complexity of relationship, and that is the challenge for every boy – and for many men who continue to struggle to move beyond the lonely satisfaction of heartless sex to the rewards of an intimate relationship.

Somewhere between heartfelt romances and heartless relationships is the story of how boys make that transition – or often pursue both simultaneously. It offers a complex picture of the inner life of boys, affirming a boy's potential to be caring and loving while acknowledging the fact that many boys are capable of hurting girls in the headlong pursuit of sexual experience. Most boys come to 'romantic' relationships with the desire to love and be loved, as well as to find sexual expression. The fact that relationships don't come easily and naturally for many – even most – boys is the result of the conflict they experience between several powerful forces in their psyches and the failure of their emotional education to prepare them for the work of intimacy and relationship.

Every man remembers the physical and emotional turmoil of his own adolescent sexuality – the twin torments of desire and anxiety – but most women don't hear about it. For most mothers, as a son begins puberty, his sexuality becomes clearly visible in one sense – facial hair, broadening shoulders, a deepening voice – but almost completely obscured in terms of the expectations, hopes, fears, and emotional conflicts that are so powerful for every boy. For most girls a boy's sexuality is clearly communicated in those physical attributes and a heightened interest in the opposite sex, but the emotion he brings to his actions is obscured and is subject to interpretation by girls whose understanding is naturally coloured by their own distinctly female sexual and emotional development. There are boys, of course, probably at least 2 per cent, who aren't attracted to girls and never will be. For them, coming of age in a homophobic environment can be a confusing and painful journey. But many will eventually end up in satisfying romantic relationships with other men. This chapter, however, is about boys who struggle with their feelings about girls.

What we see in teenage boys is a complex saga of sexuality and intimacy, one fraught with the tension of boys' fears, hopes, and longings. Theirs is a tradition of emotion, no less true today than it was four hundred years ago when Shakespeare's Romeo gave voice to adolescent boys' intensely romantic, impulsive longing for a love relationship. Like Romeo's yearning for Juliet – swift on the heels of a romance with a different girl – most boys' first experiences of a romantic relationship are full of emotional drama. In our work with boys, we see their pain, their struggles, their ignorance, how unrealistic their hopes are sometimes; we see the extent to which they lack the trust and love they would need in order to bring balance to their lives.

## What Boys Want

The moment you look into a boy's hopes and fears, you begin to understand the struggle that every boy confronts in his efforts to navigate adolescent sexuality. He is faced with a complex set of internal demands: he wants sex, he wants love, he wants to be manly – and through it all he doesn't want to get rejected or hurt. This is a daunting emotional challenge because each of these internal demands involves difficult obstacles and consequences.

### A Boy Wants to Love and be Loved

Boys yearn for emotional connection, but they are allowed very little practice at it. With their male friends, they have spent most of their time together before high school playing competitive games, teasing one another, or playing at being 'big men' in fantasy or real games. As they get older, many find a kind of artificial tenderness during times of shared intoxication. Boys want to connect with girls, but most have so little grounding in emotional communication that they can't even imagine what intimacy is. They've had few lessons in learning to 'read' others, to pick up on emotional cues through conversation, facial expression, or other subtle body language. It is hard to be empathetic when you can't understand what someone else is feeling, and because boys have not been encouraged to cultivate empathy, they misread social and sexual cues from girls: they can't figure out what a girl might think or want. They can easily become lost in the emotional complexity of an intimate relationship and choose simple sex over emotional intimacy, or just give up, saying, in effect, 'Oh, hell, this is too complicated. Let's go play basketball.'

### A Boy Wants to Satisfy His Sexual Impulses

Boys have strong sexual urges, and their first sexual lessons are private ones. A boy's own sexuality – the physical development and sensations that go with it – is a dominant feature of his life beginning before puberty. Although there are differences among boys in terms of how strong their 'sex drive' is, adolescence tends to be a time when a boy often has sex on his mind. If there is any difference between male and female sexuality, it may be that boys are more easily aroused than girls. This may be due, in part, to the fact that their world is saturated with female sexual images – from underwear catalogues or the *Sports Illustrated* Swimsuit Edition magazine, to *Baywatch* or sexy beer commercials on TV, to the siren song of Internet porn ads boys see while cybersurfing, or simply to the girls they see every day in their classroom who are proudly celebrating their emerging womanhood with short skirts and tight sweaters. It would be difficult for boys to avoid sexual thoughts even if they wanted to. To contend with this arousal, nearly all boys masturbate, and they do it regularly.

Because masturbation is such a natural part of an adolescent boy's experience, he is a veteran of sexual pleasure before he ever becomes involved in partnered sex. When he is drawn by his desire for love coupled with mature sex, a boy has to make a precarious crossing over a bridge from that intensely personal, rewarding, and predictable fantasy exercise to a real-life girl with her own unfamiliar sexual and emotional terrain. From a performance standpoint, it's almost impossible to fail at masturbation. With a girl, what was simple becomes infinitely more complicated, physically and emotionally. With complexity comes the potential for frustration or failure, and if a boy hasn't learned how to manage those feelings any other way, he may react with hostility or anger towards a girl.

## A Boy Wants to be Manly

Through all of this, a boy wants to live up to the image of competent, independent masculinity he is being sold by his peers and culture. But parts of this image are in direct conflict with the traits he will need in order to have fulfilling relationships. Fundamentally, it is this wish to be competent, strong, and independent that makes boys wary of the mutual dependence and trust that are at the heart of any intimate relationship. From a young age, and as boys progress through adolescence, the distinctly male culture of cruelty pounds home the demand that boys toughen up, that they do not appear vulnerable. Dependence on girls – being 'pussy-whipped' – is derided by the group. Boy groups will exert these pressures in order to avoid losing a member – a valued drinking companion or basketball pal. Boys in groups will also deride girls in order to appear tougher or to save face by adopting a sour-grapes 'Who needs them, anyway?' posture.

Perhaps the biggest advantage of manliness is that it allows a boy to avoid a type of searing pain for which he has insufficient balm. The reason a boy fears dependence on a girl is that he fears her rejection and the pain and humiliation that go with it. A boy's desire to be powerful isn't as much about muscle as it is about heart and the fact that if you allow yourself to be dependent on someone – for a smile, for love, for sex, for self-respect – then you can be devastated by her as well.

How a boy resolves these three challenges of his emotional life – intimacy, lust, and power – defines the quality of his intimate emotional relationships. Every boy moves towards manhood with his own unique history of emotional experience and education of the heart. There are many boys who are prepared for loving, intimate relationships because they have experienced emotional attachment through a loving relationship with a parent, and perhaps they have seen a good marriage in action in their own parents' relationship. They see it as a do-able, believable thing – something they can copy for themselves. Unfortunately, they are not the majority. The majority of boys are not prepared to manage the complexities of a loving relationship because they've been shortchanged on the basic skills of emotional literacy: empathy, conscience, the vocabulary for meaningful emotional expression, and the idea that emotional interdependence is an asset – not a liability.

To talk meaningfully about the sexual and romantic aspects of a boy's life requires that we all put aside any sexual politics, gender grudges, or defensiveness. Boys have a story of their own. In our talks with boys, we find that many of them are in awe of girls; curious about sex and baffled by girls; frightened by their own inexperience and often unsure of themselves. Their journey follows a develop-mental path that takes them from sexual awareness to relationship – from solo practice to partnership – and the inner struggle it entails. Along the way, most boys manage to dabble in some version of boy–girl relationship, from group dates to puppy love, to 'going steady', to passionate love affairs. This consummated love happens for many before they are emotionally ready for it: the average boy first has sexual intercourse while he is still a teenager, often before age sixteen. On the journey, however, some boys lose their way and become sexual drifters, half-hearted partners asking little and giving the same. Others turn to sexual exploitation of girls, becoming thoughtless, heartless partners. And still others – a great many, in fact – push on towards adult life with hopes of finding love and security but sadly limited by their own emotional illiteracy.

Whether boys become kind, devoted lovers and sexual partners, or heartless and exploitative, depends on the boy, his early experiences, his social environment, the kind of 'script' that is written for him by his peers, and the girl culture in which he lives. From his earliest gender experiences, and the adolescent stirrings of lust and curiosity, a boy develops his own sense of what relationships and sexuality are all about.

## Jonathon: A Young Man's Awakening

A college student we know to be an intelligent, caring, and thoughtful young man described his sexual career to us: 'The thirteen- and fourteen-year-old girls were "crazy horny", but being small, I wasn't in a position to act upon it. But there were stories about "Lynn" telling "Josh" that she was going to have sex with him, or this one doing it with that one. Everyone talked about everybody's sex life. This kid, John, my friend, was developmentally ready, and he had gotten a hand job or whatever in a movie theatre, and all the girls were talking about sex a lot – *a lot*. This girl, Emily, would talk about wanting it all the time, and she started going with this guy from another school, and they had sex *five times in a day*, she said, and all of this when she was fourteen. *Fourteen*.'

'What was it like in school when you got older?'

'The best-looking fifteen-year-old girls go after the older guys. The fifteen-year-old guys, you know, are still developing, or they've just finished developing and they're still in the awkward stage, and then there are the kids who have been beautiful from day one, and they're getting all the girls, and you hate them with a passion, you know. Or you have braces, and then you're really bummin'.

'I remember being in awe of girls. I was still developing and still feeling awkward about my looks, and things were changing, and it was completely inconceivable to me to have a girlfriend. I went out on a couple of dates, and not much happened. But I had a lot of guy friends who were doing just fine. My best friend, Ned, lived in the city. They were having sex by the time they were sixteen. Not me. I was, you know, out of the woman scene in school. Interested but couldn't get anything.

'Not until I got to college. And then it was a different ball game. There were more women than men, I'd gotten my braces off, and then, all of a sudden, it was like the school attitude about sex was back, only now the guys were into it, too. In my first year I must have hooked up with ten different women.'

'Everyone was sleeping with one another?'

'Well, it depended. If you were a good-looking guy or an athlete or had a funny personality, you could definitely hook up on weekends. There was this really cool dance club, and everyone pretty much ended up there at the end of the night, and you were practically guaranteed to have a really close dance with someone and get into it.'

'What is "hooking up"? Is that intercourse?'

'Hooking up is getting close with someone. Holding hands is not a hook-up. Kissing is at least a hook-up. A hook-up can be sexual intercourse as well. Some people were having sex right away. The girls I was hooking up with I wasn't having sex with right away. It was new to me to be hooking up at all. You know, I was, like, new at this whole thing.'

'What was your aim? What was your goal?'

'To get . . . to get . . .'

'To get laid? To have intercourse?'

'Yeah . . . well, not really. I wanted my first experience of sex to be meaningful because I had heard so many stories from people saying it wasn't. It's not that everyone was saying, "I want to have sex with you," but there were times, you know, I could probably have pushed it, but I wanted my first time having sex to be meaningful.'

'Was it?'

'Yes, it was awesome. It was my second year at college. I went on a camping trip, and I met this girl, Shannon, who was two years older than me. She was the head of the outing club. We hit it off right away. We fooled around that weekend in a tent, and then when we got back to school, we were kind of seeing each other off and on, fooling around. She didn't know I was a virgin, and on my birthday she made me a really nice meal, and afterwards we had some wine and we were fooling around . . . and she said to me, "Do you want me to grab a condom?" And I was about to tell her I was a virgin or about to say, "Are you sure you want to do this?" but then I was thinking this feels totally right, I love this. I really liked this girl. I was really attracted to her; she was awesome. And she was down with it; it's not like I had to persuade her. We had been totally comfortable with each other from day one. We got totally naked that first day we got back to campus, you know, completely. Even though we hadn't had sex, we were still doing a lot of other stuff. We had sex three times, all these different positions. And she said, "I'm glad that I'm with someone who knows what he's doing," and I told her it was my first time. And she didn't believe me. She said, "Yeah, whatever . . . ," and I said, "No, seriously." First she was shocked, and then she was honoured, and then she said, "I'm glad you didn't tell me because I probably wouldn't have had sex with you, knowing that it was your first time." Because girls think about it the same way, you know, the first time being a big deal.

'But then my point of view changed. A month ago I was seeing a girl just on a sex basis. I mean, that was a big part of it. She was going to San Francisco at the end of April. She knew I was graduating. I was respectful. I asked her, "Are you sure you want to be doing this, because I'm going to be going at the end of this term?" She's like, "Yeah." She's cool with it.'

'Are girls more romantic than boys?'

'Guys can get away with not having to be romantic, so a lot of guys don't bother. Because guys are at a premium there, you can get away with not having to court a woman. But it's different, once you're officially going out with a person; then I think people get a little more romantic with each other. But if you're going out with a lot of women, you don't have to be romantic.

'I was romantic with Steffi. I was totally in love with her, like so much that it was unhealthy. I thought, if she didn't love me, I'd never love anyone. She was going out with a friend in our first year. Then we had this weird relationship for the following two years: we'd fool around, but we were like really good friends who would fool around, but we weren't going out with each other. Then it got sort of complicated, so we broke it off. It was probably a good thing, because I was so hung up on her, but now I'm seeing Gail, and I'm finished seeing Ellen, whom I was having sex with. And it wouldn't break me up if all of a sudden Gail and I weren't being together.

'But that first year at college my aim was to hook up with girls. I hadn't done it before, and it was really big on my mind. I went to the clubs. I was thinking "Who can I go home with?" It was exciting, being away from home. You go to parties, and I had crazy confidence. I went to a party with my roommate, Peter, and I was pretty intoxicated, and I just sat down next to this really good-looking girl and struck up a conversation, and an hour later we were down by the pond making out on a bench, and then we went back to my room and fooled around. And then, here's the problem. She wanted to go out with me, but I was pretty clueless. Did I put a note on her door? That was the first official hook-up at school. But I didn't know the rules of the game. She was like waiting for me to ask her out, and she assumed that we would be going out, and she got really mad at me. We fooled around the next weekend, and a lot of her friends thought we were going out, but then I ended up hooking up with one of her friends three weeks later, and she freaked out and was totally crushed and whatever. I guess it was an insult or something. She was very upset. And I just didn't get it. I didn't get it. I didn't know she was looking for a relationship. I hadn't had one, and I just, you know, I don't know. Ever since then I'm just into hooking up.'

In his candid retrospective, Jonathon has described a long-term, somewhat unrequited love relationship, a very happy first experience of sexual intercourse with a girl whom he 'liked' but didn't love, and a series of 'hooking-up' experiences. His story illustrates many elements of male sexuality – his desire to show that he was 'good in bed', that he 'knew what he was doing'; his emotional cluelessness and lack of empathy after his 'first official hook-up' in college; his preference for 'just hooking up' as a withdrawal from the emotional complexity of relationships; the strength of his sexual desire; and his romanticism and capacity for love. These are a set of powerful forces that sexually active boys must contend with when they are even younger than Jonathon. Boys have a complex agenda, responding to these different forces; they want relationships, but they want to be manly as well. And those two wishes may conflict if a boy's image of masculinity precludes emotional sharing. An attractive boy who is masculine in this way can leave many girl casualties in his wake.

A medical friend of ours whose patients include many teenage girls describes them as 'emotionally unprotected' when they deal with boys, in that girls almost universally believe that the boy loves them when he says he does, they believe the boy when he says that he has never had intercourse before, and they believe that the boy will still love them after the medical crisis is over – be it pregnancy, abortion, or a sexually transmitted disease. 'Girls today are presumed to be more sexually sophisticated, more equal to boys that way than they used to be,' she says. 'But girls are still more vulnerable because they still believe in relationships.'

Boys are legendary for their casual disregard of relationships and their blatant interest in sex. As with most legends, there is a kernel of truth in it; and boys and men confirm this picture of themselves.

One man in his forties told us, 'When I think about what I did in school, I am terrified for my daughter.' Another friend, turning forty-five, said, 'I'm beginning to slow down. I don't think about sex all the time now. It is kind of a relief.' Another man, who had struggled with fidelity in his marriage, said to us with obvious relief when he turned fifty, 'I'm not thinking with my penis any more.'

That many boys pursue sex without any interest in love and end up in a cynical, exploitative place is undeniable. But for most boys, cynical or closed is not what they started out to be.

## Boys Start Out as Loving Partners

Every child, boys included, comes into this world wanting to love and be loved by his parents. Forty years of research on emotional attachment shows us that without it children die or suffer severe emotional damage. Research aside, it is also common sense and clinical wisdom that human beings almost universally want to be loved. Boy babies are as cute and beguiling and eager to please as are girl babies, and their desire to love and be loved is every bit as profound as that of girl babies.

Young boys practise being lovers on their mothers. They hug their mothers, kiss them, bring them their excitement and the things they have found. A teacher who works with primary children, self-publishing books they have written, notes that almost every child – including boys – names his mother on the dedication page, along with a simple, but earnest declaration of his love.

Boys are free to express love in a more complete way in early childhood because they do not yet have to be afraid to express a sense of dependence. The early mother–child relationship is a prologue to everything that occurs in adult intimacy, including gazing into each other's eyes, caressing, and sensual, though not sexual, pleasures of all kinds. As infants and toddlers, boys are almost totally dependent, and they do love fully and completely the woman who, as a mother, loves them back and in so doing provides a template for all their later love relationships.

Later boys start to transfer some of their love for their mother on to girls. Some boys recall having crushes on girls in kindergarten; others will tell us that, before they were thirteen, 'I couldn't have told you what a girl was.' But eventually many boys we talk with tell us they want love in their lives. They aren't hunting for trophy girlfriends; they're eager to please and thrilled at the thought that they could impress a girl and be special to her in a romantic way. The boys who are talking about dates for their graduation two months ahead of time are high with romantic hopes – not plots for sexual conquest. They are eager to fall in love.

Many boys also want the security of a committed relationship because dating scares them. One man, in looking back on a love relationship that started in school and continued through his second year of college, described his relationship with one particular woman as 'such a comfort, such a wonderful thing. Dating was so painful. I wanted to know we were committed, that we had a relationship decided. It didn't matter what the terms were about sex.'

But boys are also sexually aroused – a lot. These strong feelings are not completely welcome. It's like standing hungry and penniless outside a restaurant. Nearly all boys learn how to quell these pangs when they are alone. There is some relief in this and some shame. Many young boys yearn for an imagined day 'when they are older' and can be having sex with a real girl instead of magazine centrefolds. The headmaster of a public boys school where we have consulted spoke the 'boy truth' when he remarked, on the topic of boys' silence about their inner lives: 'Boys don't want anyone to get close to their inner lives, because their inner lives are so close to their masturbatory lives.'

The mother and father of a thirteen-year-old boy came to discuss their son's recent refusal to talk about 'personal' things. His mother asked, 'Why has he stopped talking to me? Why do I only get monosyllabic answers from him?'

When we suggested that the boy might be developing a wish for autonomy, a wish for privacy in general, and a private fantasy life connected to his masturbatory life, this intelligent, sophisticated mother said, half jokingly, 'Oh, he's not doing that yet.' Her husband thought aloud, 'Let me see, thirteen . . . Well, I had a pretty rich masturbatory life when I was his age.' The mother was embarrassed to hear her husband talk that way. But it was clear that he felt a link with what might be his son's authentic experience.

Another mother of a thirteen-year-old boy called us for advice when she discovered that her son, who had become increasingly private of late, was tapping into an 'X-rated' Internet sex site – the computer-age equivalent of hiding a copy of *Playboy* under the mattress. We do not condone Internet pornography, but when we began to explain how sexual curiosity and masturbation do fit into the grand, normal scheme of things for a male, she winced and interrupted: 'Can't we just skip all the details and get to the part where you tell me what to do about what's going on?'

We could 'skip all the details', but anyone who wants to understand boys' emergent sexuality and its effect on later love relationships – especially mothers trying to understand their sons – needs to know some details.

There is a joke among men that goes like this: studies show that 95 per cent of boys masturbate and 5 per cent of boys are liars. If a boy hasn't tried his hand at masturbation prior to reaching puberty, the likelihood is that he will discover and practise masturbation during early adolescence. When? Zella Luria at Tufts University says that most parents talk to their boys about masturbation when they are thirteen and that they are about two years too late.

A man in his late thirties recalls life at thirteen: 'I was like everyone else, I guess. Until about sixteen, I was too afraid of girls to ask for what I wanted sexually. It was easier to beat off at night and stare at girls during the day. The first time, believe it or not, it happened almost spontaneously one night while I was reading in bed. I was thirteen, and I actually believed I had invented masturbation.'

A boy's experience with masturbation means that he begins to build up a library of sexual memories in his head long before he has any partnered sexual experience in adolescence. He controls these fantasies. He can have sex every night with the most popular girl in school, the hottest movie star, his best friend's mum, or one of his teachers. All of these women are mad about him and will do whatever he wants. This desire for control of what happens in a sexual encounter is what motivates some men to pay for sex with a prostitute, an almost exclusively male activity.

By adolescence, a boy wakes up most mornings with an erection. This can happen whether he is in a good mood or a bad mood, whether it is a school day or a weekend. A boy's experience of an erection, however, is that it came to him, uninvited, but inviting – tempting him with its ability to provide sexual pleasure. Many boys even think of their genitals as having kind of an active consciousness – a penis with a mind of its own.

So boys enjoy their own physical gadgetry. But the feeling isn't always 'Look what I can do!' The feeling is often 'Look what *it* can do' – again, a reflection of the way a boy views his instrument of sexuality as just that: an object.

What people might not realize when they justly criticize men for *objectifying* sex – viewing sex as something you do rather than part of a relationship – is that the first experience of objectification of sexuality in a boy's life comes from his experience of his own body, having this penis that makes its own demands.

## Sexual Curiosity and Experimentation

Healthy male sexuality is shaped by cultural norms, but it grows from a boy's natural curiosity, biological energy, and raw enthusiasm. Healthy girls and boys come into the world with the same amount of sexual interest and curiosity. Unless a girl is taught to be inhibited, she is as interested and curious as a boy. Most girls are responsive to social cues telling them that certain behaviours are off-limits, but the limits are open to interpretation given today's highly sexualized media and culture and fairly explicit sex education lessons in schools. As a result, most adolescent girls are sexually aware, and many are sexually active, even aggressive, presenting today's boys with visions and opportunities the likes of which their forefathers could only fantasize about. Boys, traditionally less fettered by social restrictions on sexual activity, enjoy even looser limits today, and when the opportunity arises, they jump into sexual or quasi-sexual encounters.

Heightened physical camaraderie of adolescent boys and girls becomes noticeable around the time of puberty and is reflected in the ambience of middle school and secondary school.

On a visit to the campus of Saint George's School in Tacoma, Washington, several years ago, a memorable scene unfolded one warm, autumn day. A river runs right through the school campus, and on this sunny afternoon kids had taken inflatable rings up-river and were rafting down through the school campus. In each large ring were two or three high school kids draped all over one another: two boys and a girl, two girls and a boy, sometimes three girls or two boys – the boys took care to avoid crushing together with only boys. The physical ease, the pleasure in having to be pig-piled on top of one another, the casual sexuality made 'safe' by the platonic restraint required by the river clearly delighted them. For all of them this was a forerunner to more intimate sexual contact. Probably some of these kids were already sexually experienced. But for those who were not yet there, this shared group physical contact was practice for them. In any school, when kids are allowed to sit however they want, they often lean or drape themselves over one another.

On the emotional playing field, however, the gap between the emotional education of girls and that of boys begins to show itself in new ways. Through the eyes of a barely pubescent middle school boy, girls seem generally more mature, more powerful, and more confident than boys. Much of this impression is projected by their blooming sexuality.

Girls enter puberty about a year or two before boys, at around age ten to eleven. They get secondary sexual characteristics and their growth earlier than boys. Boys start developing signs of puberty at between twelve and thirteen. All you have to do is look at a class of twelve- to thirteen-year-olds – tall girls with developing breasts beside littler boys with high voices – to see the developmental gap. Often when we talk to fourteen-year-old girls in our work at schools in the US and ask them whether they are looking forward to high school, they say, 'Oh, yeah, we can't wait to get out of here and meet some real boys.'

A thirteen-year-old boy expressed dismay at the way 'girls changed' from the easy friends they were in previous years to the 'snobby, mean' creatures they had become that year. 'They used to respect other people and didn't talk like they were the best things in the entire world. Now, it's like, they think they know everything, and they act really strange. First of all, they all act exactly the same. It's like they looked at a training booklet on how to dress, how to walk, how to comb their hair. And they all do it just that way. *That's* really weird. And then they talk about who's going with who and who's mad at who, and sicker stuff – like who *kissed* who – and they do it *everywhere*. They do it right in the middle of the corridor between classes! First there's two, then five more come, and pretty soon there's this big clump of them, and they're talking in these loud voices about all this stuff. They're really screwed up.'

Boys vary in how early they become interested in girls, but by the age of thirteen or fourteen, most boys are, and any boy who doesn't at least profess interest is in danger of being labelled a 'loser' or a 'fag'. And when they're ready, if they are attractive at least, they find no shortage of interested girls, who, because of changing mores, are allowed to be more sexually assertive, something boys find both challenging and relieving.

Jonathon, the college student, recalled the mutual sexual curiosity and playfulness of his crowd of boys and girls at that age and described a typical bit of messing about, 'just stupid games we'd play when we had a couple of girls over to my friend's house'. In this mutually sexually charged wrestling play, he said, 'the girls would grab us, you know, *down there*. And guys would grab the girls' breasts, too, and it was cool, you know, it was not assault, you know. It was okay with them.'

Here, then, is the aggressive, physical play of boys and girls that serves as a preface to more direct sexual activity. But even in these early and fun-filled moments, there is a power struggle playing out, a wish by boys to dominate in order to appear in control but, more important, to avoid the risk of rejection and humiliation by girls.

## The Culture of Cruelty: Providing the Male Sexual Script

As it is for every adolescent, what boys do sexually is, to some extent, scripted for them by the peer group and by society's stereotypes about the nature of male and female sexuality. Depending on his neighbourhood, school, and ethnic or religious context, every boy has a sexual script that he is taught and that may be with him for life, whether it matches the reality of his circumstances or not. In early adolescence, before boys have really begun to have sexual experiences with partners, they begin to firm up their fantasy visions of their sexuality. Often the fantasies are connected to power – the idea that a man should be able to dominate a woman.

Much of this fantasy of domination arises from anxiety or fear of rejection, as does so much male aggression. Moreover, to boys, it's an important image to maintain, an aura of sexual pride that proves their masculinity to other boys. This is reflected in the cocky conversations we hear among boys today, reminiscent of the ones we heard among boys of our own adolescence a few decades ago, and similar to those we've seen captured in some truthful coming-of-age films about adolescent boys.

The film *This Boy's Life*, Tobias Wolff's memoir of his adolescence, shows this behaviour of boys. When two boys meet on the street, one asks the other (the fourteen-year-old Leonardo DiCaprio) about the date he had last night:

'Did you go to Wanda's last night?' the friend asks.

'Uh-huh,' DiCaprio replies.

'Did you make out?'

'Uh-huh.'

'Make out good?'

'Uh-huh.'

'How good?'

'I fucked her 'til her nose bled,' DiCaprio says.

To which the friend replies mockingly, 'Sure you did.'

They then go to the house of one of the boys and watch a *Superman* show on television. As the show comes on, DiCaprio groans theatrically, 'Oh, Lois, oh, baby, come here, I got six hot inches just waiting for you.' His friend, mockingly, says, 'You wish.' 'Lois, I want you so bad . . . I'll do better than Superman.'

The narrator's voice reflects: 'We had to talk dirty for a while. It was a formality, like crossing yourself with holy water when you went to church. After that we shut up and watched the show. We softened, we surrendered. We watched Superman have dumb adventures with dorky plots, and we didn't laugh at them.'

In the adolescent male culture of cruelty, boys feel that they have to talk about power; they have to talk about disrespecting women – they have to in order to display their strength. None of this has much to do with actually understanding or knowing girls and women. Much of it is in response to the impressive physical presence, social power, and perceived sexual aggression of adolescent girls. Adolescent boys spend a lot of time talking about impressing, dazzling, making out with, having sex with, and otherwise overpowering girls and women. Most of this boasting, as every man will later admit, is purely insecure bluster. This storytelling occurs years ahead of most boys' first experience with sexual intercourse, and most boys have no intention of actually treating girls this way.

Why do boys do this? Why is this their take on sexuality? The answers can be found in the early lessons boys get in viewing girls as foreign, in boys' tremendous performance anxiety in life, and in the culture of cruelty, where boys are punished for showing vulnerability and pressured to demean feminine qualities as a way of boosting their masculine image.

Performance anxiety dogs boys always, but perhaps most of all in their sexual endeavours. Every man knows this anxiety; a woman has to imagine it through a boy's perspective: novice though he may be, he feels that, to satisfy his partner, he has to 'do it right'. It starts out with whether or not he will be a 'good kisser'. When he gets older, the stakes get higher. He has to get it up and keep it up. He cannot come too early – which, at seventeen, is a real possibility – and he cannot come too late. In his mind, he has to be the great lover, she the passive recipient. Why? Because it has been like that in a boy's mind throughout his masturbatory career, because his fantasies of sex merge with his fantasies of power in his private sexual moments. And he thinks he has to take that act on the road and make good on it. But he can't, because he is frightened and inexperienced – and then he finds out that his partner thinks the whole deal should be collaborative. What a relief. But does that mean he's less of a man? Maybe. And what if he is good with one girl but fails to get an erection with another girl? Maybe the *girls* have the power over *him*. Maybe he's not such a big deal after all. This is what a boy is thinking. It is exhausting.

The culture of cruelty adds punishment to pain: a boy can't admit to other boys that he's anxious, hurt, or sad if that has been his lot. Angry or hostile is okay, though, evidenced by the Monday-morning bragging about sexual conquests, demeaning descriptions of girls, and 'Fuck 'em. Who needs 'em?' posturing. Performance is critical to boys; yet ironically, the endeavour in which some sort of failure is almost inevitable – sex and intimacy – is the one endeavour in which a boy can't admit failure.

Not only do boys carry around a large case of performance anxiety, but when they experience failure, in sexual or romantic terms, they have to lie about it – or at the very least keep silent about it to avoid humiliation of the worst kind.

Intimacy in a relationship with a girl demands sensitivity, respect, and tenderness. At about the time that boys are beginning to develop sexually and beginning to develop an interest in girls, they are subjected to the culture of cruelty, which is all about power, dominance, and denial of sensitivity. Here a boy is taught in a systematic way to view tender feelings as 'feminine' and to eschew them for the same reason. By portraying vulnerable qualities as alien – undesirably feminine – the boy culture promotes the view of girls and women as 'other' and defines the eventual aim of a sex relationship as domination. That is the culture of cruelty's 'power teaching'. A boy under its influence denigrates girls and women in order to control his anxiety about them. If he has to talk with them and be tender and kiss right, each of those requirements becomes a risk, and his experience with risk is that if he doesn't measure up, he'll be slammed for his failure. In the context of a boy–girl relationship, rejection is emasculating; thus, girls become the enemy because they have the power to inflict the most humiliating emotional hurt.

The culture of cruelty teaches boys that, in the male realm, feminine qualities are loathsome; to the degree that a boy buys into that belief, and loathes the qualities of tenderness and vulnerability in himself, he grows to hate parts of himself and girls as well. For that boy, and his like-minded audience of boys, girls represent the lowest caste in the social order, fair game for use or abuse. Behind that macho posturing is high anxiety about girls and women. Sometimes this hypermasculinity meets with approval: many boys can outrage and impress girls by being 'bad'. Alongside his desire, every boy harbours a fear of girls because they hold such power to reject him. Anxiety limits a boy's ability to pick up on external cues, and his anxiety about girls and about his performance with them distorts his perception of them and obscures the cues that might guide him towards a more meaningful experience in relationship. If boys are not taught empathy, then their response to rejection or frustration easily becomes devaluation of girls and women.

### *Michael with Jerry: Young Love and Betrayal*

Jerry, a man in his late forties, remembers how, when he was ten, he listened to records by Carole King and Carly Simon, but only when he was alone in his room. 'I hid the records when my friends came over because it wasn't cool,' he says. He was a boy of tender sensibilities, a romantic, but the requirement of looking cool conflicted with his interest in girls and in love even at this early age.

'I've always loved love – I love that female energy,' he says, recalling his crushes on girls from as early as six years old. He remembers his first kiss, with a nine-year-old girl, at a building construction site next to his parents' house. At thirteen, he had his first sexual experience, with a twelve-year-old girl whom he adored. The parent of a girl this age might look at this thirteen-year-old boy as predatory, but more objectively, he was a boy in love who found a girl with mutual affection and budding passion.

'I was so taken with her. I did love her,' Jerry says. 'Her parents went out a lot, and they both worked. The first time we went over to her house alone, we went up to the attic and had sex. It was great. We had sex for three years. We were very creative. Location is tough when you are that age. We talked almost every day. We were inseparable. She was a singer, and we wrote music together.'

Jerry was faithful to his girlfriend and presumed she felt the same loyalty. He was wrong.

'One day she was acting strange, and I asked her about it, and she told me that she'd slept with a friend of her brother's,' he says. 'I was so hurt. So hurt. I got drunk and challenged this big kid who'd slept with her. He mopped up the alley with me.'

Jerry was heartbroken and humiliated, and he gave up the girl rather than try to save the relationship. He didn't see her any more, and he had always thought of it as a clean break. But it wasn't really, for him, because the loss of trust, and the association of intimacy and betrayal, coloured his view of every woman thereafter who entered his life with love in mind. Jerry abandoned his previous interest in the full range of emotional intimacy: he simply sought refuge in sex and the warm, casual company of women, which he still desired. Sex was good. Music and drugs made it even better. Love? He didn't want to think about it. 'I dated a lot of girls and slept with a lot,' he says. 'I insulated myself a lot. I didn't let my guard down after that. I remember thinking "*I'm not going to let that happen again.*" I wasn't going to get attached. From sixteen to eighteen, I was involved with a lot of girls. I was definitely romantic, but I had a cold place in me. There was one girl I started to get attached to, but I pulled away from her because she was too clingy; her neediness scared me.'

What is poignant about Jerry's story is the very limited and stereotypical way he dealt with betrayal – how he had to go and physically challenge the fellow who had slept with his girlfriend and how he avoided emotional intimacy for years after that, despite his sexual relationship with numerous girls and women. He connected with women socially and sexually, but he was unable to cope with the hurt and complexity inherent in love relationships and withdrew into himself.

Some boys who can't cope with emotional hurt or the painful challenges of relationship have a different reaction: instead of turning inward, they go on the attack.

## Exploitation: Boys Who Use Girls

A friend who played football during his last year in school told us of a day another football player on the team boasted, 'I fucked a girl last night and didn't even have to kiss her.' In the moment he heard that, this friend thought, 'I'm not like that. I'm a different kind of man to that guy.' There is a difference between men who struggle with relationships, men who want intimacy and don't always achieve it, and those who exploit and prey upon women to satisfy their appetites for simple sex, to guarantee that they will be fully in control, that the power over what happens in a relationship will be in their hands. Sometimes there is an element of revenge for past hurts. And sometimes these men are imitating what they have seen other men do to women.

At one extreme are men who themselves have been sexually abused. Sexual abuse of boys is more rare than sexual abuse of girls, and although in both cases the perpetrators are more likely to be men, with boys the abuse more often carries with it the burden of silent shame. For reasons of stoicism and the shame of having had a homosexual encounter, boys are reluctant to report abuse. While it is a minority of boys who are abused this way, their sexual and intimate lives are affected by abuse, and the consequences can be lifelong. As with girls, boys who have had these experiences are predisposed towards serious mental illness, including post-traumatic stress disorder, depression, and character disorders. A sense of victimhood, the feeling that one's body is not one's own, and a profound mistrust of intimacy are all the result of abusive experiences. Because boys and men are more likely to express emotional pain in destructive ways, it is not surprising that most sex offenders were themselves victims of sex abuse at an earlier age. Not all victims grow up to inflict this trauma on others, but many continue to punish themselves by retreating from normal sex and intimacy.

Some men, as boys, were not sufficiently athletic, developed, strong, or conventionally attractive to be a big draw for girls, especially in middle school or early secondary school. The boys who were not so conventionally attractive may have had to wait until they could become attractive to girls, and they may have had to develop other ways of communicating with or becoming attractive to girls. Boys who are athletes, who fit the conventional model of good-looking and powerful, are in an easy position to exploit their popularity. While this is natural, inevitable, and for the most part harmless, it can take a boy athlete down a road that leads to a destructive attitude towards women.

The most terrible situations occur when empathy is systematically trained out of boys, when they are taught to see themselves as dominating, when they find themselves repeatedly in situations in which they do not have to empathize with girls, or when they are systematically taught to exploit girls. This is the 'entitled prince' scenario played out in the sexual realm, and it is an ugly drama. Though many boys might be tempted by this idea – remember the masturbatory fantasies of domination that are so common for boys – it is the athletes, especially prominent and successful athletes at the secondary school or college level, who are most often trained to think of themselves as entitled to the sexual attention of girls and women.

Taken to its worst extreme, the culture's worship of boy athletes can result in the situation described in Bernard Lefkowitz's *Our Guys: The Glen Ridge Rape and the Secret Life of the Perfect Suburb*.[1] The book explores an actual case in which five American high school football players were charged with the gang rape of a mentally retarded girl whom they had known all of their lives. The girl was lured into a cellar, coerced into performing oral sex, and then penetrated with several objects, including a baseball bat. In the wake of disclosure that the boys had been involved in such an incident, many of the leading adults in the community – as well as many parents, educators, ministers, girlfriends, and others – aggressively defended the perpetrators as 'good boys', whose lives would be marred by this 'tragedy'. Lefkowitz observed that very few people jumped to the defence of the girl, nor did many people question the moral character of the boys who had carried out the rape. Most adults excused them on psychological grounds: the boys were 'hyper'; the girl was flirtatious. The message: boys are not responsible for what happens when a girl goes down into a cellar with them, not even when the girl is retarded.

These boys were, in their small town, 'the Jocks', the reigning kings of the town social set. They weren't great athletes, but they were the most celebrated ones in town; they weren't great students either, but their athletic credentials bought them safe passage through their teachers' report books. Mediocre in so many ways, they nonetheless excelled at creating a caste system in which they used certain 'types' of girls to further their agendas of sexual conquest and social status. They had sexual access to a class of insecure girls – many of them thirteen- and fourteen-year-olds – who were desperate for their attention in order to advance their own social hopes. These girls were taken upstairs at parties to provide oral sex and other sexual services. Downstairs were the popular girls, called the 'Little Mothers', socially adept cheerleaders who doted on these boys but weren't expected to satisfy their sexual demands. Lefkowitz writes:

If you were a Jock, these girls [the Little Mothers] were perfect. Unlike real mothers and sisters, they weren't censorious or judgemental. Because they were cast in the maternal role, they were not usually regarded as potential sex partners. For a teenage guy who might be insecure about his sexual performance, the last thing he wanted was to have to perform with a girl who could tell everybody he knew about his shortcomings in the sack. [pp 145–147]

But even the Little Mothers were disregarded at the deepest levels. One of them said about the Jocks' casual disregard of them, 'That was something you had to accept when you were with these guys . . . It was like [they] didn't know how to treat someone.' [pp 145–147] But because they were Jocks, they didn't have to learn how to treat someone in a respectful or intimate way. And the fact that no one required them to act responsibly, morally, or with character gave them the licence to think that they could do what they wanted, with whom they wanted.

The aura of entitlement around athletes is a uniquely powerful setting for sexual exploitation, but no class of boys has a corner on exploitative behaviour. Almost any day in the newspapers you can find evidence of this worst-case mentality at work. As Lefkowitz notes: 'For a lot of boys, acting abusively towards women is regarded as a rite of passage. It's woven into our culture.' [pp 145–147]

Less extreme, but similar, conditions exist for every boy and contribute to incidents of coercive sex, or what is sometimes called 'date rape'. Date rape is a frequent and much-discussed problem on campus because young people, trying to work out their intimacy and their sexual drives, can often find themselves in situations where a girl can be exploited. Most often, those situations arise when one or the other or both people have drunk so much that their judgement is impaired, and the self-doubt and second-guessing can come the morning after, when a young woman wakes up and feels that she has been taken advantage of.

The young man may have been following his own script of power and conquest, oblivious in the moment or in general to the visual and emotional cues that a young woman may give. If his peer or community culture holds him to no higher standard of conduct, then even a boy of conscience can get into situations in which he feels a cultural licence to engage in sexually aggressive behaviour. Perhaps the girl has been drinking. Perhaps their conversation has been flirtatious and seems to invite sex. Perhaps he's drunk or under the influence of drugs. Perhaps he is sexually aroused and wants swift gratification more than he wants to stop himself. Perhaps his pals are waiting to hear the score. Under these circumstances the recipe for exploitation is available to everybody, and a boy who gets a steady diet of it knows he has no limits.

When people say that a boy 'should know' when a girl doesn't want sex, they ask too much – and not enough – of boys. If a boy's emotional education has left him blind to emotional cues and awareness, then a different, more direct kind of tutoring is necessary to communicate the basics: when you get aroused, you don't just rape girls. If you know drinking makes you lose control, then don't drink or don't drink so much. If a girl's judgement is influenced by drink, drugs, or emotional vulnerability, don't exploit the opportunity. Boys and girls in middle school and secondary school, as well as young men and women in college, need to discuss these situations with each other *before* they occur in order to develop empathy for each other's experience.

It is the responsibility of people who raise boys to train them specifically to be good, empathic partners to girls and women. It can be done, by fathers who model respect for women in the family and in the wider world, by mothers who help sons understand a girl's point of view, and by anyone in a boy's life who helps him see his connectedness to others as a positive thing. What will not work is to ignore this need for guidance, leaving boys to their own devices, winking at their dominating and reckless behaviour, and forcing girls and women to pay the price for this cultural and parental negligence. It serves a boy poorly, too, setting him up to play a dead-end role in relationships and condemning him for taking bad turns, when that is where all the signs in his life were pointing.

### Guilt and Growth: Movement towards Maturity

Like many men, Geoff, a political consultant in his early forties, recalls his exploitation of girls as 'a phase I went through'. He was a boy who liked being around girls and knew how to relate to them, and they were attracted to him as a result.

'I knew how to talk to girls, and I knew how to listen,' Geoff says. 'I figured, if that's what they want, then give it to them. What could be easier? What I wanted mostly was sex, but I never met a girl or a woman who wouldn't reward a good listener. The hard part was talking after sex. Even listening after sex was excruciating. They thought I was being intentionally mean by not talking to them afterwards, but the truth is, I just wanted them to shut up. What was left to say? Especially when my failures were too humiliating – times when I was either impotent or came too soon. I was embarrassed and angry. I knew I had blown it. Here I was in my last years of school perfecting my image of a cool, in-control kind of guy, and then something like this would happen, and there was no way I could pretend I was in control. So naturally, I took it out on the girl. I'd withdraw and refuse to talk. And when I did talk, I said mean things, things I'm embarrassed to remember. Even to girls I cared about. Whenever feelings got complicated for any reason, I felt cornered, and I lashed out – nothing physically violent, but saying something hurtful or cruel. Anything to fight my way out of that uncomfortable spot. I never wanted to hurt anyone. When I look back now at how I've treated some of the girls I dated in my teens, I'm really ashamed. I wish I could go back and apologize to them. I was such a moral midget!'

Even so, Geoff eventually ceased to be such an overt manipulator. In part, the change was due to his simply growing up. All therapists clearly see that human beings are motivated to become better than they are. Without this motivation, psychotherapy would be almost impossible. If an adolescent boy is not too damaged psychologically, he will continue to become more mature as he moves into his twenties and thirties. It is a well-known fact in the field of criminology that most criminals (the vast majority of whom are male) stop committing crimes against society as they move into their thirties. No one is completely sure why this happens, but the same occurs for 'relationship crimes'. As boys grow, most tend to be less exploitative and heartless in their relationships with girls.

Another man, now a caring husband and father, describes a similarly exploitative adolescence with delayed regret, explaining, 'Satisfying myself was all I knew about, and sex was the most satisfying thing around. It was uncomplicated if you didn't get emotionally involved. It was simple at a time when a lot of other things at school and at home weren't simple. The sex, the beer, the music: it was everything I wanted!'

So why did he give it up?

'I don't know,' he says. 'My focus started to shift.'

Just as boys whose parents raise them to be emotionally whole men grow sooner towards that light, we believe that there is, within every person, every boy, something that pushes for growth, that wants to be better. Along the way, some men come down on the side of power, others on the side of intimacy, and many struggle in between. Some learn the lessons of relationship; others never do. Some of the lessons are clear and simple; others are more complex. But it is imperative that boys be taught, so that they may share the essence of human experience, the joy that comes from a loving relationship, without hurting others along the way.

# 11. Anger and Violence

The greatest remedy for anger is delay.

Seneca

We see a lot of angry boys. Some of them we see in therapy, sent by teachers or parents concerned about their aggressive behaviour or about underlying themes of anger or violence in their school writings. We also hear about a lot of angry boys from their victims. We see other angry boys just out and about: the young bully who torments other children at the park, the punk who shouts abusive taunts at passers-by in the shopping centre, and the silent, brooding boy who looks like a powder keg ready to blow.

The most powerful expression of anger is violence, and like everyone else, we see the worst of that in the news. There are few images more heartbreaking than those of the recent past involving boys who shot, strangled, stabbed, or in some other way inflicted violence on others, including children, teachers, and their own parents. Whether the stories come from rural Jonesboro, Arkansas, where two boys, eleven and thirteen years old, armed with guns, ambushed classmates in their playground, or from Chicago's inner city, where two boys, ten and eleven years old, dropped a five-year-old boy out of a fourteenth-floor flat window to his death on the asphalt below, each act of violence adds to the disturbing picture developing of boys as a class of violent offenders.

Everyone has a theory about what makes children violent. Some blame the frightening rise in violence by children on the glorification of violence in the popular culture, easy access to guns, growing up in an economically disadvantaged violent neighbourhood, and more hours of inadequate supervision brought about by the disappearance of the two-parent family. Certainly, those are significant factors. Criminologists and other social scientists have learned a lot about factors that place people 'at risk' for becoming violent criminals. However, all this knowledge still does little to help us anticipate if and when a *specific* person will hurt someone else or destroy property. And these truths stop short of addressing the clear pattern of young *male* violence.

In previous chapters we have highlighted a number of boy–girl differences that define the emotional miseducation of boys and the damage it does. Compared to girls, boys tend to experience and create more problems in primary school; boys draw harsh discipline like a magnet and thereby learn lessons of shame and domestic violence; as teenagers, they drink sooner and harder, and drive drunk more frequently; their suicide rate is higher. But nowhere is this difference between boys and girls more extreme than when it comes to physical violence – against people or against property. Nowhere is it clearer that the emotional education our culture gives boys is failing them – and all of us.

Dramatic statistics confirm that boys, as a group, are more aggress-ive and violent.[1] Of all killings committed by juveniles, about 95 per cent are committed by boys. In the recent past, there have been dramatic increases in the rates of the types of violent juvenile crimes that, in the United States, are committed almost exclusively by boys – homicide, aggravated assault, and forcible rape. The problem is not restricted to the United States. In Europe juvenile rates for these crimes are on the increase.[2] Canada has its own set of horror stories, the most chilling one to date being that of three thirteen- to fifteen-year-old boys beating a minister and his wife to death with a baseball bat. For every one of the tragic stories we read about in the paper, there are many others, less sensational, but most share the common denominator of angry boys hurting those around them or destroying property.

Sometimes in the archaeology of the life of a violent boy, we uncover extreme conditions, such as years of unspeakable abuse. Other such boys – whether killers, fighters, or vandals – will have experienced a breach of trust by someone close; a loss they could not mourn, be it from death, divorce, or leaving; shame from harsh or critical parents or teachers; humiliation at the hands of cruel peers or in the ebb and flow of social interactions, sports, or academic performance. In short, they suffer the trials and tribulations of life imposed on many of us at one time or another. The difference between them and us is that they lack sufficient psychological resources to control their emotional reactions.

Despite the clear pattern suggesting a serious problem, our society tends to overlook boy violence until dramatic episodes such as the playground shootings capture public attention. Even then, there is a kind of cultural denial, an aroused yet ineffectual talk-show mentality that does little to address the problem and only reinforces the sense of societal helplessness in the presence of violent boys. A worried mother in Colorado, in a letter to the editor of *USA Today*, wrote that she was concerned about the escalating violence and its impact on her own son:

If we are ever to have an effective dialogue about violence, the crux of the problem must be identified and targeted and that, friends, is that we have a nation of boys who do not control their anger. Before anyone cries 'male-bashing', I have an 11-year-old boy and I am concerned about him and the level of escalating violence from the schoolyards of Arkansas and Kentucky to the basketball courts of the so-called professionals . . . We must teach boys that to control one's anger is not to be a sissy but to be a civilized human being.[3]

What's to be done? Some respond that we need to get tougher about how we raise our boys – spank them more often – in much the same way that death penalty advocates respond to rising crime rates. But as we know from research and our therapy experience with boys, the 'big-stick' approach to discipline doesn't work; it only makes boys more prone to meanness.

Our work takes us into the inner life of boys, where they absorb the hand that life has dealt: how their parents treat them, the neighbourhood they live in, how well they learn at school, the way their friends act and then react to it. This is where you find the difference between a boy who acts violently and one who does not.

Thus, we return to the story with which we began this book – the biblical tale of Cain. Here we find many of the same themes that characterize the emotional lives of boys today who use violence as a response to conditions in modern life. In the story from Genesis, Cain's anger is triggered by his perception that God, the heavenly father whom he so strove to please, holds him in disregard, while Abel is clearly favoured. Cain, naturally, is disappointed, and his reaction to disappointment is anger.

The next lines in this brief story are subject to a wide range of interpretations, but at the heart of it, God admonishes Cain for dwelling in self-pity and anger:

> Why are you distressed,
> And why is your face fallen?
> Surely, if you do right,
> There is uplift.
> But if you do not do right,
> Sin crouches at the door;
> Its urge is toward you,
> Yet you can be its master.
>
> (Genesis 4:6)

We won't try to second-guess the biblical intent of God's words, but we find there an expressed challenge to Cain to think through his angry impulse, and although the desire to act on it might feel urgent, 'Yet you can be its master'. Count to ten. Think about it. Choose to 'do right'.

But Cain isn't listening, or more precisely, he isn't hearing the non-violent option. He slays Abel, and God's response is to decree that Cain live in the shadow of his act for the rest of his life, working the soil without gain and being banished to the land of Nod to become a 'ceaseless wanderer on earth'.

Cain is stricken with remorse – 'My punishment is greater than I can bear,' he cries – but it's too late. The deed is done, the damage unalterable.

This is the story of so many boys today whose shame becomes anger, and whose anger moves so swiftly to violence. These boys, too, need fuller emotional resources to deal with the distress they experience from a teacher's criticism, a parent's harsh comment, a classmate's taunt, or a girl's rejection.

Our challenge as parents and teachers is to teach the lessons of emotional literacy that enable a boy to bend under emotional trials without breaking into violent revenge:

· Life isn't always fair. Learn to deal with it.
· You can't just go around hurting people every time you get angry.
· You need to consider how your actions affect others.
· Don't see threats where they don't exist.
· You need to know that controlling your anger does not make you a sissy.

Instead, it is the legacy of Cain that we see in aggressive boys we have known, and it is one borne out in research on delinquency and violence. A boy who has been disappointed or feels disrespected, who has been shamed or frustrated, grows angry and lashes out. Like Cain, he doesn't pause to consider the consequences to either himself or his victim. Many of these boys are sorry afterwards, but by then the damage has been done, and the contrition is of little use to anyone. Their violent actions have inflicted irreparable harm on their victims and wounded the hearts of all who care. And the boys themselves are diminished by those violent actions. Like an axe that is dulled as it chops a tree, the boys are hurt by the social and psychological consequences of what they have done.

The mechanism of cause and effect can be seen when we look at the world of sports and the lessons it teaches about the value of self-restraint. For instance, Alonzo Mourning, a multimillionaire basketball star for the Miami Heat, was interviewed about an on-court altercation in which he was the main attraction. At the very end of the game, an angry Mourning had punched Larry Johnson, an opponent who Mourning thought was playing too rough. Johnson returned the punch; both men were suspended for two games. Unfortunately for Mourning, his suspension coincided with the final of an important play-off series. As it turned out, his team, which — had he been in the line-up — would have been heavily favoured to win, was roundly trounced, and the season was finished. One instant of bad judgement helped erase a whole season of hard work by an entire team, disappointing a legion of fans. Mourning said later that he shouldn't have thrown the punch. That he had let down his teammates. That he was stupid. The man he hit, Larry Johnson, who was suspended because he retaliated, said, 'I should have known better. I should have been a punk and walked away.'

Most boys don't want to risk being seen as a wimp – a 'punk'. And many boys don't know when to walk away. Too often there is too little buffer between an angry feeling and a violent response. The line between throwing a punch and walking away is sometimes very thin. Violence could have been prevented had there been a little more empathy, a bit more self-control, a better reading of the situation, a little less anger, a decision to use words instead of actions – or had a man possessed the maturity to walk away from a fight without thinking of himself as a 'punk'. These are the things that we, as parents and educators, must teach our boys.

In order to teach those lessons, it helps to understand three things about the way a boy interprets incoming signals – real and imagined – and why he responds to his life and our lessons the way he does:

1. *In boys the motivation for aggression is more 'defensive' rather than offensive or predatory.* The aggression that boys display is usually in response to a perceived threat or a reaction to frustration or disappointment. Violent boys are not testosterone-laden beasts, as some would suggest; they are vulnerable, psychologically cornered individuals who use aggression to protect themselves.

2. *Boys are primed to see the world as a threatening place and to respond to that threat with aggression.* Because they are caught in the trap of trying to satisfy the impossible requirements of the traditional masculine self-image, boys are sensitive to any perceived disrespect. Furthermore, their experience in the culture of cruelty leaves them expecting hostility in their interactions with others. Last, boys, because of their emotional illiteracy, are bad at reading emotional cues in social situations. As a result, they are more likely to interpret neutral situations as threatening.

3. *Boys often don't know or won't admit what it is that makes them angry.* This is the flip side of their difficulty in reading emotional cues in others. Because of their emotional miseducation, boys are often unaware of the source or intensity of their bottled-up anger. As

a result, they are prone to engage in explosive outbursts or direct their violence towards a 'neutral' target – usually a person who is not the real source of the anger.

## Violence as Armour

There is a long history of behavioural research with animals that has classified physical aggression by variety and examined the different brain structures involved in each type. The research shows, for instance, how different neural pathways are involved in different kinds of aggression.[4] An example: the brain processes aggression that is directed at killing an animal for food along different pathways than it does violence that is part of a display of male dominance. Only some of this is relevant to human aggression. The most significant point is the distinction between the more predatory or offensive type of fighting and aggression that is reactive or defensive. From our experience with 'normal' boys, we feel that much of their physical aggression is reactive. That is to say, a boy will perceive a threat, either real or imagined, and react like a cornered animal. It is aggression triggered by the need for protection or as a reaction to pain.

Boys feel extremely vulnerable in their efforts to live up to the 'Big Impossible', and there is much emotional inner territory that they need to protect. There is, for example, the impossible self-image of manliness to uphold. But perhaps most problematic is their low threshold for emotional pain. Boys who do not have well-developed psychological resources for managing their feelings tend to be very vulnerable to emotional pain. They are not adept at recognizing or coping with anxiety and sadness – feelings that often accompany close human relationships – so they must be vigilant in protecting themselves. When they do feel the emotional pain, it is often intensely acute – like a hammer slamming a thumb – and accompanied by a howl of anger and a lashing out at the most convenient target.

Many circumstances can trigger anger, but one that is common-place in the male adolescent culture of cruelty is the feeling of inferiority or being devoid of social status. There is little scientific evidence to support the admittedly popular idea that boys with high testosterone levels are aggressive and yet have higher social status. Our clinical experience also refutes the notion of such a biological imperative. It is not the virile class leader who is usually the bully or the one getting into fights after school. It is the boy who is further down the social ladder, one who feels rejected or ashamed, who expresses his hurt through aggressive action.

Clinical evidence tells us that boys who have the genetic defect Kleinfelter's syndrome tend to be aggressive. Kleinfelter's is a clinical condition caused by an extra female chromosome (XXY), and affected boys have small genitalia and a testosterone deficiency. Clinicians who work with these boys report that they tend to be self-conscious because, especially for those on the cusp of puberty who must shower together after gym class, penis size is a visible measure of manhood. These boys tend to get into trouble fighting, perhaps to protect themselves against the pain of this shame and perhaps in part to validate their manliness.

Research directed by Richard Tremblay at the University of Montreal with normal thirteen-year-old boys also verifies the observation that it is the rejected, unpopular boy who is most aggressive. Tremblay studied a large group of boys from the time they were in kindergarten. Those who had been consistently rated by teachers and peers as physically aggressive also tended to be boys who were having academic problems and were generally unpopular. This is not news; other studies have confirmed this finding. But what is most notable about Tremblay's work is that he found that these boys had *lower* levels of testosterone than the more popular, tough, but not physically aggressive, school leaders.[5]

### Dan with Leif: Passing Around the Pain

Leif was a boy who seemed to have a lot going for him – a caring mother, comfortable economic circumstances, a good school to attend. And he was talented, very bright, athletic, and possessed of a very nice boy's version of his mother's good looks, blond, with a classic Nordic face. Until he was around eight years old, Leif did nothing to suggest that he was other than happy, and his fighting was limited to garden-variety messing about with a brother who was two years his junior.

But at the start of the school year when he was eight, a new boy joined Leif's class. Jeffrey was a superstar. He was smart as a whip and soon eclipsed Leif as the brightest kid in class. In the playground no one could touch Jeffrey. He could run faster, throw a football farther, and beat anyone easily in one-on-one basketball, an honour that was once Leif's. If that had been where it ended, Leif could probably have survived. But Jeffrey also wanted to be at the centre of their school year's society, and he had the social and political skills to pull it off. He was adept at forming coalitions and advancing his popularity while subtly undermining that of his rivals. This talent, together with the popularity afforded Jeffrey by his intellectual and athletic gifts, meant he could dictate what was cool and what wasn't. And with Leif as his primary rival for male leader status, Jeffrey began to consciously try to undermine him. If Leif thought one baseball player stood out, Jeffrey would counter with another. If Leif brought a Smashing Pumpkins CD to school, Jeffrey would see to it that Green Day, his favourite band, was acknowledged as superior.

Leif got mad, and his sometimes immature responses did little to help his popularity. He would lose his cool with Jeffrey and say things that Jeffrey would use to mock him. As Leif began to lose friends, his aggressiveness only mounted. His mum brought him in to see me because he had started to fight with his little brother all the time. The straw that broke the camel's back was when she found herself in the emergency room watching her younger son getting three stitches in his lower lip.

Leif was a deeply angry, defensive, and clearly pained boy. His fall from grace had left him defensive and hard to reach. And just around the time he started seeing me, things got even worse for him at home. His very uninvolved father – his parents had never been married – moved back to the city where Leif lived and decided that, if he had to pay child support, he wanted to get his money's worth. So he set about obtaining joint custody and having Leif and his brother visit him on weekends. This might have been nice had his motivation not been primarily spiteful. Leif told me that, when they went to the father's flat, his dad usually just rented a video for them and spent most of the time hanging out drinking wine with one of his girlfriends.

Because it was hard to get Leif to talk about his feelings, I spent a lot of time talking sports with him. He enjoyed these conversations, but at another level sports was a 'hot-button' issue. It revealed his need to be better than he was. Leif had become focused on athletic ability as the key to his happiness. His unspoken assumption was clear: he thought that if he could beat Jeffrey at basketball, he'd be popular. Because Leif no longer felt that he had control over his life at school or at home, he wanted to be more powerful. Who could be more powerful than the sports gods he had been taught to worship? He began to fabricate wild stories that he fervently wanted me to believe. He would say that he could 'almost' dunk a basketball on a regulation rim. The fact that he was under five feet tall would have made this highly unlikely. Wanting desperately to appear tough, he would tell me about fights in which he supposedly 'destroyed' some older kid. Whenever I began to make progress with Leif and he would start to exaggerate less, or he wouldn't get into so much trouble at school, his father would engineer his removal from therapy, only to return him in a few months when his behaviour deteriorated.

By the time he was ten, his parents decided to transfer Leif to a school in his father's neighbourhood. The change would do him good, they said, and the cheaper tuition was attractive. But instead of flowering in his new school, his grades got worse, and he became a disruptive force in class. In my experience, it often takes a whole year for a boy to become fully integrated into a new class. Leif didn't have the patience to weather the initial storm. Because he was so hurt and raw, and had lost interest in pleasing his teachers or working hard, and because he wasn't readily accepted by the 'nice' kids, he started to hang around with the 'bad' kids. He told me about their practice of taking keys and gouging deep scratches into cars or stealing their registration number plates. He got caught once and had to pay for some damage to the owner of a Cadillac, but Leif showed no real remorse. As he got older, his vandalism escalated. He told me stories about defacing public property with spray paint, and he had started making pipe bombs at home out of match tips and gunpowder he extracted from numerous smaller firecrackers.

When his father switched to an HMO-based health insurance plan, Leif left therapy with me and started being seen at his local health centre, where he was allowed far fewer therapy sessions. Not surprisingly, his destructive behaviour worsened.

Leif was the recipient of large doses of some of the worst kind of pain for a boy: rejection by his friends, an inconsistent and generally disinterested father, and a narrowing of opportunities to share his painful feelings. Since Leif could neither understand his inner turmoil nor find solace in friendship or family, his pain became anger and his expression of it became violent, in a perpetual cycle of social and emotional distress.

## When Boys See the World as Threatening

We have said that much of boys' aggressiveness is reactive rather than inborn. That is, a boy perceives a threat of some kind and responds with aggression, either to keep the threat at bay or as a reaction to pain. In order to understand how this happens, it helps to understand what it is that boys find threatening – or more specifically, why boys often see other people as threatening regardless of whether they actually are.

Although men don't challenge one another to duels as they did in centuries past, a cornerstone of the traditional masculine belief system is that a man must uphold his image as strong and deserving of respect. As a matter of honour, boys feel compelled to defend themselves against being 'dissed'.

Boys who have endured the teasing, the taunting, and the perpetual 'dissing' of the culture of cruelty become habitually on their guard against attack. Like a simple textbook case of psychological conditioning, boys come to associate peer relationships with hostile strikes, most often verbal but also physical.

Scott, an MBA candidate in his mid-twenties, entered therapy with the short-term goal of helping him make some decisions about career and relationships. During one of our sessions, he mentioned that he had recently been at a party with his fiancée, and she had noticed that he would flinch slightly when someone near him made a sudden arm movement. In talking with her about it, he remembered that when he was thirteen all the boys at school had a ritual of hitting one another in the balls whenever they could surprise a boy with the quick assault. He recalled always walking down the school corridors holding a thick textbook to protect himself below the belt, should he become the target of a sneak attack.

In addition to the physical harassment at school, Scott had two older brothers at home with whom he wrestled nonstop through childhood and well into his teens. One brother in particular used to smack him in the stomach almost every time he was within arm's reach. Scott eventually came to realize that he reflexively tightened his stomach muscles whenever he passed another man on a pavement or in a hallway. 'It's crazy,' he said. 'It's like I was abused or something. I can't believe that I'm still affected by stuff that happened so long ago.'

Unfortunately, he is not alone. The culture of cruelty leaves this kind of legacy in the lives of many boys and men.

The culture of cruelty and boys' emotional miseducation teach them not only to startle at shadows but to see threats where none exist. This emotional myopia blurs emotional cues and makes boys more likely to miss or misunderstand the meaning of others' actions or words. Michael Holley, a sports columnist for the *Boston Globe*, relates a story about baseball star Alber Belle – 'the angriest brother in America' – who when approached by a sportswriter asking 'What's up?' heard 'You suck.'[6] When someone like Mr Belle perceives the world to be this hostile, his resulting violent actions are a little more understandable.

Aggression researcher Ken Dodge and his colleagues show how aggressive boys often misinterpret the intentions of others, see hostility of intent where it doesn't exist, respond to that perceived threat with hostility, and feel that their aggression is justified in response to the incoming hostile action.[7]

The reactions of one boy – we'll call him Jack – provide a good illustration of the Dodge experiments.

Jack is nine years old. He and the rest of the boys in his class have agreed, with parental permission, to take part in the study. As soon as school is over for the day, instead of heading home, he is escorted by a young man to a small room with a TV monitor. Jack is told that he is going to watch a videotape of some boys doing different things together and then answer some questions about what he sees.

In the first scene, there is a boy about Jack's age seated on the floor building a tower with large wooden blocks. Jack is told by the researcher to imagine that he is this child. In the video scene another child enters the room. He walks by the block tower and knocks it over. Most of us, watching this tape, would find it hard to tell whether his action was the result of carelessness, purely accidental, or intentional. But see how Jack responds when he is asked:

'What happened in this story?'

'The kid knocked his tower over.'

'Can you tell me anything else about it?'

'Yeah. He just came and knocked it over for no reason. Maybe he didn't like the other kid.'

'How could you tell what happened in the story?'

'Well, he just walked by and did it. You could see him do it.'

'How do you know he did it on purpose?'

'He didn't like the other kid.'

'How do you know?'

'He knocked his tower over.'

'What should the other boy do?'

'He should never let him play with him again. Or he should wait and wreck his tower if he makes one.'

Not all boys see malicious intent in this tape. Some see the incident as accidental, or they don't respond with hostility even if they suspect malice on the part of the tower-toppling boy. But aggressive boys do tend to interpret neutral events as hostile actions.

In life, just as in this study, at least three factors contribute to boys' emotional response to aggression. First, in viewing the tape, they don't take in or use enough information about the other boy's intent. Aggressive boys like Jack make less use of relevant information — that is, they rely more on what they expect to see happen than on relevant social cues, such as the boy's facial expression or tone of voice. Second, they are more likely to see a hostile intent in an ambiguous situation. In other tapes in which a boy is shown trying to be helpful but failing – something bad happens anyway, such as paint spilling on an art project – aggressive boys also typically fail to recognize the positive effort that was being made by the helpful boy; they see only the damage and interpret it as the result of a hostile intent against them. Last, these boys generate more hostile reactions to these situations. Rather than come up with what the researchers call 'socially competent responses' – talking about the problem and reaching a compromise or better understanding, for instance – they are more likely to come up with hostile responses to the other child.

Patterns in how a boy perceives these videotapes predict how that boy will behave in response to an actual provocation. A child who expects others to act in hostile ways, sees hostile intent in others' actions, connects with that hostility, and returns it completing the circuit that powers aggressive behaviour. In experiments that confront boys with what seems to be a real threat, those boys who are wired for aggression react with even greater hostility.

### Dan with Seth: The Safety of the Black Belt

Seth was a tall, angular fifteen-year-old. When I first saw him that September after school started, I hardly recognized him. He had grown at least six inches over the holiday and now was one of the tallest boys in his class. He had been lifting weights religiously over the summer in anticipation of football try-outs and was beginning to look less like a boy and more like a man.

I had known Seth since his arrival at the school when he was thirteen. I had seen him for several months at that time when his parents had separated, but now they were back together, and although I hadn't really been seeing him 'officially', we often seemed to find ourselves in the same place – hanging around outside at lunch, watching a game, or as part of an informal group that seemed to materialize in the same place many days after school. Sometimes, as was the case on this particular day, he would just grab me when I was walking down the hall and ask if I had a few minutes to talk. As chance would have it, I was planning a quick escape to a nearby coffee shop for a wake-up cup of coffee. I invited him to come along.

Seth was not the most popular boy among the teachers. He was very smart, which helped, but like his father, a successful trial lawyer, he had an incisive argumentative facility that he would employ at times just for fun – often against an unsuspecting teacher. In a fit of frustration at Seth's repeated challenges, an English teacher had once hurled an eraser at him. The school took disciplinary action against the teacher, but a mitigating factor was that he had missed hitting Seth. The teacher was allowed to remain on the faculty, but the incident continued to create tension between Seth and him.

Similarly, some of Seth's fellow students thought he was a pain in the ass. There were a few who were especially put off by Seth's constant bragging about his competence in tae kwon do, which he had been taking since the age of seven. As we sat down in the restaurant, I asked, 'What's on your mind?'

'Nothing, really. I just wanted to get out of that hellhole for a while. Thanks for the coffee. I need it. I was up until one in the morning working on that stupid government paper for Mr Mauck.'

'What's it on?'

'Immigration. Like whether we should have quotas or whatever. Mr Mauck is so liberal it makes me puke. It's like the fucking foreigners are gonna take over the country, and all he wants to do is let in whoever wants to come and give them whatever they want. Man, what we really need is to build a huge wall across the whole Mexican border and put machine gun towers up there and give the guys infra-red glasses. So like every time they see someone trying to cross the border, they could just mow 'em down.'

'Why do they bother you so much?'

'Man, it's like they're gonna take over. They come here, they're not Americans, they don't have any money, they don't speak English, they just drain the economy and have a million kids. It's ridiculous. They just want to come here and live off us.'

Anger comes out in all kinds of ways, and Seth's racism was one more symptom, an affectation, of his anger looking for a target.

'Okay, that's enough racism for me today. How about we change the topic. What did you do this weekend?'

'I went to that party at Marty's.'

'Did you have a good time?'

'Yeah, I hung out with this girl, Brenda. Like she was really hot for me. We didn't do anything, but I'm gonna call her tonight. She used to be Bill's girlfriend, but she doesn't like him any more 'cause he's such a loser. He like practically stalks her now cause he's so whipped. She told me that he still like calls her all the time, and she just kind of says, "Whatever," and talks to him for like two seconds and says, "Gotta go." He's gonna be wicked pissed when he finds out I'm boffing her. He'll probably go nuts and try to kill me. Like he could. Man, I can just see it.'

At this point Seth is looking pretty excited, and he stands and begins to act out a hypothetical scene between Bill and himself.

'"Hey, Seth, I hear you're goin' out with Brenda."

'"Yeah, like so what? Leave me alone."

'Then he starts to come at me, then – bam!'

Seth demonstrates his best tae kwon do kick, followed by two rapid punches that would probably have disabled Bill if he really had been at the receiving end of them.

So the stage was set. With Seth's preconceived assumption of hostility on Bill's part, the chances of their ever having a reasonable discussion about the situation were next to zero. Seth would ignore the reality of the situation and eventually shape it to his expectations.

Seth was damaged goods. His perceptions were skewed by his life experience, and he routinely misperceived most cues as hostile. Seth's angry responses to the world of people around him would not change with harsh punishment: his life had already dealt him harsh blows. To defuse that anger would be an 'inside job' – helping Seth recognize his feelings as anger, tracking the anger to its source, and developing more successful strategies for coping with those circumstances and managing his feelings.

## Looking Inwards: Reading One's Own Emotions

If an angry boy has difficulty accurately reading other people's emotional signals, it is the flip side of trouble that stems from his inability to read his own emotions. As we have discussed before, boys who have been emotionally miseducated can have an inner landscape that is as foreign to them as the dark side of the moon. As a result, boys who are angry or sad or afraid often don't really know why. They may have a general sense that they are upset, but they often cannot identify the emotion and are even more blind to its real cause. In cases such as these, the human tendency is to look to the immediate environment for a cause. The blame may be inappropriately assigned to a certain teacher, a sister, a coach, or a girlfriend. This becomes particularly dangerous in cases where there is a reservoir of strong unconscious negative emotion, because it is continually seeking outlets.

### Dan with Dale: Anger under Wraps

In a school a therapist's office may often be a makeshift affair. Most schools cannot afford to hold a designated spot for a psychologist who is only around one day a week. Today I was seeing Dale in an old, rarely used room in the back of the main administration building. It was small, with only a few pieces of odd furniture, but Dale and I had made a home of sorts there. The best part about it was that three of its walls were composed of a series of long, vertical windows. It was late in the school year and a beautiful day, so we had opened many of them and were enjoying the fresh air and sunshine.

Dale was seventeen and nearing the end of his junior year (lower sixth). He was one of the brightest boys in the all-honours programme at this competitive school. His grades were generally quite good except in his Spanish class. He was at odds with his teacher, who had the reputation of being something of a martinet, and Dale had just finished serving a suspension for swearing at him in class. His mandatory visits to see me were part of the deal that had been worked out to keep him from being thrown out of school.

Dale's father was a successful research chemist, and like him Dale showed a strong aptitude for the sciences. But unfortunately for Dale, his father didn't want to have much to do with him. He had ended his marriage to Dale's mum in a bitter divorce, when Dale was about six years old. He had remarried and had had two children with his new wife, Eleni. She and Dale didn't get along at all, and she discouraged her husband from spending any time with him, usually using their own children as the wedge to drive between Dale and his father.

Making matters worse, Dale's mother had also remarried, to a man fifteen years her senior who had never been a parent before and probably never should have been one. He did not understand kids. He expected unquestioning obedience from both Dale and his mother. She was devoted to him, Dale thought mostly out of fear, and she generally supported him against Dale. An irritable man to begin with, Dale's stepfather didn't like the peace of his household disrupted by Dale's music or his friends or, especially when Dale was younger, the boy's efforts to get some attention from him. It was clear that Dale had gotten a raw deal, and he was rightly sad and angry about what had happened to him. But to talk with him, Dale seemed indifferent to it. He often gave a one-word, nebulous response to my questions: 'Whatever' – as if to say, 'It's no big deal.' During one session I tried to get him to open up by asking him leading questions:

'Wow, your stepdad sounds like a nightmare. Doesn't it bother you?'

(*Laughing*) 'Not really.'

'But he doesn't let you do anything. He's always on your case.'

'Whatever.'

'Whatever what?'

'Just whatever.'

At this point a rather large wasp flew into the room. Dale looked at it and said, 'You know, when I was a kid, we used to take hair spray and a butane lighter and toast wasps. You could get them as they were flying and just napalm the shit out of them.'

'Excuse me, Dale, sorry to be the shrink here, but back in psychology school, they taught us that sometimes things that seem unrelated are actually connected. Like our discussion about your stepfather and your memory about torching wasps. It makes me think that you might actually be angry at him and not the wasp.'

'Whatever.'

Over time, through our discussions, Dale was able to move beyond 'whatever' and begin to articulate his anger. Still, he minimized the power it held in his life. He had to or risk feeling overwhelmed by it. To make progress, however, he would need to confront the full measure of his feelings. In an unusual therapeutic move, but appropriate in this case, I took Dale on a walk to an abandoned Victorian house nearby. It was in the process of being demolished to make way for a shopping centre, but some of it remained standing. There was even one unbroken window. I gave Dale permission to vent his anger. I told him to think about his father, his stepfather, and his mother and take it out on the house. At first he just tossed rocks at the window, but after a short time, his face got red and his countenance changed. When I picture the scene now, I remember how his physical restraint fell away and he exploded with anger directed at this wreck of a house. He picked up a large tree branch and started slamming a corner of the building; he kicked at the walls and stabbed them with his lance. I thought I caught the glimmer of tears, but he suppressed them. After a while he began to tire, and his fury began to subside. He dropped the branch and sighed, wiped his face.

'Okay, Dale, why don't you try to cool down. We have to get back to school in a minute.'

He nodded quietly and appeared to be a little surprised with himself.

'I think you got a little something out of your system. Maybe you are a little angry at them after all.'

'It kinda looks like it, huh? Or maybe I just didn't like the architecture.'

Over time Dale came to recognize the true source of his anger, and he took it out less on his teachers. Life was still no bed of roses for him, but he had accomplished one of my primary goals for him: he now acknowledged what made him mad. He had also learned that his rage was of a piece – it could be identified, understood, managed – and he didn't have to be overwhelmed by it. This is an unconscious fear that many boys have, and it contributes to their effort to bottle up their anger. Because they have not been taught the skills to deal with strong emotions, they try to deny or stifle them. At least now Dale was more emotionally conscious, so his anger had less power over him. He could look at his anger in the light of day.

## Alcohol: The Match to the Fuse

With boys, the combination of anger and alcohol is a recipe for violence.[8] Crime statistics clearly show the relationship. Battered women certainly know that alcohol intoxication can frequently be the spark that sets off the blaze of physical abuse. And no urban police officer would be surprised to hear the statistic that half of all murders are committed by men under the influence of alcohol. It should come as no surprise that, when boys and men are drunk, they are more likely to get into fights. For example, a drunk teenager is twice as likely to get in a fight if he's a boy. But we do not know how much the relationship between alcohol and fighting might be mediated by biology and how much might be due to learned factors.

There is evidence, for example, that there is a certain type of problem drinker who first begins drinking heavily as a teenager and when drunk is far more prone to fight. This is sometimes referred to as the 'male-limited' type of alcoholic, because nearly all who display this pattern are men. Furthermore, studies of adopted men with this type of alcoholism in their pedigree find that it has a genetically heritable component. But as we discussed previously, inherited predispositions are never the full explanation for human behaviour. The relationship between the bottle and the boy's fighting is complex and not fully understood. What a boy expects to occur when he is drunk, how fervently he feels that he has to maintain a strong masculine image, and, most important, what he has been taught about controlling his anger all contribute to whether he will fight, drunk or sober.

## Strategies and Circuit Breakers: Teaching Boys to Defuse Anger

The image of the kindergarten mother or primary school teacher admonishing a young boy to 'use your words' has become a familiar sight and sound in the cultural landscape. Most often it pops up at the moment of conflict, when a boy's frustration or anger is fast-forwarding him to aggressive action against another child. The reminder not only urges him to recognize and express his feelings verbally but, in doing so, helps him hit the 'pause button' on his angry physical reaction.

It is no coincidence that a consistent finding in research on delinquency is that boys who aren't adept with verbal expression are at increased risk for aggression and delinquency. A recent comprehensive review of all psychological studies that have examined the verbal ability–aggression/delinquency relationship strongly confirms the connection.[9]

Why?

One straightforward interpretation is that verbal processes – talking through a problem – can act as a buffer between feeling and action, a brake on impulsive, aggressive action. Maximizing a boy's ability to express his thoughts in words and making him practise expressing himself, especially when it comes to his emotions, can help protect him from acting on impulse.

As with many of the issues raised in this book, when male violence is viewed through a different lens, we can come to understand boys better. When an act of vandalism or a violent outburst is seen as a protective response against anticipated pain rather than a biological imperative, we can seek to quell that fear. For too many angry, violent men, the internal damage from too many years of fear, too much broken trust, lives lived too long in adverse circumstances, is too often beyond the reach of our limited psychological remedies. If we are to protect boys from becoming men like these, we need to try not only to remove the sources of adversity but also to open boys to their inner world in order that they may learn ways to avoid acting violently.

As therapists, we know the deeper healing that 'using words' can accomplish: even in small, inarticulate doses, talking about feelings releases emotional pressure and weakens the grip of anger and hostility. If you can get a boy talking, it raises his anger to the conscious level, and once it becomes conscious, it loses some of its power. If you can get a boy to figure out what it is he's mad about, then he's in a position to begin to change the destructive pattern of responses in his life.

## 12. What Boys Need

What is the normal child like? Does he just eat and grow
and smile sweetly? No, that is not what he is like. The
normal child, if he has confidence in mother and father,
pulls out all the stops. In the course of time he tries out
his power to disrupt, to destroy, to frighten, to wear down,
to waste, to wangle, and to appropriate . . . At the start
he absolutely needs to live in a circle of love and strength
(with consequent tolerance) if he is not to be too fearful
of his own thoughts and of his imaginings to make progress
in his emotional development.

Donald W. Winnicott, *The Child, the Family,*
*and the Outside World*

We were talking with a mother recently. She is a warmhearted and
wise woman who is clearly beloved by her four children and her
husband. She has been a hands-on mum all along, generous with
affection and always on duty as a ready listener and trustworthy
confidant. Her son, thirteen, lately seems to have begun an exit – first,
from home, by virtue of the fact that his school and extracurricular
activities keep him busy elsewhere for all but the very final hours of
his day, and second, from their relationship, which once felt warm
and collaborative and now feels stiff and even adversarial at times.
They don't chat any more around the kitchen table as they once
did; now he seems to prefer that any communication with her occur
through his closed bedroom door.

'The older he gets,' she says, 'the more mysterious he seems to
me. I'd like to hear that this is only a phase – that we'll be able to
be close again some day. And I'd like to know that the things I do
– like teaching respect, responsibility, and just loving him – will
make a positive difference in his life.'

We know, from research and in our practice, that it is within the power of every parent – every adult in a boy's life – to give him the emotional grounding he needs to make his way in the world. What do boys need to develop strong, flexible emotional lives, to be the empathic human beings that they *themselves* would wish to become?

What boys need, first and foremost, is to be seen through a different lens than that which tradition prescribes. Individually, and as a culture, we must discard the distorted view of boys that ignores or denies their capacity for feeling, the view that colours even boys' perceptions of themselves as above or outside a life of emotions. We must recognize the harm in asking 'too much and not enough' of them – in demanding more at times than they are developmentally able to give while unnecessarily lowering expectations of self-control, empathy, emotional honesty, and moral responsibility. We bristle when we hear destructive or disappointing boy behaviour excused with 'boys will be boys', when the truth of those words – boys *will* be boys – could instead be used to advance the understanding that boys struggle in uniquely male ways at times, and they need 'boy-friendly' adult love, support, and guidance to develop a broad range of emotional responses to life's challenges. They do not need to be excused from the struggle to be good people. It has been our hope throughout this book that the reader would see boys anew through our experiences as therapists to boys and would, as a result, be moved to examine his or her deepest assumptions about boys.

How can parents and teachers do this? In one sense, the answers defy generalization, so individual are the circumstances of any one boy's life – his physical and emotional issues and the family, school, and community context of his life. Does this boy 'need' more sports in his life? Does that one need more music? Does he need less time on computer? Different games? Different friends? Advanced schoolwork to challenge him as a learner, or a lighter academic load to allow for greater diversity in his pursuits? More routine or less structure? We know these are the real questions with which parents and teachers struggle in daily life with boys, and you won't find the answers on a list of 'rules' for raising 'good' boys. There are many ways to be a good boy, many definitions of it, and a great many different paths by which boys may travel to a meaningful and satisfying life.

The following seven points have the potential to transform the way you nurture and protect the emotional life of the boy in your life. The points aren't snappy one-liners, which we feel ignore the complexity of real lives. We are psychologists, therapists, after all; we believe in the substance, not slogans, of emotional awareness and growth. Every boy's internal life and journey are unique, but in these seven ways, their needs are precisely the same. These are the foundations of parenting, teaching, and creating communities that respect and cultivate the inner life of boys:

1. *Give boys permission to have an internal life, approval for the full range of human emotions, and help in developing an emotional vocabulary so that they may better understand themselves and communicate more effectively with others.*

The simple idea here is that you consciously speak to a boy's internal life all the time, whether he is aware of it or not. You respect it, you take it into account, you make reference to it, you share your own. There is something of the prophecy fulfilled here. That is, if you act as if your son *has* an internal life – if you assume that he does, along with every other human being – then soon he will take it into account.

Instead of saying, 'You can try out for soccer or be in the school play this autumn. Which do you want to do?' you might say, 'I know you were disappointed about not getting a part in the play last year. Do you want to take the risk and try out again? I also know that soccer has been an old friend to you, but I've sensed you were losing interest in it these last two seasons. What do you think you want to do this autumn? How are you going to choose between the two?' The question assumes pain, internal conflict, risk, courage, complexity.

We know a school, an all-boys school, that has traditionally had a very strong athletic department and a 'winning tradition'. At the beginning of the last season, the football coach stood up and asked his players, 'What is my job as coach?' The boys said a number of things: to teach us skills, to motivate us, to make us work hard. When they had exhausted their suggestions, the coach said, 'Well, it is all of those things, but I'll tell you what my real job is. It is to love you. No matter what happens during the season, my job is to love you.' Many boys squirmed in discomfort when he said this; they did not know what to make of it. However, following an up-and-down season with some spectacular wins and some dreadful losses, the two captains of the teams spoke at the final athletic banquet, and they announced that they felt great about the season and had really loved their teammates. Everyone there was moved by this declaration and admired the fact that these two 'tough' football captains had said such a thing at an athletic banquet. How many people realized that it was the football coach, through his own choice of words and his coaching style, who had given them 'permission' to speak in that way, modelled the way a man can say such a thing?

A much-loved teacher said to us, 'Boys will be open about their feelings if you create a safe environment for it.'

We see this happening in classrooms where students are asked to keep journals, write essays, create art, or engage in discussions about feelings – their own or others', or those of characters in history or literature. It is not at all unusual for a boy who 'never talks about his feelings' and struggles to hide his own vulnerability to talk easily about the vulnerability and fears that a fictional boy feels. This is valuable talk; this is one way a boy learns the emotional vocabulary he needs to eventually understand and express his own feelings.

A school in Virginia published an account that a thirteen-year-old boy named Casey Johnson had written in English class about his life as a very successful soccer goalie. He entitled it 'Being a Goalie'. It is a clear reflection of a boy's constant emotional processing of life – even when all those around would swear he's just out there keeping goal:

People say that a goal is not the goalie's fault; it's the team's. But we all know they really think it's the goalie's fault. I know that if the other team scores, it's my fault. Waterford kicked off. As they brought the ball down the field, I yelled, telling my defenders to cover the open men. The Waterford player with the ball faked out his defender, took two more strides and shot. I dove. I heard cheering. I knew they had scored. I rolled over and saw the ball in the back of the goal. I had failed my team again. I got up and wiped the mud off my hands and legs. One of my teammates said, 'It's not your fault, Casey. It was the team's.' I knew he thought it was my fault, but I said 'thanks' anyway.

After the Waterford team scores one more, and then a final goal, the boy writes:

I could not get up off the ground. My face was wet with tears and mud. My teammates did not even bother to look at me. They looked as if they didn't want anything to do with me. The only thing that was of any comfort to me was a comment from the player who had scored.

'Nice try,' he said.

A teacher had made it safe for Casey to write the essay, the school made him feel proud of writing it, and he got a lot of positive feedback from children and parents. He was twice a hero, not just because he was a soccer goalie but because he had written about his internal experience in a heartfelt and direct way.

What is a 'safe environment', and how does a parent create one? In a family, anything that is a ritual provides the possibility for emotional 'safety' because it is a familiar niche of time – a protected space – in which there is no pressure to perform, no pressure to measure up, and no threat of judgement. Many mothers tell us that they go to see their sons at bedtime, giving the familiar back rub or enjoying a chat about the day, especially in the early years before adolescence. Perhaps they prepare breakfast for their boys or share an interest in reading, music, sports, or outdoor activities. Fathers tell us of doing gardening with their sons or going for haircuts, going bowling, bicycling or hiking, or building models. Mother or father, you might drive your son to soccer practice or stay for the games; you might read the sports pages together in the morning or do puzzles on Sunday afternoons. If in that shared time together a parent communicates openness, acceptance, and affection, then a boy learns these values of relationship.

Many people think that the only way to hold the interest of boys is to offer them stereotypical 'boy' entertainment and role models: tough-guy movie stars and 'iron-man' athletes. If you want boys to listen at a school assembly or banquet, a professional athlete is almost always a sure bet because athletes instantly command boy respect. But does that mean that athletes are the *only* people boys will listen to? To capture the hearts and minds of boys, do you have to cater to conventional boy interests? To assume that is to trivialize and underestimate the spiritual and intellectual interests of boys.

We know the head of a boys school who invited a Franciscan monk to speak to the school body. Before the assembly began, the monk said to his host, 'I'd like to do a brief meditation before I start to speak, and I'd like to take questions at the end.' The head of the school did everything he could to politely discourage the monk from doing either of those two things, because he was afraid that the boys wouldn't respond well. But boys love novelty, they love risk taking, they love courage; this monk had all three.

He stood up and said, 'Before I speak, I'd like to conduct a meditation. Would you all close your eyes and put your hands on your knees.' They all did, and he led them through a meditation. He then spoke about some important moral and spiritual issues and concluded, asking, 'Do you have any questions for me?' There was a long silence, and the head of the school was acutely uncomfortable, fearing that no boy would evince any interest at all and the school would be embarrassed. But the monk was completely unfazed by the silence. He stood quietly and waited. Finally, a hand went up. The boy, showing that admirable boy quality of directness, asked the question that must have been on the mind of every boy in that assembly room: 'Why would *anyone* want to become a monk?' When the monk answered the question with authenticity and directness, twelve hands went up with additional questions. Many boys wanted to know what was going on in the monk's mind. It was unlikely that any of these boys would go on to choose a life of spiritual contemplation, but their curiosity about the inner life was evident.

As a parent, one of the most important things you can do is talk about an inner life with boys. If you reveal your struggles and your thoughts, they may or may not respond instantly with insight, but they will absorb the experience and be shaped by it. These often are the moments they remember the most. Boys may talk about sports with their fathers, and years later they may remember fondly going to a game, but what they tell us about in therapy are the times when the parental curtain parted, when they saw their mother's courage, or their father's tenderness or tears, or the time that their father shared with them the story of some terrifying struggle, acknowledging fear as a 'real man' emotion.

No, a parent cannot successfully regale a son with stories of her or his college years. An adolescent boy is too interested in his own life to listen to such stories for long. But a mother or father can, in a relevant moment, share deep feelings about a moral dilemma she or he faced. If your fifteen-year-old seems disinterested in the moment, drop it, but don't give up. Despite the look on a teenage boy's face, his disinterest or cynicism won't last for ever, and he has a hungry mind that wants and needs to know how to deal with the emotional challenges of life as well as the technological and athletic challenges.

*2. Recognize and accept the high activity level of boys and give them safe boy places to express it.*

We visited a Montessori school in Minneapolis, Minnesota, that was housed in a large, old school building with high ceilings and spacious halls. Outside every classroom there was a space on the floor, marked off by tape, inside which lay a skipping rope. Any student who felt restless was allowed to go there to skip. Because the Montessori method relies so much on individual work and creative expression, a class is rarely all working on the same thing at the same time.

In this school, therefore, a child could leave the room and exercise as a matter of self-regulation. Boys were the most frequent users. Is this possible in every school? Almost certainly not; the group-based instruction and activities of most classes, and traditional policies regarding the need for safety and monitoring, would preclude such a solution in the vast majority of schools. However, the principle of allowing boys to exercise when they need to during a school day is a powerful one. The head of one small prep school in Pennsylvania said to us, 'It is amazing how much work boys will get done when going outside is the reward.'

If you ask boys in school what their favourite part of the school day is, they often answer, 'You mean, besides P.E.?' Boys need space for their jumping, their energy, their exuberance. They need it in school, and they need it at home. Isn't the finished basement the home version of the school gym? Isn't an excessively neat and orderly home, a home without some safe free-play space, something of a torment for a boy?

Anne Roche Muggeridge, a mother of four sons, wrote a piece entitled 'Boys Should Be Boys', in which she declares:

Don't treat your boys with tranquillizers. Like those old-fashioned head-masters, simply wear them out. My husband made a rink every winter in our garden, and all the neighbourhood boys played there night and day. They used to come in to use the bathroom, in their skates. They played floor hockey using their baby sister as a goal. They broke the bottom landing while competing in how many steps they could clear in jumping over her. I miss them. They grew up to be kind, gallant, honest, funny, devout, stoic, brave and generous. I miss them. [The Roxbury Latin School Newsletter, Roxbury, Massachusetts]

Here is someone who appreciates and has faith in boys. Many parents of boys do embrace the physicality of boys in this way; some do not. Most teachers of boys also love boys; some, unfortunately, do not. Boys are tremendously sensitive to adults who do not have a reasonable tolerance level for boy energy, and when they do sense that a person has a low threshold of boy tolerance, they usually respond to it as a challenge.

Activity level isn't just an issue with little boys. Teenage boys bump and push. When we sit down with a group of adolescent boys in almost any school setting, there is an inevitable physicality even to something as simple as finding a place to sit and sitting in it. If there are desks and chairs, then those get jostled about with plenty of scraping and bumping; if there is a couch, then there will be a moment of scuffling to see who sits where; if it's on the floor, then there will be the pig-pile of boys, and others rooting about for the right spot. We're not talking about physical aggression, just a vibrant, active body language that's always in use. They knock one another's hats off; they sprawl across furniture and occupy dinner tables and family room floors in a way that seems larger than necessary. Sometimes they don't watch where they are going, and sometimes they just enjoy throwing their weight around. Wouldn't you, if two years ago you used to weigh 100 pounds and now you weigh 175? When you are a boy, it is just plain fun being big!

And if – as was the case two winters ago at the school where one of the authors works – there is a fresh snowfall on the hill outside the headmaster's office and he has left his two children's sleds outside the house, why, then, you start to sled, and then two of you sled, and then three get on a sled in a giant pile, and who cares if you're wearing grey flannel trousers and blue blazers and the temperature is ten degrees? You take off the blue blazer, hang it on a fence post, and you are ready to sled. And then you try and miss trees by a close margin, and then you try to push a friend off mid-hill. And older teachers are appalled: they think the standards are slipping – boys didn't used to do this (but of course, they did). They did, they do, and they always will. Boys need to learn how to manage their physicality to do no harm, but they need not be shamed for exuberance.

*3. Talk to boys in their language – in a way that honours their pride and their masculinity. Be direct with them; use them as consultants and problem solvers.*

Because boys are miseducated to fear excessive feeling and vulnerability, it is important to communicate with them in a way that honours their wish for strength and does not shame them. They often act as if they were allergic to direct emotional appeals of the kind that might work with girls. As therapists, to engage a boy in conversation, we often need to communicate differently with him than we would with a girl.

With girls we can ask, 'How are you feeling?' and most of the time they can tell us.

More often with boys our questions must be more specific: 'How angry are you about being sent here?' 'Why do you think you were sent here?' 'What are your parents so worried about?' 'Do you think the situation warrants your seeing a therapist?'

Boys may be reluctant to talk about their feelings, but they love problem solving; they love to be consulted. We have had many boys refuse to come to family therapy, some even refusing to get out of the car and walk into the building. What usually works is to walk out to the car park and say to a boy, 'Look, I understand that you don't want to be here and you don't believe in this stuff, but I am giving your parents advice on how to manage you and I feel acutely uncomfortable doing it without your input.' We have had boys come to sessions and say they will not talk, but they talk if you present them with problems, if you don't saddle them with the entire weight of talking. In our work with boys, we often find that we need to lead with our feelings and allow a boy to pick or choose between options. For example, if a boy describes a situation that seems terrifying or full of grief, we will say, 'I don't know you well enough to know how you felt, but it seems to me that you were in a pretty scary situation there. I would have been frightened had I been in your shoes.' A boy can always say, 'No, that's not true of me,' at which point he is also likely to correct our misimpression with additional thoughts we can then explore.

One doesn't say to a boy, 'I'm sure you must have been scared.' If, in response to the adult's laying his or her emotional cards on the table, a boy says, 'Well, maybe I was scared a little,' the therapist, or any adult, can then reply with real empathy, 'I can sure understand that.' That experience, repeated briefly hundreds of times, can make a boy feel that his feelings are valid, that many other boys and adults share his sense of vulnerability.

If you want to know something about your son's emotional responses, ask him about how his friends feel, whether it was an unnerving situation for someone else:

• How did he help his friend?
• Could he have used help in that situation?
• What does he think of the way the adults handled the situation?
• What would he have liked to see you do had you been in a position of authority?
• Does he think that a woman might have handled the situation differently to a man?

Boys like to discuss what is masculine and what is feminine – so do girls, for that matter – what is innate and what is learned. Boys are happy to discuss what is true of them and what is not. We've never met a boy who wouldn't respond to a series of yes-no questions.

The problem with boy—adult conversation is that adults get exasperated because they expect a different kind of communication. Adults expect much of adolescent boys because boys look big and want adult privileges. But if they haven't had much practice talking, or they think it isn't manly to talk, berating them or being disappointed in them won't help. It only discredits the adult in the eyes of the boy.

Using a son as a consultant does not mean doing everything he wants. Absolutely not! But it does mean giving him a hearing. It helps if you have been doing it since he was young, because the practice you have shared together of talking, listening, and consulting will have helped your son know what is good judgement and what is not. If you listen to him seriously, he'll listen to himself seriously.

Is communicating with boys sometimes difficult? Yes, it often is. Is it impossible? Almost never. Only with the most angry, contemptuous, and suspicious boys is conversation impossible. If you are willing to ask consultative questions, put your emotional cards on the table, and not be disappointed with brief answers, you can communicate with boys. Above all, you have to convey your respect for a boy's psychological defences, his wish to be strong, and his need to appear stronger than he feels. There is no need to berate him for his desire to be a competent boy, a respected boy among his peers and in his own mind. If you honour that, he can feel that he does not need to be so guarded, and he will talk.

*4. Teach boys that emotional courage is courage, and that courage and empathy are the sources of real strength in life.*

If you ask a boy about courage, he's likely to use the word *bravery* in his answer somewhere, and if you ask him to give you an example of bravery, he's likely to turn to popular movies or perhaps an act of physical heroism that he's seen covered in the news or read about for school, or maybe a classmate's willingness to stand up to a bully. Popular movies aimed at boys seem to prize only one kind of courage: standing up to a physically larger opponent. The willingness to fight an enemy, to outwit a dinosaur, to defeat an alien monster, to look into the eye of a villain with a gun, is the media's definition of male courage.

Adventure and war stories are as old as time, and boys show a special fascination for them. Watch little boys act out their dramas of courage and they are typically situations of warfare. But that is not all that boys want to see or all they want to know about. Boys and girls are hungry for stories of emotional courage.

Each January, when the life and times of Martin Luther King, Jr, become the topic of class discussion in most American schools, boys and girls are impassioned by their study of the slain civil rights leader. They hear King's courage in his stirring speeches, in books or documentary films about his non-violent marches for civil rights. They also witness the courage, not only of King, but of the many other 'ordinary people' of that period who took a stand against racism within the landscape of their own lives and communities. Students encounter a similar message of emotional courage as courage in their study of American slavery, the Holocaust, the suffrage movement in the United States, and in the present, the international human rights movement and environmental activism.

Boys are not half-hearted in their interest in these topics. They love heroes; they all have dreams of greatness. Boys are open to inspiration. What kind of models are we offering them?

Outside the studies of emotional courage in school, we find a sad dearth of such images or opportunities for recognizing emotional courage in daily life for boys. Men, in particular, are rarely celebrated for moral or emotional courage. Men in the news are almost always there because they represent power, skill, or wealth; men in entertainment programming are either dominators like Arnold Schwarzenegger, who is fearless, or good-natured nitwits like Tim Allen on *Home Improvement*, where the context of sitcom life simply doesn't include emotional courage.

Most important, boys need models of emotional courage in their own lives, not just in the media. We need to recognize and identify for them emotional courage in the lives of women and men, in our families and in the lives of children and others around us. In life and art, we need to provide boys with models of male heroism that go beyond the muscular, the self-absorbed, and the simplistically heroic. Many adults display emotional courage in their work or personal lives, but rarely do we allow our children to witness our private moments of conscience or bravery. We need to speak of it, and we need to recognize out loud the emotional courage of those people around us who, in small ways daily, exhibit personal courage – to make a class speech, to be active despite handicaps, to learn a new language, to step forward to help when it would be easier to look away. When we give emotional courage a face and a form – our own or someone else's – we leave an indelible impression. Boys can and will respond to the complexity of real courage.

Mark Twain's description of courage, which we quoted in chapter 5, bears repeating: 'Courage is resistance to fear, mastery of fear – not absence of fear.' Boys need to learn that it is part and parcel of true emotional courage in a man to accept fear and other feelings of vulnerability in himself and others.

A father was putting his seven-year-old son, Charlie, and the son's friend Jeff to bed on a sleepover night at Charlie's house. Charlie was going through a period in which his sense of vulnerability was heightened: he had fears of many things. Charlie was focused on tornadoes, because he had heard a news report about the tornadoes that had hit Nashville, Tennessee, very hard and because his family had close friends who lived in Tennessee. Even with Jeff in the room, Charlie expressed his fears without hesitation:

'Dad, I'm not going to be able to go to sleep because of the tornadoes.'

'Charlie, there won't be any tornadoes tonight, I promise.'

'But Dad, there are tornadoes.'

'I know, Charlie, but not in Boston.'

'I'm not going to be able to go to sleep, Dad, I'm sure I'm not.'

Jeff, the friend who had been listening to this exchange and who had undoubtedly experienced fears in his young life, spoke to Charlie across the dark room. 'Charlie, I just banged the wall by mistake. Maybe that's the sound that scared you.'

'No, Jeff. It wasn't that. It's the tornadoes.'

Charlie appreciated the effort to reassure him, but he couldn't take comfort in Jeff's words because it wasn't the sound in the room that had frightened him; it was the sound of the fear in his heart, and his thoughts were not so much about killer winds as about loving friends he worried were in the path of danger.

The father heard the friend's effort to calm Charlie and realized that his own efforts to persuade had been pointless. So he asked, 'Would it help if I lay down with you and put my arm around you?'

'Yes, Dad, but you have to stay.'

The father stretched out beside his son and put an arm around his shoulder. 'I will stay until I'm sure you are asleep. Will that be okay?'

'Yes, Dad. Can you hug me tighter?'

We hope this book has shown you that boys have fears – not just 'developmentally appropriate' ones about thunder and dark rooms, but fears about everyday situations as they grow up; in this respect they are no different from anyone. Boys have fears, boys have needs, boys are vulnerable, and boys have a capacity for powerful inner feelings. Acknowledging boys' fear will not make them weak; it will free them from shame and make them stronger. Boys are prisoners of those feelings as long as they have to deny the truth of them or require themselves to be fully in control of them. When boys and men rigidly deny their fears, they are less than fully human; besides, the effort of trying to deny fears is exhausting. We need to acknowledge and empathize with those fears, which are universal, and we need to teach boys to honour their own fears and respect the fears of others. That is empathy, and as Charlie's friend, Jeff, demonstrated, every boy has the capacity for empathy. Boys need to have the experience of being empathized with, be able to display their own capacity for empathy, and be asked to be empathic.

Do boys need special training to be empathic? We do not believe they need *special* training, but they do need opportunities to display their empathy. For the most part, boys only need to be encouraged to display their natural capacity for empathy. Watch any boy with his dog or cat; in a classroom where there are pet gerbils or frogs or snakes, watch boys vie for the chance to be the caregiver, to tend to the needs of the class pet.

There are many ways to give boys the opportunity to learn to be empathic. Tending pets is one way. Tending people and tending community is another. Boys of all ages need the chance to take care of animals, babies, the needy, older people, the environment. We see boy empathy in schools where community service is a regular part of the curriculum; we see boy empathy in families where brothers and sisters need care and help.

We know of a school in Chicago where, in the spring of their final year, students are given the opportunity to go off campus and do a community service project. Most of the students enjoy the project, but every year at least a few boys are deeply moved by it, and they say so in the assembly at which they share their experience and how it has helped them 'see the world in a new way'.

'At first I resented having to take care of this retarded boy because he wouldn't do anything I said and it was frustrating,' a boy said in one recent presentation. As he continued to tell the story, it turned out that the retarded child had become attached to him, and at the end of their six weeks at the job, the child had hugged him. As he described this moment, he started to choke up in front of the school. Obviously, it had been enormously meaningful to him to have made a difference in the life of a handicapped child.

How many of our graduating schoolboys have had the experience of taking care of a disabled child or an elderly person? Too few, we venture to guess. Boys who have such experiences become more empathic. The more such experiences they have, the more empathic they become.

Because of the training our culture gives boys, they may, at times, need limits on their competitiveness and the rush for individual achievement. We know a soccer coach who makes the entire team run laps if anyone on his team criticizes or is contemptuous of a teammate or an opponent during a game. He requires them all to participate in the reminder because he wants them all to know how negatively he feels about a win-at-all-costs mentality, and he wants boys to use peer pressure to soften one another's criticisms. Athletics and team sports give us a chance to teach empathy in a situation in which boys are highly motivated to learn it. Anyone who has ever doubted the empathic nature of boys should witness the kind of caring, camaraderie, and loyalty boys display in a team sport setting – in the face of defeat and injury, as well as in the flush of victory.

*5. Use discipline to build character and conscience, not enemies.*

Sooner or later, every boy gets into trouble, whether as a result of his impulsivity, his activity level, or just because he's human: it is a normal part of growing up. What happens to boys in the disciplinary encounter will form the moral underpinnings of their later behaviour. We believe that boys need discipline that is clear, consistent, and not harsh. The best discipline is built on the child's love for adults and his wish to please. If that impulse is respected and cultivated, children will continue to be psychologically accessible through their love and respect. If they are unduly shamed, harshly punished, or encounter excessive adult anger, they will soon react to authority with resistance rather than with a desire to do better.

The truth is that children who are well disciplined early in life – that is, well guided rather than punished – need less and less overt discipline as they get older. In our work with troubled boys, we often see the effects of harsh discipline, which are simply more trouble and lasting emotional scars. We also know from our work with boys that even experienced 'troublemakers' can find inspiration in discipline that consists of genuine guidance and empathy.

Listen to the words of Mack, a fourteen-year-old boy who was the class speaker at his graduation from a small, public school in Middleburg, Virginia. In his earlier years, Mack was one of those regular visitors to the headmaster's office, a boy with a penchant for impulsive, disruptive behaviour.

'I was always the – I guess you could say "unique" one,' Mack said. 'I was different: I liked playing different games, I liked watching different TV shows, and I had different interests. But that was okay. I had fun.

'There was really one person who understood me and supported my different interests and views,' he continued, referring to the headmaster, Mr Gilford, who, he said, was 'not at all like a stereo-typical headmaster,' but rather, 'seemed to know me before I had even come to school the first day.'

Mack recalled a day in his first year at the school when he was sent to Mr Gilford's office: 'As I was walking down the hallway to his office for the first time, I thought I was taking my last steps, just thinking, "What will he do?" When I sat down, the first thing he said to me was, "Well, hello, Mack. How's your day been going so far?"

'This startled me for two reasons. One, he was calm, gentle, and friendly. Two, was actually what he said. I thought he was going to react like a madman! We finished the meeting in a casual and enjoyable conversation rather than in condemnation.'

Here is a boy, seven years after the fact, remembering *not* being yelled at, remembering *not* being punished. His speech is a measure of how much boys expect punishment and how transformative reasonable dialogue can be for the vast majority of them.

*6. Model a manhood of emotional attachment.*

Boys imitate what they see. If what they see is emotional distance, guardedness, and coldness between men, they grow up to emulate that behaviour. While it is rare in the United States, it is common in many other cultures for men to express physical affection, both in private and in public. We know a man who always greeted his best friend with a hug, and this scene played out in the son's presence year after year. Any effect on the boy was not immediate. The son, like many boys, went through a period in his adolescence when he wouldn't touch or be touched by any adult, neither his father nor anyone else. But now, in his early twenties, he hugs both his father and, when they chance to meet, his father's friend. What do boys learn when they do not see men with close friendships, when there are no visible models of intimacy in a man's life beyond his spouse?

In our experience as therapists, we see many men lonely for the company of other men, and they have been so since school or since the end of their college days. Many men do not know how to initiate or maintain significant friendships; too many men do not know how to open up to other men. Aaron Beck, a psychiatrist and depression researcher from the University of Pennsylvania, said he played on a tennis foursome for twenty years with great enjoyment, but he and his partners did not disclose much information to one another. One day he came home to get prepared for tennis, and his wife said, "Joe just called and said he may not be able to play tennis tonight." "Why not?" Beck asked. "Well, he's getting divorced, and because of the financial arrangement, he may not be able to afford to keep up his club membership." Beck's reply was, "He's getting divorced? I didn't know that!" Even if, as we believe, male friendship may not need to be measured by the yardstick of personal disclosure, it is sad when a man cannot tell his partners of twenty years that he is getting divorced.

The loneliness of men has to be addressed in the lives of boys. Boys need to be encouraged to initiate friendships, maintain them, and experience the conflicts that arise in male friendship from different levels of athletic skill, from teasing, and from competition for the attention of girls. Too often boys lack both the resources and the will to resolve those conflicts and preserve friendships.

When we talk to mothers and other women about boys' need for a model of a manhood of emotional attachment, we often get a dry laugh. 'What does that look like in a man?' they want to know. And how can they possibly contribute to this as women?

First, encourage and support those friendships. Then recognize and accept that men's friendships don't always look the way you might expect them to look, or would like them to look, and that is because some of men's attachments aren't as close, aren't as reliable, are too infected with competition compared to what women enjoy, and many of their friendships are just different from yours.

A colleague of ours was firm in her belief that girls' friendships were better than boys'. She had to question her assumptions one day when she watched four boys fishing at a nearby reservoir. As she sunbathed and watched the boys, they stood there, almost shoulder to shoulder, fishing for two to three hours, and they hardly talked. They certainly didn't have a sustained conversation. But watching them for some time, she came to realize that there was a tremendous closeness between those boys – and between many boys and many men – that transcends conversation. She saw how intimate these boys were without conversation, how trustworthy was the silence between them. They loved being in one another's presence, and that was what counted.

Most boys love being in the presence of men. They like watching their dads, they like being with them, they like playing with them. But they also need them to speak of closeness from time to time, and that can be hard for dads to do. There are so many men who report that, as boys, they never heard their fathers say, 'I love you.' So sometimes it has to be arranged.

'Daddy and Me' seminars, of the kind sponsored periodically by schools, religious congregations, and community recreation centres, offer a great model. These may range from the simplest kindergarten event to sophisticated travel adventures, or spiritual retreats for adult sons and their fathers, but the good ones share some important common denominators: they carve out a time for father and son to be together. They put the two in a situation that takes Dad out of the boss's seat and makes father and son partners instead. They include unstructured time for wandering and exploration, as well as some structured time for activities that are designed to help strengthen the bond — not the competition or friction — between father and son. When we see fathers and sons in these situations, we typically see sons beaming at the undivided and uncritical attention they are getting from their dads, and we see how grateful the fathers are to have this organized, sanctioned chance to be this way with their sons. It is beautiful. That it is a planned event takes nothing away from it. The experience of emotional connection is genuine, and it shapes a boy in a genuine way.

7. *Teach boys that there are many ways to be a man.*

Over the years of our work at two all-boys schools, Belmont Hill School and Saint Sebastian's School, we have had many boys come into our office, sit down, and say, 'I'm not really a Saint Sebastian's [or Belmont Hill] boy.' That a boy feels he must start off a session by announcing that he is different or sensitive or not as athletic as the ideal makes us sad, because it means that he is measuring himself against a standard of idealized masculinity. Very few boys or men are tall, handsome, athletic, successful with women, endlessly virile, and physically fearless. If our culture is, as Mary Pipher, the author of *Reviving Ophelia*, says, toxic for girls because it teaches them that there is only one definition of female beauty — and if that drives girls towards diets, eating disorders, and chronic low self-esteem — then we need to re-examine the messages we send to girls. That has been the great achievement of the last twenty-five years of research into the stress points in the lives of girls. Boys suffer from a too-narrow definition of masculinity, and it is time to re-examine that message, too.

A loving, kind, middle school teacher we know confided, 'You worry throughout your childhood about whether or not you are going to be a man. Then, once you are a man, you spend the rest of your life wondering whether *they* think you made it.' The Big Impossible. We can do better.

Sometimes the key to reaching a boy is simply for a man to communicate his own intense interest in a subject. A school teacher said to us, 'So many boys come to my class hating poetry. They don't want to have anything to do with it. But when I show them that poetry has meaning for me, some of them start to warm to it, even to love it.'

There's got to be something for everybody.

We have to teach boys that there are many ways to become a man; that there are many ways to be brave, to be a good father, to be loving and strong and successful. We need to celebrate the natural creativity and risk taking of boys, their energy, their boldness. We need to praise the artist and the entertainer, the missionary and the athlete, the soldier and the male nurse, the store owner and the round-the-world sailor, the teacher and the chief executive. There are many ways for a boy to make a contribution in this life.

Our boys are going to grow up to be many sizes, to possess many skills, and to do a wide variety of things. We must not disregard their many offerings; we must not make them feel that they do not measure up, that we disdain their contributions. We have to ask a lot of them, morally and spiritually, and we have to support them in their efforts to please us. And if they try to please us, we must communicate to them that they are not a disappointment to us. The only thing that will make growing up psychologically safe for our sons is for them to know that we value them and that we love them, and that we have every confidence that they will grow naturally into good men.

The human personality and human philosophy are formed by repeated experiences, sometimes minuscule ones. That's why most people, if they are going to be helped by therapy, usually require long-term therapy. Their problems have been so long in the making.

Boys come to conclusions about the way they should be, what constitutes masculinity, and whether or not they are good and worthwhile boys as the result of hundreds, or even hundreds of thousands, of moments of hearing, observing, and reacting to messages about what makes a boy and a man. Much of what they see and hear is painful and distorting; much of what they experience makes them want to hide their true selves and only show the world their most conventional and acceptable self, so that the culture will neither be outraged by them nor attack them.

The only way to make a difference with a boy is to give him powerful experiences that speak to his inner life, that speak to his soul and let him know that he is entitled to have the full range of human experience. That permission is given to boys by teachers, by parents, by ministers, by aunts and uncles. And they do it by affirming for a boy that his vulnerability is human and acceptable. Once you understand that to be human is to be vulnerable – whether you are a boy or a girl – then you can go on and be brave, confident, and productive from a solid foundation. You don't have to hide your vulnerability from yourself, and so you are not deeply afraid or fragile.

In all our years as therapists, we have never met a boy who didn't crave his parents' love and others' acceptance and who didn't feel crippled by their absence or redeemed by their abundance. Strong and healthy boys are made strong by acceptance and affirmation of their humanity. We all have a chance to do that every day, every time we are in the presence of a boy and we have a chance to say to him, 'I recognize you. You are a boy – full of life, full of dreams, full of feeling.'

# Notes

## 1. The Road Not Taken

1. The work of Carroll Izard and his colleagues greatly influenced our thinking on this point. They have outlined some of the important developmental aspects of emotional knowledge and how a lack of this knowledge can lead to a disruption of normal social relationships. For example, 'Deficits in the understanding of emotion expressions and emotion experience could contribute to developmental deficiencies in adaptive social behavior and to the emergence of behavior problems.' From C. Izard, D. Schultz, and B. P. Ackerman, 'Emotion Knowledge, Social Competence, and Behavior Problems in Disadvantaged Children' (paper presented at the biennial meeting of the Society for Research on Child Development, Washington, DC, April 1997), 4.

2. For an excellent discussion of how boys move from being emotionally reactive as infants to emotionally unexpressive by the time they are teenagers, see L. R. Brody, 'Gender, Emotional Expression, and Parent–Child Boundaries', in *Emotion: Interdisciplinary Perspectives*, ed. R. D. Kavanaugh, B. Zimmerberg, and S. Fein (Mahwah, NJ: Lawrence Erlbaum, 1996), 139–70. For example, she discusses a study that used adult raters who had been misinformed about the baby's gender, and boys were still rated as more expressive of emotions. She writes, 'There seems to be a developmental shift in which males become less facially expressive of emotions with age, whereas females become more so ... [This is because] the socialization of emotions by both parents and peers differs for boys and girls' (140).

3. These authors are concerned with how feelings of empathy develop. They distinguish between feelings of sympathy that usually lead to attempts to help or comfort a suffering person, and personal distress, where another's distress upsets a person and causes him to try to avoid the distressing situation. They feel that whether a person feels sympathy or is distressed may be related to his ability to regulate emotional arousal. Their results provided evidence for that view: 'Boys who tended to others' distress by acting out tended to evidence more personal distress ... Boys who were less well-regulated ... also tended to escape the crying infant by turning the speaker off ... Thus boys who appeared to be better regulated were more likely to comfort the infant than those who were less regulated'

(1689). R. A. Fabes, N. Eisenberg, M. Karbon, D. Troyer, and G. Switzer, 'The Relations of Children's Emotion Regulation to Their Vicarious Emotional Responses and Comforting Behaviors', *Child Development* 65 (1994): 1678–93.

4. One very interesting line of research on the effects of the environment on the brain regards how prolonged stress affects the hippocampus, a brain structure involved in both stress regulation as well as memory. In a review of research on the destructive and protective aspects of adrenal steroids in the central nervous system (CNS), McEwen and his colleagues (B. S. McEwen, J. Angulo, H. Cameron, H. M. Chao, D. Daniels, et al., 'Paradoxical Effects of Adrenal Steroids on the Brain: Protection versus Degeneration', *Biological Psychiatry* 31 [1992]: 177–99) note that the hippocampus, unlike some other brain structures, is very vulnerable to stress-related adrenal steroid damage, containing the highest number of corticosteroid binding sites in the brain. One effect of this damage is to minimize the ability of the hippocampus to regulate the response to stress through the hypothalamic-pituitary-adrenal (HPA) axis. In rats with hippocampal damage, there is a tendency for the HPA axis to hypersecrete steroids during moderate stress and a less efficient shutdown of the HPA axis in the aftermath of stress (R. Sapolsky, L. Krey, and B. S. McEwen, 'The Neuroendocrinology of Stress and Aging: The Glucocorticoid Cascade Hypothesis', *Endocrinology Review* 7 [1986]: 284–301). Memory dysfunction is a classic neuropsychological manifestation of hippocampal damage with research finding both visual–spatial and verbal memory deficits (see A. Diamond, 'Rate of Maturation of the Hippocampus and the Developmental Progression of Children's Performance on the Delayed Non-Matching to Sample and Visual Paired Comparison Tasks', *Annals of the New York Academy of Sciences* 608 [1990]: 394–426; and R. P. Kesner, B. L. Bolland, and M. Dakis, 'Memory for Spatial Locations, Motor Responses, and Objects: Triple Dissociation among the Hippocampus, Caudate Nucleus, and Extrastriate Visual Cortex', *Experimental Brain Research* 93 [1993]: 462–70). A real-life example of this was shown in an important study that linked post-traumatic stress disorder, hippocampal damage, and memory dysfunction in a sample of combat veterans (J. D. Bremmer, P. Randall, T. M. Scott, R. A. Bronen, J. P. Seibyl, et al., 'MRI-Based Measurement of Hippocampal Volume in Patients with Combat-Related Post-traumatic Stress Disorder', *American Journal of Psychiatry* 152 [1995]: 973–81).

5. There is quite a bit of research literature on this subject, much of it inspired by the seminal work by Eleanor Maccoby and Carol Jacklin in *The Psychology of Sex Differences* (Stanford, CA: Stanford University Press, 1974). Two more current general sources are: D. Blum, *Sex on the Brain: The Biological Differences Between Men and Women* (New York: Viking,

1997) and E. E. Maccoby, *The Two Sexes: Growing Up Apart, Coming Together* (Cambridge, MA: Belknap Press of Harvard University Press, 1998). References concerning specific sex differences are found in the notes for chapter 2.

6. This is taken from J. Shibley, E. F. Hyde, and S. J. Lamon, 'Gender Differences in Mathematics Performance: A Meta-analysis', *Psychological Bulletin* 107 (1990): 139–55.

7. This is from R. E. Tremblay, B. Schaal, B. Boulerice, L. Arseneault, R. Soussignan, and D. Perusse, 'Male Physical Aggression, Social Dominance and Testosterone Levels at Puberty: A Developmental Perspective', in *Biosocial Bases of Violence*, ed. A. Raine, P. A. Brennan, D. P. Farrington, and A. S. Mednick (New York: Plenum Press, 1997), 271–91, 274. See also J. Archer, 'The Influence of Testosterone on Human Aggression', *British Journal of Psychology* 82 (1991): 1–28. Archer writes, 'Although it has been established in a wide range of vertebrate groups that testosterone facilitates aggression, there is little or no conclusive evidence for primates' (3). And further, 'Experimental studies of mice and pigeons have also shown that the animal's previous experience of fights can override manipulations of its testosterone levels. Thus even in birds and rodents, social experience has to be taken into account when considering the influence of testosterone on aggression' (2). Finally, 'We can conclude therefore that most of the limited evidence regarding a possible influence of prenatal androgens on aggression in humans is negative' (5).

8. These were eighteen highly aggressive pre-pubertal males who were admitted to the children's unit of Bronx Children's Psychiatric Center for violent or unmanageable behaviour. All had longer than six-month histories of ongoing highly aggressive and oppositional behaviours. Most had used weapons to attack family members or peers, and a number had made attempts to seriously injure infant siblings. Rather than finding differences in serum testosterone (none of the children had values outside the normal range or had levels different from matched control children), the authors note that most of the children had a previous history of abuse and neglect. The authors write: 'As far as hormonal influences are concerned it is possible to view the elevated mean testosterone levels that previously have been reported in aggressive adolescents and adults as *effects* rather than causes of aggressive behavior' (1221) and 'The findings suggest simply that great caution be used in drawing inferences about causality (or biological determination) from adult studies that link testosterone to aggressive human behavior' (1222). J. N. Constantino, D. Grosz, P. Saenger, D. W. Chandler, R. Nandi, and F. J. Earls, 'Testosterone and Aggression in Children', *Journal of the American Academy of Child and Adolescent Psychiatry* 32 (1993): 1217–22.

9. There are many books and articles on cultural influences on aggressive

behaviour. Those that most influenced our thinking are J. L. Briggs, *Never in Anger: Portrait of an Eskimo Family* (Cambridge, MA: Harvard University Press, 1970); D. P. Fry, 'Intercommunity Differences in Aggression among Zapotec Children', *Child Development* 59 (1988): 1008–19; R. K. Denton, 'Surrendered Men: Peaceable Enclaves in the Post Enlightenment West', in *The Anthropology of Peace and Nonviolence*, ed. L. E. Sponsel and T. Gregor (London: Lynne Rienner, 1994), 69–108; C. A. Robarchek, 'Ghosts and Witches: The Psychocultural Dynamics of Semoi Peacefulness', in *The Anthropology of Peace and Nonviolence*, ed. L. E. Sponsel and T. Gregor (London: Lynne Rienner, 1994), 183–96; and C. M. Turnbull, 'The Politics of Non-Aggression', in *Learning Non-Aggression: The Experience of Non-Literate Societies*, ed. A. Monagu (New York: Oxford University Press, 1978), 161–221.

10. There are numerous publications based on this study. Two that influence our thinking are: J. H. Pleck, F. L. Sonenstein, L. C. Ku, and L. C. Burbridge, *Individual, Family, and Community Factors Modifying Male Adolescents' Risk Behavior 'Trajectory'* (Washington, DC: Urban Institute, 1996), J. H. Pleck, F. L. Sonenstein, and L. C. Ku, 'Masculinity Ideology: Its Impact on Adolescent Males' Heterosexual Relationships', *Journal of Social Issues* 49 (1993): 11–29. For other publications, go to the Urban Institute Web site: http:www.urban.org/.

11. This is discussed in M. E. Lamb, R. D. Ketterlinus, and M. P. Fracasso, 'Parent Child Relationships', in *Developmental Psychology: An Advanced Textbook*, 3rd ed., ed. M. H. Bornstein and M. E. Lamb (Hillsdale, NJ: Lawrence Erlbaum, 1992), 465–518. For example, parents (especially fathers) describe their sons with terms like *sturdy, handsome*, and *strong*, and their daughters with terms like *dainty, pretty*, and *fragile* (492).

12. These issues are discussed in S. Denham, D. Zoller, and E. A. Couchoud, 'Socialization of Preschoolers' Emotion Understanding', *Developmental Psychology* 30 (1994): 928–36; J. Dunn, J. R. Brown, and M. Maguire, 'The Development of Children's Moral Sensibility: Individual Differences and Emotion Understanding', *Developmental Psychology* 31 (1995): 649–59; and J. Dunn, J. R. Brown, and L. Beardsall, 'Family Talk about Feeling States and Children's Later Understanding of Others' Emotions', *Developmental Psychology* 27 (1991): 448–55. A recent meta-analysis, that is, a statistical analysis of the results of a large group of studies as if they were all from one study, reveals two interesting findings: that mothers talked more and used more supportive speech with daughters than with sons. In addition, mothers' talk with sons was more direct and informational in content than it was with daughters. C. Leaper, J. Anderson, and P. Sanders, 'Moderators of Gender Effects of Parents' Talk with Their Children: A Meta-Analysis', *Developmental Psychology* 43 (1998): 3–27.

13. This is from C. A. Cervantes and M. A. Callanan, 'Labels And Explanations

in Mother–Child Emotion Talk: Age and Gender Differentiation', *Developmental Psychology* 34 (1998): 88–98. In this study, eighty-four children aged two, three, and four were studied along with their mothers in a joint storytelling session. They had a dolls' house and some plastic people and were told to play out a story that had four features: parents going away and leaving a child with another caregiver, father falling down and getting hurt, dog getting lost, and parents coming back. The researchers were interested in how many emotional words mothers and children used and whether these were labels ('He is sad') or explanations ('He is sad because he lost his dog'). Previous work has shown a direct connection between the frequency of parent–child emotional conversation and later understanding of emotions. Also, previous work has shown that mothers use emotional labelling more with girls and explanation more with boys. This has been interpreted to mean that boys are more socialized to problem-solve about emotions or to have control over emotions ('The boy is sad because he lost his dog; let's go find it'). In contrast, in emphasizing direct references to emotional states with girls, mothers might be encouraging girls to focus on the emotional states themselves and orienting them towards an interpersonal approach involving emotional sensitivity. Consistent with previous work, mothers used more emotional explanations with boys across all age groups. Here is a nice example:

> *Mother (M) and three-year-old son (S)*
> M: How do you feel about them [the parents] going away?
> S: Um, he's afraid.
> M: He's afraid? What makes him afraid?
> S: He's not afraid.
> M: He's not afraid? Does he know that Sam will take good care of him [while his parents are gone]?
> S: [nods]

Notice how she avoids the discussion of fear and his feeling of it. She explains it away for him. These results about the quality of the mother's talk could not be explained by child talkativeness, general language competence, or the child's use of emotional language.

14. The heart of this story is told in a few lines in chapter 4 (verses 2–16) of the Book of Genesis, ending with 'Then Cain went out from the Lord's presence and settled in the land of Nod to the east of Eden.' Oxford Study Edition of the New English Bible (New York: Oxford University Press, 1976). A detailed discussion of this story can be found in E. Weisel, 'Cain and Abel: The First Genocide', in *Messengers of God: Biblical Portraits and Legends* (New York: Random House, 1976), 37–68.

## 2. Thorns among Roses

1. See K. L. Alexander and D. R. Entwisle, 'Achievement in the First 2 Years of School: Patterns and Processes', *Monographs of the Society for Research in Child Development* 53, 2 (1988), serial 218.

2. Diane Halpern gives a cogent discussion of this in 'Sex Differences in Intelligence: Implications for Education', *American Psychologist* 52 (1997): 1091–1102. She reviews the literature and although she finds a few differences between boys and girls on aspects of intelligence, rather than discuss these as part of the nature–nurture debate, she adopts a psychobio-social model wherein the inextricable links between the biological bases of intelligence and environmental events are emphasized. From the article: 'A predisposition to learn some behaviors and concepts more easily than others is determined by prior learning experiences, the neurochemical processes that allow learning to occur (release of neurotransmitters) and change in response to learning [such as] changes in areas of the brain that are active during performance of a task' (1092).

3. These findings are discussed in J. Huttenlocher, W. Haight, A. Bryk, M. Seltzer, et al., 'Early Vocabulary Growth: Relation to Language Input and Gender', *Developmental Psychology* 27 (1991): 236–48: and S. E. Shaywitz, B. A. Shaywitz, J. M. Fletcher, and M. D. Escobar, 'Prevalence of Reading Disability in Boys and Girls: Results of the Connecticut Longitudinal Study', *Journal of the American Medical Association* 264 (1990): 998–1002.

4. Gender differences in activity level are reviewed in G. A. Kohnstamm, 'Temperament in Childhood: Cross-cultural and Sex Differences', in *Temperament in Childhood*, ed. G. A. Kohnstamm, J. E. Bates, and M. K. Rothbart (New York: Wiley, 1989), 483–508; and E. E. Maccoby, *The Two Sexes: Growing Up Apart, Coming Together* (Cambridge, MA: Belknap Press of Harvard University Press, 1998).

5. There has been a recent debate about whether boys really have a higher prevalence of ADHD than girls, especially for the primarily inattentive (i.e. non-hyperactive) type of ADHD. But when the prevalence statistics include only the impulsive-hyperactive type of ADHD, boys are shown to have a higher prevalence. This is discussed in a recent review: E. A. Acia and K. C. Connors, 'Gender Differences in ADHD?' *Developmental and Behavioral Pediatrics* 19 (1998): 77–83; and a recent epidemiological study in Tennessee: M. L. Wolraich, J. N. Hannah, T. Y. Pinnock, A. Baumgaertel, and J. Bown, 'Comparison of Diagnostic Criteria for Attention-Deficit Hyperactivity Disorder in a County-Wide Sample', *Journal of the American Academy of Child and Adolescent Psychiatry* 35 (1996): 319–24.

6. This is discussed in J. Kagan and N. Snidman, 'Infant Predictors of Inhibited and Uninhibited Profiles', *Psychological Science* 2 (1991): 40–44.

7. See J. M. Safer, W. Zito, and L. Fine, 'Increased Methylphenidate Usage for Attention Deficit Disorder in the 1990's', *Pediatrics* 98 (1996): 1084–88.

8. The 'official' diagnostic criteria for ADHD can be found in American Psychiatric Association, *Diagnostic and Statistical Manual of Mental Disorders*, 4th ed. (DSM-IV) (Washington, DC: American Psychiatric Association, 1994). See also N. Hallowell and J. Ratey, *Driven to Distraction* (New York: Pantheon, 1994).

## 3. The High Cost of Harsh Discipline

1. In chapter 11 of *The Myth of Male Power: Why Men are the Disposable Sex* (London: Fourth Estate, 1994), Warren Farrell writes about his view that 'the system protects women', citing these justice department statistics and adding that in North Carolina convictions of second-degree murder result in an extra 12.6 years of prison sentence for men and that sentences are longer even when crime and offence history are equated.

2. This is taken from Table E of J. Austin, B. Krisberg, R. DeComo, S. Rudenstine, and D. Del Rosario, 'Juveniles Taken into Custody: Fiscal Year 1993' (Washington, DC: Office of Juvenile Justice and Delinquency Prevention, 1995). This table shows that boys are detained by the courts at higher rates than girls for all offences. For drug offences, 37 per cent of boys are detained compared with 26 per cent of girls. This ratio of a 1.5 times higher detention rate for boys holds for all crimes (22 per cent males, 15 per cent females). Interestingly, these gender differences are of the same magnitude as the detention differences between white and non-white delinquency cases (17 per cent for whites, 26 per cent for non-whites).

3. These data are taken from the U.S. Office for Education, Office for Civil Rights, Elementary and Secondary School Civil Rights Compliance Report, as discussed in J. Gregory, 'Three Strikes and They're Out: African-American Boys and American Schools' Responses to Misbehavior', *International Journal of Adolescence and Youth* 7 (1997): 25–34.

4. Perhaps the most outspoken critic of spanking is Murray Strauss, who has written extensively on its harmful effects. His 1994 book, *Beating the Devil Out of Them: Corporal Punishment in American Families* (New York: Lexington Books), lists problems caused by spanking and other forms of corporal punishment: increased risk of depression and suicide, criminality, substance abuse, and engaging in masochistic sex practices as adults. In the book Strauss reports on the findings of the National Family Violence

Surveys of 1975 and 1985, from which these statistics were taken. In another article, M. A. Strauss, D. B. Sugerman, and J. Giles-Sims, 'Spanking by Parents and Subsequent Antisocial Behavior of Children', *Archives of Pediatrics and Adolescent Medicine* 151 (1997): 761–67, Strauss describes the decrease in the prevalence of corporal punishment since the 1950s but claims that even today its practice is commonplace. The findings from the survey of residents of Ontario, Canada, were reported in H. L. MacMillan, et al., 'Prevalence of Child Physical and Sexual Abuse in the Community', *Journal of the American Medical Association* 278 (1997): 131–35.

5. This is taken from sociologist Phillip Davis's report summarizing more than three hundred hours of first-hand observations he and his graduate students made of 'naturally occurring threats' happening mostly in shopping centres between 1989 and 1991. P. W. Davis, 'Threats of Corporal Punishment as Verbal Aggression: A Naturalistic Study', *Child Abuse and Neglect* 20 (1996): 289–304.

6. This is taken from P. K. Trickett and L. Kuczynski, 'Children's Misbehaviors and Parental Discipline Strategies in Abusive and Nonabusive Families', *Developmental Psychology* 22 (1986): 115–23.

7. This was written to the 'Ask Beth' column and published in the *Boston Globe* on September 12, 1997 (D15). The columnist responded with excellent advice to this mother, including warning about both the futility and harmful effects of yelling at her sons.

8. This is from G. H. Elder, J. K. Liker, and C. E. Cross, 'Parent–child Behavior in the Great Depression: Life Course and Intergenerational Influences', *Life-Span Development and Behavior* 6 (1984): 109–58.

9. The work of Grazyna Kochanska and Martin Hoffman has greatly influenced our thinking about conscience development, including the role of different memory processes. This is discussed in M. L. Hoffman, 'Discipline and Internalization', *Developmental Psychology* 30 (1994): 26–28; also, G. Kochanska, 'Toward a Synthesis of Parental Socialization and Child Temperament in the Development of Conscience', *Child Development* 64 (1993): 325–47.

10. From A. P. Goldstein, *Delinquents on Delinquency* (Champaign, IL: Research Press, 1990), 38.

11. This is from Z. Strassberg, K. A. Dodge, G. S. Petit, and J. E. Bates, 'Spanking in the Home and Children's Subsequent Aggression Toward Kindergarten Peers', *Development and Psychopathology* 6 (1994): 445–61.

## 4. The Culture of Cruelty

1. There is a growing body of literature that discusses the boys who feel the most extreme effects of the culture of cruelty: those who are systematically bullied or rejected. Although rejection or bullying at any age can lead to behavioural problems such as aggression or sadness, by the age of twelve or thirteen, high levels of loneliness become a salient feature for submissive boys who are rejected by their peers. In part, it is the fear of ending up like these boys that makes all boys this age feel vulnerable. See D. Olweus, *Aggression in the Schools: Bullies and Whipping Boys* (New York: Wiley, 1978); D. S. J. Hawker and M. J. Bolton, 'Peer Victimisation and Psychosocial Adjustment: Findings with a British Sample' (paper presented at the biennial meeting of the Society for Research on Child Development, Washington, DC, April 3, 1997); and J. T. Parkhurst and S. R. Asher, 'Peer Rejection in Middle School: Subgroup Differences in Behavior Loneliness and Interpersonal Concerns', *Developmental Psychology* 28 (1992): 231–41.

2. Aspects of this are discussed in T. Alferi, D. N. Ruble, and E. T. Higgins, 'Gender Stereotypes during Adolescence: Developmental Changes and the Transition to Junior High School', *Developmental Psychology* 32 (1996): 1129–37. These authors note that even though their increased cognitive maturation should allow them greater flexibility in their thinking about gender, adolescent boys become more rigid about gender roles in part because there is increased pressure to be sexually attractive. The initial transition into the very new realm of middle school requires quite a bit of adaptation, and as a result there is increased flexibility in thinking about gender roles. But entrance into middle school also includes a concomitant exposure to older adolescents who have begun to date. This makes gender more salient, and rigidity about gender roles increases into high school.

3. This is taken from D. Gilmore, *Manhood in the Making: Cultural Concepts of Masculinity* (New Haven: Yale University Press, 1990), 15.

4. For more information on growing up gay we recommend E. Bass and K. Kaufman, *Free Your Mind: The Book for Gay, Lesbian, and Bisexual Youth and Their Allies* (New York: HarperCollins, 1996), and E. Marcus, *Is It a Choice? Answers to 300 of the Most Frequently Asked Questions about Gays and Lesbians* (San Francisco: HarperCollins, 1993).

5. The full reference is M. Signorile, *Queer in America: Sex, Media, and the Closets of Power* (New York: Bantam Doubleday Dell, 1993). He discusses his gang experiences in chapter 2 of that book.

6. This is from an article by N. R. Kleinfield entitled 'Friends, from Boys to Men', *New York Times*, June 3, 1997, B1.

## 5. Lost Fathers, Lost Sons

1. This article by Patricia Cohen appeared on July 11, 1998, on pages A1 and A15 of *The New York Times*.
2. The October 1996 meeting was the Conference on Father Involvement sponsored by the National Institute of Child Health and Human Development (NICHD) Family and Child Well-Being Network, held in Bethesda, Maryland, on October 10 and 11.
3. The conference paper was: G. J. Duncan, M. Hill, J. Yeung, 'Fathers' Activities and Child Attainments' (paper presented at the NICHD Family and Child Well-Being Network's Conference on Father Involvement, Bethesda, Maryland, October 10–11, 1996). For more on the Panel Study of Income Dynamics see M. Hill, *The Panel Study of Income Dynamics* (Newbury Park, CA: Russell Sage, 1992).
4. The full citation is: K. M. Harris, F. F. Furstenberg Jr., and J. K. Kramer, 'Paternal Involvement with Adolescents in Intact Families: The Influence of Fathers Over the Life Course', *Demography* 35 (1998): 201–16.
5. This is the continuation of the Patterns of Child Rearing study begun in the 1950s by Robert Sears and Eleanor Maccoby. The current study was published as R. Koestner, C. Franz, and J. Weinberger, 'The Family Origins of Empathic Concern: A 26-Year Longitudinal Study', *Journal of Personality and Social Psychology* 58 (1990): 709–17.
6. See K. M. Harris and S. P. Morgan, 'Fathers, Sons and Daughters: Differential Paternal Involvement in Parenting', *Journal of Marriage and the Family* 53 (1990): 531–44; and K. M. Harris, F. F. Furstenberg Jr., and J. K. Kramer, 'Paternal Involvement with Adolescents in Intact Families: The Influence of Fathers Over the Life Course', *Demography* 35 (1998): 201–16.
7. This information on changes in the level of father involvement in child care is taken from an excellent review of father involvement research: J. H. Pleck, 'Paternal Involvement: Levels, Sources, and Consequences', in *The Role of the Father in Child Development*, ed. M. E. Lamb (New York: Wiley, 1997), 68–103. Two other good general sources on research on fathers can be found in the volume edited by Michael Lamb in which the Pleck article appears and in R. D. Parke, *Fatherhood* (Cambridge, MA: Harvard University Press, 1996).
8. The full citation is: T. DeLong and C. C. DeLong, 'Managers as Fathers: Hope on the Homefront', *Human Resource Management* 32 (1992): 178. This piece and related work are also discussed in J. A. Levine and T. L. Pittinsky, *Working Fathers: New Strategies for Balancing Work and Family* (New York: Addison-Wesley, 1997), especially chapter 6.
9. This material is a summary of pages 122–28 of E. Erikson, *Identity Youth and Crisis* (New York: W. W. Norton, 1968).

10. This is from R. Larson and M. Richards, *Divergent Realities: The Emotional Lives of Mothers, Fathers, and Adolescents* (New York: Basic Books, 1994).
11. This is from J. Youniss and J. Smollar, *Adolescent Relations with Mothers, Fathers and Friends* (Chicago: University of Chicago Press, 1985).

## 6. Mothers and Sons

1. There is a voluminous literature in psychology on characteristics and consequences of mother–child attachment. Many studies have shown that disordered attachment, such as an insecure or disorganized mother–child bond, contributes to later problems in the child, such as disruptive behaviour in school, depression/anxiety, and poorer cognitive functioning. Some recent articles on this topic are: K. Lyons-Ruth, M. A. Easterbroks, and C. D. Cibelli, 'Infant Attachment Strategies, Infant Mental Lag, and Maternal Depressive Symptoms: Predictors of Internalizing and Externalizing Problems at Age 7', *Developmental Psychology* 33 (1997): 681–92; and E. A. Carslon, 'A Prospective Longitudinal Study of Attachment Disorganization/Disorientation', *Child Development* 69 (1998): 1107–28.
2. Scientists have known for more than forty years that laboratory animals that were stroked and handled for even fifteen minutes a day during the newborn period ended up being smarter and better able to handle stress. More recently it has been shown (see D. Liu et al., 'Maternal Care, Hippocampal Glucocorticoid Receptors and Hypothalamic-Pituitary-Adrenal Responses to Stress', *Science* 277 [1997]: 1659–62) that mother rats who naturally engage in more licking and grooming of their pups have offspring that when they are adults show healthier stress responses than the adult offspring of mother rats who lick and groom less. In a commentary on the Liu et al. article, Robert Sapolsky (R. M. Sapolsky, 'The Importance of a Well-groomed Child', *Science* 277 [1998]: 1620–21) suggests that the findings are directly relevant to humans: 'Although specific licking and grooming do not tend to humans the broader point emphasizing the importance of early experience does' (1620–21).

## 8. Boys' Struggle with Depression and Suicide

1. According to 'The Emergence of Youth Suicide: An Epidemiologic Analysis and Public Health Perspective' by M. Rosenberg, J. Smith, L. Davidson, and J. Cohn (*Annual Review of Public Health* 8 [1987]: 420), the suicide rate for adolescents (ages 15–24) has gone up from under 4 per cent in 1950 to nearly 15 per cent in 1986 (see also R. F. Diekstra and N.

Garnefski, 'On the Nature, Magnitude and Causality of Suicidal Behaviors: An International Perspective', *Suicide and Life Threatening Behaviors* 25 [1995]: 36–57). Between 1979 and 1991, suicide rates for young people ages fifteen to nineteen rose nearly 34.5 per cent, but for younger children (ages ten to fourteen) during this same period, suicide rates climbed 75 per cent (in C. W. Sells and R. W. Blum, 'Morbidity and Mortality among U.S. Adolescents: An Overview of Data and Trends', *American Journal of Public Health* 86 [1996]: 513–19). The recent trend for the suicide rate among fifteen- to nineteen-year-old males has nearly tripled, going from 6 per 100,000 in 1965 to 17.8 per 100,000 in 1992 (see D. Shaffer, M. Gould, P. Fisher, et al., 'Psychiatric Diagnosis in Child and Adolescent Suicide', *Archives of General Psychiatry* 53 [1996]: 339–48).

2. This is taken from B. Birmaher et al., 'Childhood and Adolescent Depression: A Review of the Past 10 Years. Part I', *Journal of the American Academy of Child and Adolescent Psychiatry* 35 (1996): 1427–39. These authors discuss the epidemiology of both dysthmic disorder (DD) and major depressive disorder (MDD). At a given point in time, studies have found that the number of children with MDD ranges between 0.4 per cent and 2.5 per cent; and between 0.4 per cent and 8.3 per cent in adolescents. The figures for DD are similar: 0.6 per cent to 1.7 per cent in children and 1.6 per cent to 8.0 per cent in adolescents. The lifetime prevalence for MDD among teenagers (number of teens reporting whether they have ever had MDD whether or not they currently have it) has been estimated to be between 15 per cent and 20 per cent.

3. These figures are taken from National Center for Health Statistics, 'Deaths for 72 Selected Causes, by 5 Year Age Groups, Race and Sex: United States 1979–1995, Trend B', Table 291A (1997).

4. Gary Remafedi, *Death by Denial: Studies of Suicide in Gay and Lesbian Teenagers* (Boston: Alyson Publications, 1997).

5. See H. Z. Reinherz et al., 'Early Psychosocial Risks for Adolescent Suicidal Ideation and Attempts', *Journal of the American Academy of Child and Adult Psychiatry* 34 (1995): 599–611.

## 9. Drinking and Drugs

1. This is taken from J. A. Webb, P. E. Baer, and R. S. McKelvey, 'Development of a Risk Profile for Intentions to Use Alcohol among Fifth and Sixth Graders', *Journal of the American Academy of Child and Adolescent Psychiatry* 34 (1995): 772–78. They report in their study of 136 10–12-year-old students in Houston, Texas, that 89 per cent of the 10–11-year-olds say they have no intention of drinking beer while they are in middle school. That number dropped slightly for 11–12-year-olds.

2. These statistics are taken from L. B. Johnston, J. Bachman, and P. O'Malley, *Monitoring the Future: National High School Drug Use Survey* (Washington, DC: National Institute on Drug Abuse. Data for 1975–1995 were available at the time of this writing).

3. This is reported in M. D. Slater, D. Rouner, K. Murphy, F. Beauvais, J. Van Leuven, et al., 'Male Adolescents' Reactions to TV Beer Advertisements: The Effect of Sports Content and Programming Context', *Journal of Studies on Alcohol* 57 (1996): 425–33.

4. Ethanol's effects on the brain are reviewed in R. O. Pihl and J. B. Peterson, 'Alcoholism: The Role of Different Motivational Systems', *Journal of Psychiatry and Neuroscience* 20 (1995): 372–96.

5. The full citation is G. Canada, *Reaching Up for Manhood: Transforming the Lives of Boys in America* (Boston: Beacon Press, 1998): 72.

6. This is taken from an article entitled 'A Way of Life at College and One Drunken Death', by William Glaberson, published in *The New York Times*, midwest edition, page A17, on November 3, 1997.

7. See the discussion in L. P. Ellickson, K. A. McGuigan, V. Adams, R. M. Bell, and R. D. Hays, 'Teenagers and Alcohol Misuse in the United States: By Any Definition It's a Big Problem', *Addiction* 91 (1996): 1489–1503.

8. This information comes from several sources: on drunk driving, binge drinking, and fighting, see L. P. Ellickson, K. A. McGuigan, V. Adams, R. M. Bell, and R. D. Hays, 'Teenagers and Alcohol Misuse in the United States: By Any Definition It's a Big Problem', *Addiction* 91 (1996): 1489–1503. For alcohol arrests, see H. N. Synder, 'Juvenile Arrests for Driving Under the Influence, 1995', OJJDP Fact Sheet 67, Washington, DC: U.S. Department of Justice, 1997. For sexual behaviour, see L. L. Langer and J. G. Tubman, 'Risky Sexual Behavior among Substance-Abusing Adolescents: Psychosocial and Contextual Factors', *American Journal of Orthopsychiatry* 67 (1997): 315–22. For special risks associated with beginning drinking at a young age, see E. Gruber, R. J. DiClemente, M. M. Anderson, and M. Lodico, 'Early Drinking Onset and Its Association with Alcohol Use and Problem Behavior in Late Adolescence', *Preventive Medicine: An International Journal Devoted to Practice and Theory* 25 (1996): 293–300.

9. The primary sources for this section are J. C. Froehlich, 'Opiod Peptides', *Alcohol Health and Research World* 21 (1997): 132–35; and R. O. Pihl and J. B. Peterson, 'Alcoholism: The Role of Different Motivational Systems', *Journal of Psychiatry and Neuroscience* 20 (1995): 372–96.

## 10. Romancing the Stone

1. This is from pages 145–147 of B. Lefkowitz, *Our Guys: The Glen Ridge Rape and the Secret Life of the Perfect Suburb* (Berkeley: University of California Press, 1997).

## 11. Anger and Violence

1. These data are taken from reports from the Office of Juvenile Justice and Delinquency Prevention: H. N. Synder and M. Sickmund, 'Juvenile Offenders and Victims: A Focus on Violence', Pittsburgh, PA, National Center for Juvenile Justice, 1995; H. N. Synder, 'Juvenile Arrests: 1996', OJJDP Juvenile Justice Bulletin, Washington, DC, U.S. Department of Justice, November 1997. For example, the data from 1996 showed that of the 2,900 arrests of juveniles for murder or non-negligent manslaughter, 93 per cent were male. Eighty-five per cent of the 1996 juvenile arrests for violent crimes – murder, forcible rape, robbery, and aggravated assault – were male.
2. Alan Cowell, 'Now, Teenagers Turn to Crime', *New York Times*, March 25, 1998, E1.
3. This is from a letter published in *USA Today* on March 27, 1998, 12A.
4. The primary source of this information comes from John Archer, *The Behavioral Biology of Aggression* (Cambridge: Cambridge University Press, 1988).
5. The full citation is B. Schaal, R. E. Tremblay, R. Soussignan, and E. J. Susman, 'Male Testosterone Linked to High Social Dominance but Low Physical Aggression in Early Adolescence', *Journal of the American Academy of Child and Adolescent Psychiatry* 34 (1996): 1322–30.
6. Michael Holley, column in the *Boston Globe*, November 26, 1998, E1.
7. Dodge has published extensively in this area. Two primary sources for us were: K. A. Dodge, G. S. Pettit, C. L. McClaskey, and M. M. Brown, 'Social Competence in Children', *Monographs of the Society for Research in Child Development*, serial 213, 51, no. 2 (1986); and K. A. Dodge and D. R. Somberg, 'Hostile Attributional Bias among Aggressive Boys Are Exacerbated under Conditions of Threat to Self', *Child Development* 58 (1987): 213–24.
8. Three sources used for this section on drinking and male violence are K. A. Miczek, E. M. Weerts, and J. F. DeBold, 'Alcohol Aggression and Violence: Biobehavioral Determinants', in *Alcohol and Interpersonal Violence: Fostering Multidisciplinary Perspectives*, ed. S. E. Martin (NIAAA Research Monograph 24), Rockville, MD: National Institutes of Health,

1993, 83–119; R. O. Pihl and J. B. Peterson, 'Alcohol, Serotonin, and Aggression', Special Issue: Alcohol, Aggression, and Injury, *Alcohol Health and Research World* 17 (1993): 113–16; and C. R. Cloninger, S. Sigvardsson, T. R. Przybeck, and D. M. Svrakic, 'Personality Antecedents of Alcoholism in a National Area Probability Sample', *European Archives of Psychiatry and Clinical Neuroscience* 245 (1995): 239–44.

9. A review of the research literature on this topic can be found in T. E. Moffitt, 'The Neuropsychology of Juvenile Delinquency: A Critical Review of Research and Theory', in *Crime and Justice: A Review of Research*, vol. 12, ed. M. Tonry and N. Morris (Chicago: University of Chicago Press, 1990).

# References

Much of what we have said in this book comes from our experience as therapists to boys and as consultants to schools. We have also made much use of scientific research and other scholarly work. The references that follow are selected books and research articles that have influenced our thinking.

## 1. The Road Not Taken

Archer, J. 'The Influence of Testosterone on Human Aggression'. *British Journal of Psychology* 82 (1991): 1–28.

Beal, C. R. *Boys and Girls: The Development of Gender Roles*. New York: McGraw Hill, 1994.

Blum, D. *Sex on the Brain: The Biological Differences Between Men and Women*. New York: Viking, 1994.

Bremmer, J. D., P. Randall, T. M. Scott, R. A. Bronen, J. P. Seibyl, et al. 'MRI-Based Measurement of Hippocampal Volume in Patients with Combat-Related Posttraumatic Stress Disorder.' *American Journal of Psychiatry* 152 (1995): 973–81.

Briggs, J. L. *Never in Anger: Portrait of an Eskimo Family*. Cambridge, MA: Harvard University Press, 1970.

Brody, L. R. 'Gender, Emotional Expression, and Parent–Child Boundaries.' In *Emotion: Interdisciplinary Perspectives*, ed. R. D. Kavanaugh, B. Zimmerberg, and S. Fein. Mahwah, NJ: Lawrence Erlbaum, 1996, 139–170.

Campbell, L., K. J. Anderson, and P. Sanders. 'Moderators of Gender Effects on Parents' Talk to Their Children: A Meta-Analysis.' *Developmental Psychology* 34 (1998): 3–27.

Cervantes, C. A., and M. A. Callanan. 'Labels and Explanations in Mother–Child Emotion Talk: Age and Gender Differentiation.' *Developmental Psychology* 34 (1998): 88–98.

Constantino, J. N., D. Grosz, P. Saenger, D. W. Chandler, R. Nandi, and F. J. Earls. 'Testosterone and Aggression in Children.' *Journal of the American Academy of Child and Adolescent Psychiatry* 32 (1993): 1217–22.

Denham, S., D. Zoller, and E. A. Couchoud. 'Socialization of Preschoolers'

Emotion Understanding.' *Developmental Psychology* 30 (1994): 928–36.

Denton, R. K. 'Notes on Childhood in a Nonviolent Context.' In *Learning Non-Aggression: The Experience of Non-Literature Societies*, ed. A. Monagu. New York: Oxford University Press, 1978, 94–143.

———. 'Surrendered Men: Peaceable Enclaves in the Post Enlightenment West.' In *The Anthropology of Peace and Nonviolence*, ed. L. E. Sponsel and T. Gregor. London: Lynne Rienner, 1994, 69–108.

Diamond, A. 'Rate of Maturation of the Hippocampus and the Developmental Progression of Children's Performance on the Delayed Non-Matching to Sample and Visual Paired Comparison Tasks.' *Annals of the New York Academy of Sciences* 608 (1990): 394–426.

DiGeorge, A. M. 'Disorders of the Gonads.' In *Textbook of Pediatrics*, 10th ed., ed. V. C. Vaughn III, R. J. McKay, and W. E. Nelson. Philadelphia: W. B. Saunders, 1975, 1347–54.

Dunn, J., J. R. Brown, and L. Beardsall. 'Family Talk about Feelingstates and Children's Later Understanding of Others' Emotions.' *Developmental Psychology* 27 (1991): 448–55.

Dunn, J., J. R. Brown, and M. Maguire. 'The Development of Children's Moral Sensibility: Individual Differences and Emotion Understanding.' *Developmental Psychology* 31 (1995): 649–59.

Eron, L. D. 'Gender Differences in Violence: Biology and/or Socialization?' In *Of Mice and Women: Aspects of Female Aggression*, ed. K. Bjorkqvist and P. Niemela. New York: Academic Press, 1992, 89–97.

Fabes, R. A., N. Eisenberg, and L. Eisenbud. 'Behavioral and Physiological Correlates of Children's Reactions to Others in Distress.' *Developmental Psychology* 29, no. 4 (1993): 655–33.

Fabes, R. A., N. Eisenberg, M. Karbon, D. Troyer, and G. Switzer. 'The Relations of Children's Emotion Regulation to Their Vicarious Emotional Responses and Comforting Behaviors.' *Child Development* 65 (1994): 1678–93.

Fivush, R. 'Emotional Content of Parent–Child Conversations about the Past.' In *Memory and Affection Development: The Minnesota Symposium on Child Psychology*, ed. C. A. Nelson. Hillsdale, NJ: Lawrence Erlbaum, 1993, vol. 26, 39–78.

Fry, D. P. 'Intercommunity Differences in Aggression among Zapotec Children.' *Child Development* 59 (1988): 1008–19.

Hort, B. E., B. I. Fagot, and M. D. Leinbach. 'Are People's Notions of Maleness More Stereotypically Framed Than Their Notions of Femaleness?' *Sex Roles* 23 (1990): 197–212.

Izard, C., D. Schultz, and B. P. Ackerman. 'Emotion Knowledge, Social Competence, and Behavior Problems in Disadvantaged Children.' Paper presented at the biennial meeting of the Society for Research on Child Development, Washington, DC, April 1997, 4.

Kesner, R. P., B. L. Bolland, and M. Dakis. 'Memory for Spatial Locations, Motor Responses, and Objects: Triple Dissociation among the Hippocampus, Caudate Nucleus, and Extrastriate Visual Cortex.' *Experimental Brain Research* 93 (1993): 462–70.

Lamb, M. E., R. D. Ketterlinus, and M. P. Fracasso. 'Parent Child Relationships.' In *Developmental Psychology: An Advanced Textbook*, 3rd ed., ed. M. H. Bornstein and M. E. Lamb. Hillsdale, NJ: Lawrence Erlbaum, 1992, 465–518.

Leaper, C., J. Anderson, and P. Sanders. 'Moderators of Gender Effects of Parents Talk with Their Children: A Meta-Analysis.' *Developmental Psychology* 43 (1998): 3–27.

Maccoby, E. E. *The Two Sexes: Growing Up Apart, Coming Together.* Cambridge, MA: Belknap Press of Harvard University Press, 1998.

Maccoby, Eleanor, and Carol Jacklin. *The Psychology of Sex Differences.* Stanford, CA: Stanford University Press, 1974.

McEwen, B. S., J. Angulo, H. Cameron, H. M. Chao, D. Daniels, et al. 'Paradoxical Effects of Adrenal Steroids on the Brain: Protection versus Degeneration.' *Biological Psychiatry* 31 (1992): 177–99.

Oxford Study Edition of the New English Bible. New York: Oxford University Press, 1976.

Pleck, J. H., F. L. Sonenstein, and L. C. Ku. 'Masculinity Ideology: Its Impact on Adolescent Males' Heterosexual Relationships.' *Journal of Social Issues* 49 (1993): 11–29.

Pleck, J. H., F. L. Sonenstein, L. C. Ku, and L. C. Burbridge. *Individual, Family, and Community Factors Modifying Male Adolescents' Risk Behavior 'Trajectory.'* Washington, DC: The Urban Institute, 1996.

Robarchek, C. A. 'Ghosts and Witches: The Psychocultural Dynamics of Semoi Peacefulness.' In *The Anthropology of Peace and Nonviolence*, ed. L. E. Sponsel and T. Gregor. London: Lynne Rienner, 1994, 183–96.

Rosenblatt, N. H., and J. Horwitz. 'Cain and Abel: Confronting the Beast of Rage Within.' In *Wrestling with Angels*, ed. N. Rosenblatt and J. Horwitz. New York: Delacorte, 1995, 52–64.

Sapolsky, R., L. Krey, and B. S. McEwen. 'The Neuroendocrinology of Stress and Aging: The Glucocorticoid Cascade Hypothesis.' *Endocrinology Review* 7 (1986): 284–301.

Shibley, J., E. F. Hyde, and S. J. Lamon. 'Gender Differences in Mathematics Performance: A Meta-analysis.' *Psychological Bulletin* 107 (1990): 139–55.

Tremblay, R. E., B. Schaal, B. Boulerice, L. Arseneault, R. Soussignan, and D. Perusse. 'Male Physical Aggression, Social Dominance and Testosterone Levels at Puberty: A Developmental Perspective.' In *Biosocial Bases of Violence*, ed. A. Raine, P. A. Brennan, D. P. Farrington, and A. S. Mednick. New York: Plenum Press, 1997, 271–91.

Turnbull, C. M. 'The Politics of Non-Aggression.' In *Learning Non-Aggression:*

*The Experience of Non-Literate Societies*, ed. A. Monagu. New York: Oxford University Press, 1978, 161–221.

Weisel, E. 'Cain and Abel: The First Genocide.' In *Messengers of God: Biblical Portraits and Legends*, ed. E. Weisel. New York: Random House, 1976, 37–68.

Wintre, M. G., J. Polivy, and M. A. Murray. 'Self-Predictions of Emotional Response Patterns: Age, Sex, and Situational Determinants.' *Child Development* 61 (1990): 1124–33.

## 2. Thorns among Roses

Acia, E. A., and K. C. Connors. 'Gender Differences in ADHD?' *Developmental and Behavioral Pediatrics* 19 (1998): 77–83.

Alexander, K. L., and D. R. Entwisle. 'Achievement in the First 2 Years of School: Patterns and Processes.' *Monographs of the Society for Research in Child Development* 53:2 (1988), serial 218.

American Psychiatric Association. *Diagnostic and Statistical Manual of Mental Disorders*, 4th ed. (DSM-IV). Washington, DC: American Psychiatric Association, 1994.

Cantwell, D. P. 'Attention Deficit Disorder: A Review of the Past 10 Years.' *Journal of the American Academy of Child and Adolescent Psychiatry* 35 (1996): 978–87.

Hallowell, N., and J. Ratey. *Driven to Distraction*. New York: Pantheon, 1994.

Halpern, D. F. 'Sex Differences in Intelligence: Implications for Education.' *American Psychologist* 52 (1997): 1091–1102.

Huttenlocher, J., W. Haight, A. Bryk, M. Seltzer, et al. 'Early Vocabulary Growth: Relation to Language Input and Gender.' *Developmental Psychology* 27 (1991): 236–48.

Jackson, A. W. and D. W. Hornbeck. 'Educating Young Adolescents: Why We Must Restructure Middle Grade Schools.' *American Psychologist* 44 (1989): 831–36.

Kagan, J. and N. Snidman. 'Infant Predictors of Inhibited and Uninhibited Profiles.' *Psychological Science* 2 (1991): 40–44.

Kohnstamm, G. A. 'Temperament in Childhood: Cross-cultural and Sex Differences.' In *Temperament in Childhood*, ed. G. A. Kohnstamm, J. E. Bates, and M. K. Rothbart. New York: Wiley, 1989, 483–508.

Luria, A. R. *The Role of Speech in the Regulation of Normal and Abnormal Behavior*. London: Pergamon Press, 1961.

Maccoby, E. E. *The Two Sexes: Growing Up Apart, Coming Together*. Cambridge, MA: Belknap Press of Harvard University Press, 1998.

Rothbart, M. K. 'Temperament in Childhood: A Framework.' In *Temperament in Childhood*, ed. G. Kohnstamm, J. Bates, and M. Rothbart. New York: Wiley, 1989, 59–73.

Safer, J. W., W. Zito, and L. Fine. 'Increased Methylphenidate Usage for Attention Deficit Disorder in the 1990's.' *Pediatrics* 98 (1996): 1084–88.

Shaywitz, S. E., B. A. Shaywitz, J. M. Fletcher, and M. D. Escobar. 'Prevalence of Reading Disability in Boys and Girls: Results of the Connecticut Longitudinal Study.' *Journal of the American Medical Association* 264 (1990): 998–1002.

Wolraich, M. L., J. N. Hannah, T. Y. Pinnock, A. Baumgaertel, and J. Bown. 'Comparison of Diagnostic Criteria for Attention-Deficit Hyperactivity Disorder in a County-Wide Sample.' *Journal of the American Academy of Child and Adolescent Psychiatry* 35 (1996): 319–24.

## 3. The High Cost of Harsh Discipline

Austin, J., B. Krisberg, R. DeComo, S. Rudenstine, and D. Del Rosario 'Juveniles Taken into Custody: Fiscal Year 1993.' Washington, DC. Office of Juvenile Justice and Delinquency Prevention, 1995.

Chamberlin, P., and G. R. Patterson. 'Discipline and Child Compliance in Parenting.' In *Handbook of Parenting Applied and Practical Parenting*, vol. 4, ed. Marc H. Bornstein. Mahwah, NJ: Lawrence Erlbaum Associates, 1995, 205–25.

Conger, R., X. Ge, G. H. Elder, F. O. Lorenz, and R. L. Simons. 'Economic Stress, Coercive Family Processes and Developmental Problems of Adolescents.' *Child Development* 65 (1994): 541–61.

Davis, P. W. 'Threats of Corporal Punishment as Verbal Aggression: A Naturalistic Study.' *Child Abuse and Neglect* 20 (1996): 289–304.

Dishion, T. J., T. E. Duncan, M. Eddy, B. I. Fagot, and R. Fetrow. 'The World of Parents' and Peers' Coercive Exchanges and Children's Social Adaptation.' *Social Development* 3 (1994): 255–68.

Elder, G. H., J. K. Liker, and C. E. Cross. 'Parent–Child Behavior in the Great Depression: Life Course and Intergenerational Influences.' *Life-Span Development and Behavior* 6 (1984): 109–58.

Farrell, Warren. *The Myth of Male Power: Why Men are the Disposable Sex.* London: Fourth Estate, 1994.

Goldstein, A. P. *Delinquents on Delinquency.* Champaign, IL: Research Press, 1990.

Gregory, J. 'Three Strikes and They're Out: African American Boys and American Schools' Responses to Misbehavior.' *International Journal of Adolescence and Youth* 7 (1997): 25–34.

Hoffman, M. L. 'Discipline and Internalization.' *Developmental Psychology* 30 (1994): 26–28.

Hyman, I. A. *Reading Writing and the Hickory Stick.* Lexington, MA: Lexington Books, 1990.

Kochanska, G. 'Children's Temperament, Mothers' Discipline, and Security of Attachment: Multiple Pathways to Emerging Internalization.' *Child Development* 66 (1995): 597–615.

——. 'Toward a Synthesis of Parental Socialization and Child Temperament in the Early Development of Conscience.' *Child Development* 64 (1993): 325–47.

MacMillan, H. L., et al. 'Prevalence of Child Physical and Sexual Abuse in the Community.' *Journal of the American Medical Association* 278 (1997): 131–35.

Patterson, G. R., B. D. DeBaryshe, and E. Ramsey. 'A Developmental Perspective on Antisocial Behavior.' *American Psychologist* 44 (1989): 329–35.

Schoen, C., K. Davis, C. DesRoches, and A. Shekhdar. *The Health of Adolescent Boys: Commonwealth Fund Survey Findings.* Boston, MA, June 1998.

Strassberg, Z., K. A. Dodge, G. S. Petit, and J. E. Bates. 'Spanking in the Home and Children's Subsequent Aggression toward Kindergarten Peers.' *Development and Psychopathology* 6 (1994): 445–61.

Strauss, M. A. *Beating the Devil Out of Them: Corporal Punishment in American Families.* New York: Lexington Books, 1994.

Strauss, M. A., D. B. Sugerman, and J. Giles-Sims. 'Spanking by Parents and Subsequent Antisocial Behavior of Children.' *Archives of Pediatrics and Adolescent Medicine* 151 (1997): 761–67.

Trickett, P. K., and L. Kuczynski. 'Children's Misbehaviors and Parental Discipline Strategies in Abusive and Nonabusive Families.' *Developmental Psychology* 22 (1986): 115–23.

## 4. The Culture of Cruelty

Alferi, T., D. N. Ruble, and E. T. Higgins. 'Gender Stereotypes during Adolescence: Developmental Changes and the Transition to Junior High School.' *Developmental Psychology* 32 (1996): 1129–37.

Anthony, E. *American Manhood: Transformation in Masculinity from the Revolution to the Modern Era.* New York: Basic Books, 1993.

Faludi, Susan. 'The Naked Citadel.' *The New Yorker*, September 5, 1994, 62–81.

Gilmore, D. *Manhood in the Making: Cultural Concepts of Masculinity.* New Haven: Yale University Press, 1990.

Grossman, D. *On Killing: The Psychological Cost of Learning to Kill in War and Society.* Boston: Little, Brown, 1995.

Hawker, D. S. J., and M. J. Bolton. 'Peer Victimisation and Psychosocial Adjustment: Findings with a British Sample.' Paper presented at the biennial meeting of the Society for Research on Child Development, Washington, DC, April 3, 1997.

Olweus, D. *Aggression in the Schools: Bullies and Whipping Boys.* New York: Wiley, 1978.

Parkhurst, J. T., and S. R. Asher. 'Peer Rejection in Middle School: Subgroup Differences in Behavior Loneliness and Interpersonal Concerns.' *Developmental Psychology* 28 (1992): 231–41.

Signorile, M. *Queer in America: Sex, Media, and the Closets of Power.* New York: Bantam Doubleday Dell, 1993.

Stapley, J. C., and J. M. Haviland. 'Beyond Depression: Gender Differences in Normal Adolescents' Emotional Experiences.' *Sex Roles* 20 (1989): 295–308.

Wolff, Tobias. *This Boy's Life: A Memoir.* New York: Harper & Row, 1989.

## 5. Lost Fathers, Lost Sons

DeLong, T., and C. C. DeLong. 'Managers as Fathers: Hope on the Homefront.' *Human Resource Management* 32 (1992): 178.

Duncan, G. J., M. Hill, and J. Yeung. 'Fathers' Activities and Child Attainments.' Paper presented at the NICHD Family and Child Well-Being Network's Conference on Father Involvement, Bethesda, Maryland. October 10–11, 1996.

Erikson, E. *Identity Youth and Crisis.* New York: W. W. Norton, 1968.

Harris, K. M. and S. P. Morgan. 'Fathers, Sons and Daughters: Differential Paternal Involvement in Parenting.' *Journal of Marriage and the Family* 53 (1991): 531–44.

Harris, K. M., F. F. Furstenberg Jr., and J. K. Kramer. 'Paternal Involvement with Adolescents in Intact Families: The Influence of Fathers Over the Life Course.' *Demography* 35 (1998): 201–16.

Hill, M. *The Panel Study of Income Dynamics.* Newbury Park, CA: Russell Sage, 1992.

Koestner, R., C. Franz, and J. Weinberger. 'The Family Origins of Empathic Concern: A 26-Year Longitudinal Study.' *Journal of Personality and Social Psychology* 58 (1990): 709–17.

LaRossa, R. *The Modernization of Fatherhood: A Social and Political History.* Chicago: University of Chicago Press, 1997.

Larson, R., and M. Richards. *Divergent Realities: The Emotional Lives of Mothers, Fathers, and Adolescents.* New York: Basic Books, 1994.

Levine, J. A., and T. L. Pittinsky. *Working Fathers: New Strategies for Balancing Work and Family.* New York: Addison-Wesley, 1997.

Osherson, S. *Finding Our Fathers: The Unfinished Business of Manhood.* New York: Free Press, 1986.

Parke, R. D. *Fatherhood.* Cambridge, MA: Harvard University Press, 1996.

——. 'Father Involvement: A Developmental Psychological Perspective.'

Paper presented at the NICHD Family and Child Well-Being Network's Conference on Father Involvement, Bethesda, Maryland, October 10–11, 1996.

Pleck, J. H. 'Paternal Involvement: Levels, Sources, and Consequences.' In *The Role of the Father in Child Development*, ed. M. E. Lamb. New York: Wiley, 1997, 68–103.

Yogman, M. W., and D. Kindlon. 'Pediatric Opportunities with Fathers and Children.' *Pediatric Annals* 27 (1998): 16–22.

Yogman, M. W., D. Kindlon, and F. Earls. 'Father Involvement and Cognitive/ Behavioral Outcomes of Premature Infants.' *Journal of the American Academy of Child and Adolescent Psychiatry* 34 (1995): 58–66.

Youniss, J., and J. Smollar. *Adolescent Relations with Mothers, Fathers and Friends*. Chicago: University of Chicago Press, 1985.

## 6. Mothers and Sons

Carslon, E. A. 'A Prospective Longitudinal Study of Attachment Disorganization/ Disorientation.' *Child Development* 69 (1998): 1107–28.

Elium, D., and J. Elium. *Raising a Son: Parents and the Making of a Healthy Man*. Berkeley, CA: Celestial Arts, 1994.

Fagot, B. I., and M. Gauvin. 'Mother–Child Problem Solving: Continuity through the Early Childhood Years.' *Developmental Psychology* 33 (1997): 480–88.

Liu, D., et al. 'Maternal Care, Hippocampal Glucocorticoid Receptors and Hypothalamic-Pituitary-Adrenal Responses to Stress.' *Science* 277 (1997): 1659–62.

Lyons-Ruth, K., M. A. Easterbroks, and C. D. Cibelli. 'Infant Attachment Strategies, Infant Mental Lag, and Maternal Depressive Symptoms: Predictors of Internalizing and Externalizing Problems at Age 7.' *Developmental Psychology* 33 (1997): 681–92.

Resnick, M. D., et al. 'Protecting Adolescents from Harm: Findings from the National Longitudinal Study on Adolescent Health.' *Journal of the American Medical Association* 278 (1997): 823–32.

Ross, J. M. *What Men Want: Mothers, Fathers and Manhood*. Cambridge, MA: Harvard University Press, 1994.

Sapolsky, R. M. 'The Importance of a Well-groomed Child.' *Science* 277 (1998): 1620–21.

Silverstein, O., and B. Rashbaum. *The Courage to Raise Good Men*. New York: Penguin Books, 1994.

## 7. Inside the Fortress of Solitude

Askew, S., and C. Ross. *Boys Don't Cry: Boys and Sexism in Education.* Philadelphia: Open University Press, Milton Keynes, 1988.

Cole, P. M., C. Zahn-Waxler, and K. D. Smith. 'Expressive Control during a Disappointment: Variations Related to Preschoolers' Behavior Problems.' *Developmental Psychology* 30 (1988): 835–46.

Davis, T. L. 'Gender Differences in Masking Negative Emotions: Ability or Motivation?' *Developmental Psychology* 31 (1995): 660–67.

Gjerde, P. F. 'Alternate Pathways to Chronic Depressive Symptoms in Young Adults: Gender Differences in Developmental Trajectories.' *Child Development* 66 (1995): 1277–1300.


## 8. Boys' Struggle with Depression and Suicide

American Psychiatric Association. *Diagnostic and Statistical Manual of Mental Disorders*, 4th ed. (DSM-IV). Washington, DC: American Psychiatric Association, 1994.

Anderson, R. N., K. D. Kochanek, and S. L. Murphy. 'Report of Final Mortality Statistics.' *Centers for Disease Control and Prevention/National Center for Health Statistics*, vol. 45, June 12, 1997.

Birmaher, B., et al. 'Childhood and Adolescent Depression: A Review of the Past 10 Years. Part I.' *Journal of the American Academy of Child and Adolescent Psychiatry* 35 (1996): 1427–39.

Birmaher, B., et al. 'Childhood and Adolescent Depression: A Review of the Past 10 Years. Part II.' *Journal of the American Academy of Child and Adolescent Psychiatry* 35 (1996): 1575–83.

Centers for Disease Control and Prevention, National Center for Injury Prevention and Control. 'Suicide in the United States 1980–1992.' Violence Surveillance Summary Series, No. 1, 1995.

Diekstra, R. F., and N. Garnefski. 'On the Nature, Magnitude and Causality of Suicidal Behaviors: An International Perspective.' *Suicide and Life Threatening Behaviors* 25 (1995): 36–57.

Fleming, J. E., and D. R. Offord. 'Epidemiology of Childhood Depressive Disorders: A Critical Review.' *Journal of the American Academy of Child and Adolescent Psychiatry* 29 (1990): 571–80.

Moscicki, E. K. 'Epidemiology of Suicidal Behavior.' *Suicide and Life Threatening Behavior* 25 (1995): 22–35.

National Center for Health Statistics. 'Deaths for 72 Selected Causes, by 5 Year Age Groups, Race and Sex: United States 1979–1995, Trend B.' Table 291A (1997).

Reinherz, H. Z., et al. 'Early Psychosocial Risks for Adolescent Suicidal Ideation and Attempts.' *Journal of the American Academy of Child and Adolescent Psychiatry* 34 (1995): 599–611.

Remafedi, Gary. *Death by Denial: Studies of Suicide in Gay and Lesbian Teenagers.* CITY: Alyson Publications, 1997.

Rosenberg, M., J. Smith, L. Davidson, and J. Cohn. 'The Emergence of Youth Suicide: An Epidemiologic Analysis and Public Health Perspective.' *Annual Review of Public Health* 8 (1987): 420.

Sells, C. W., and R. W. Blum. 'Morbidity and Mortality among U.S. Adolescents: An Overview of Data and Trends.' *American Journal of Public Health* 86 (1996): 513–19.

Shaffer, D., M. Gould, P. Fisher, et al. 'Psychiatric Diagnosis in Child and Adolescent Suicide.' *Archives of General Psychiatry* 53 (1996): 339–48.

## 9. Drinking and Drugs

Barros, H. M. T., and K. A. Miczek. 'Neurobiological Characteristics of Alcohol-Heightened Aggression.' In *Aggression and Violence: Genetic Neurobehavioral and Biosocial Perspectives*, ed. D. M. Stoff and R. B. Cairns. Mahwah, NJ: Lawrence Erlbaum, 1996, 237–63.

Canada, G. *Reaching Up for Manhood: Transforming the Lives of Boys in America.* Boston: Beacon Press, 1998.

Cloninger, C. R., S. Sigvardsson, T. R. Przybeck, and D. M. Svrakic. 'Personality Antecedents of Alcoholism in a National Area Probability Sample.' *European Archives of Psychiatry and Clinical Neuroscience* 245 (1995): 239–44.

Cloninger, R. C. 'Neurogenetic Adaptive Mechanisms in Alcoholism.' *Science* 236 (1987): 410–16.

Ellickson, L. P., K. A. McGuigan, V. Adams, R. M. Bell, and R. D. Hays. 'Teenagers and Alcohol Misuse in the United States: By Any Definition It's a Big Problem.' *Addiction* 91 (1996): 1489–1503.

Froehlich, J. C. 'Opiod peptides.' *Alcohol Health and Research World* 21 (1997): 132–35.

Gruber, E., R. J. DiClemente, M. M. Anderson, and M. Lodico. 'Early Drinking Onset and Its Association with Alcohol Use and Problem Behavior in Late Adolescence.' *Preventive Medicine: An International Journal Devoted to Practice and Theory* 25 (1996): 293–300.

Johnston, L. B., J. Bachman, and P. O'Malley. *Monitoring the Future: National High School Drug Use Survey.* Washington, DC: National Institute on Drug Abuse, 1995.

Langer, L. L., and J. G. Tubman. 'Risky Sexual Behavior among Substance-Abusing Adolescents: Psychosocial and Contextual Factors.' *American Journal of Orthopsychiatry* 67 (1997): 315–22.

Liu, X., and H. B. Kaplan. 'Gender-Related Differences in Circumstances Surrounding Initiation and Escalation of Alcohol and Other Substance Use/Abuse.' *Deviant Behavior: An Interdisciplinary Journal* 17 (1996): 71–106.

Masse, L. C., and R. E. Tremblay. 'Behavior of Boys in Kindergarten and the Onset of Substance Use during Adolescence.' *Archives of General Psychiatry* 54 (1997): 62–68.

Pihl, R. O., and J. B. Peterson. 'Alcoholism: The Role of Different Motivational Systems.' *Journal of Psychiatry and Neuroscience* 20 (1995): 372–96.

——. 'Alcohol, Serotonin, and Aggression.' Special Issue: Alcohol, Aggression, and Injury. *Alcohol Health and Research World* 17 (1993): 113–16.

Slater, M. D., D. Rouner, K. Murphy, F. Beauvais, J. Van Leuven, et al. 'Male Adolescents' Reactions to TV Beer Advertisements: The Effect of Sports Content and Programming Context.' *Journal of Studies on Alcohol* 57 (1996): 425–33.

Synder, H. N. 'Juvenile Arrests for Driving Under the Influence, 1995.' OJJDP Fact Sheet 67, Washington, DC: U.S. Department of Justice, 1997.

Webb, J. A., P. E. Baer, and R. S. McKelvey. 'Development of a Risk Profile for Intentions to Use Alcohol among Fifth and Sixth Graders.' *Journal of the American Academy of Child and Adolescent Psychiatry* 34 (1995): 772–78.

## 10. Romancing the Stone

Brooks, G. *The Centerfold Syndrome*. San Francisco: Jossey-Bass, 1995.

Brooks, G. R., and R. Levant. *Men and Sex*. New York: Wiley, 1997.

Camarena, P. M., P. A. Saragiani, and A. C. Petersen. 'Gender-Specific Pathways to Intimacy in Early Adolescence.' *Journal of Youth and Adolescence* 19 (1990): 19–31.

Lefkowitz, B. *Our Guys: The Glen Ridge Rape and the Secret Life of the Perfect Suburb*. Berkeley: University of California Press, 1997.

Osherson, S. *Wrestling with Love: How Men Struggle with Intimacy*. New York: Fawcett Columbine, 1992.

Simon, W., and J. Gagnon. 'On Psychosexual Development.' In *Handbook of Socialization Theory and Research*, ed. D. A. Goslin. Chicago: Rand McNally, 1969.

## 11. Anger and Violence

Archer, John. *The Behavioral Biology of Aggression*. Cambridge: Cambridge University Press, 1988.

Cloninger, C. R., S. Sigvardsson, T. R. Przybeck, and D. M. Svrakic.

'Personality Antecedents of Alcoholism in a National Area Probability Sample.' *European Archives of Psychiatry and Clinical Neuroscience* 245 (1995): 239–44.

Dodge, K. A., G. S. Pettit, C. L. McClaskey, and M. M. Brown. 'Social Competence in Children.' *Monographs of the Society for Research in Child Development* 51, no. 2 (1986), serial 213.

Dodge, K. A., and D. R. Somberg. 'Hostile Attributional Bias among Aggressive Boys are Exacerbated under Conditions of Threat to Self.' *Child Development* 58 (1987): 213–24.

Miczek, K. A., E. M. Weerts, and J. F. DeBold. 'Alcohol Aggression and Violence: Biobehavioral Determinants.' In *Alcohol and Interpersonal Violence: Fostering Multidisciplinary Perspectives*, ed. S. E. Martin (NIAAA Research Monograph 24). Rockville, MD: National Institutes of Health, 1993, 83–119.

Moffitt, T. E. 'The Neuropsychology of Juvenile Delinquency: A Critical Review of Research and Theory.' In *Crime and Justice: A Review of Research*, vol. 12, ed. M. Tonry and N. Morris. Chicago: University of Chicago Press, 1990, 99–169.

Pihl, R. O., and J. B. Peterson. 'Alcohol, Serotonin, and Aggression.' Special Issue: Alcohol, Aggression, and Injury. *Alcohol Health and Research World* 17 (1993): 113–16.

Schaal, B., R. E. Tremblay, R. Soussignan, and E. J. Susman. 'Male Testosterone Linked to High Social Dominance but Low Physical Aggression in Early Adolescence.' *Journal of the American Academy of Child and Adolescent Psychiatry* 34 (1996): 1322–30.

Sickmund, M., H. N. Synder, and E. Poe-Yamagata. 'Juvenile Offenders and Victims: 1997 Update on Violence.' Pittsburgh, PA: National Center for Juvenile Justice, 1997.

Synder, H. N. 'Juvenile Arrests: 1996.' OJJDP Juvenile Justice Bulletin. Washington, DC: U.S. Department of Justice, November, 1997.

Synder, H. N., and M. Sickmund. 'Juvenile Offenders and Victims: A Focus on Violence.' Pittsburgh, PA: National Center for Juvenile Justice, 1995.